SECOND EDITION

# MOTOR LEARNING & CONTROL

## for Practitioners

*Cheryl A. Coker*

PLYMOUTH STATE UNIVERSITY

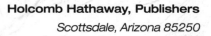

**Holcomb Hathaway, Publishers**

*Scottsdale, Arizona 85250*

**Library of Congress Cataloging-in-Publication Data**

Coker, Cheryl A.
  Motor learning & control for practitioners / Cheryl A. Coker.
    p.  cm.
  Includes bibliographical references and indexes.
  ISBN 978-1-890871-95-6
1. Motor learning.  I. Title. II. Title: Motor learning and control for
practitioners.
  [DNLM: 1. Motor Skills. 2. Learning. 3. Physical Education and
Training—methods. 4. Physical Therapy Modalities. WE 103 C682m 2009]
  BF295.C645 2009
  152.3'34—dc22

                                                    2009017100

Holcomb Hathaway, Publishers, Inc.
8700 E. Via de Ventura Blvd., Suite 265
Scottsdale, AZ 85258
480-991-7881
www.hh-pub.com

10 9 8 7 6 5 4

ISBN 978-1-890871-95-6

Printed in the United States of America.

# contents

# Behavioral Theories of Motor Control    51

# Neural Mechanisms: Contributions and Control    79

# 5 Stages of Learning    111

# The Learner: Pre-Instruction Considerations    135

# Skill Presentation    155

## 8 Principles of Practice Design    181

## 9 Practice Schedules    207

## 10 Diagnosing Errors   227

# 11 Correcting Errors    245

# Epilogue: Teaching Scenarios    269

*Please note:*  The author and publisher have made every effort to provide current website addresses in this book. However, because web addresses change constantly, it is inevitable that some of the URLs listed here will change following publication of this book.

# preface

**H**uman movement is a complex phenomenon. For practitioners concerned with movement enhancement, that complexity presents a constant challenge. The key to meeting this challenge lies in understanding how people learn. *Motor Learning and Control for Practitioners, Second Edition,* introduces practitioners to the processes that underlie human movement learning. Bridging the gap between research and practice, this text provides practitioners with the necessary tools to build a solid foundation for assessing performance, providing effective instruction, and designing practice, rehabilitation, and training experiences that will optimize skill acquisition and performance.

## Approach

The purpose of this textbook extends beyond simply presenting the concepts and principles of motor learning and control. The intent of *Motor Learning and Control for Practitioners* is to provide readers with the opportunity to become actively engaged with its content through an applications-based approach. Before readers can be challenged to apply theoretical constructs, however, they must first understand them. To facilitate this understanding, material is presented in an easy-to-read manner that incorporates a wide range of examples from everyday life, teaching, coaching, and rehabilitation. Readers have abundant opportunities to interact with the book's key concepts, principles, and basic terminology and then apply that information to real-life situations.

## Audience

This text is designed for practitioners in physical education, kinesiology, exercise science, athletic training, physical and occupational therapy, dance, and coaching. Special care has been taken to accommodate the diverse needs of this multifaceted audience, as reflected in the great variety of examples, scenarios, and activities provided throughout the text. Readers in each specific content area will have numerous opportunities to apply principles and concepts to their area of specialization and to develop a working knowledge of motor learning and control as it applies to their chosen profession.

## Organization

The focus of Chapters 1 through 4 is on the behavioral and neurological processes that influence performance. The text begins by introducing readers to the foundational concept that human movement is a complex phenomenon that is a function of the interaction of the learner, the task, and the environment in which the task is performed (Chapter 1). Readers' working knowledge of this interaction is further developed in Chapter 2, which introduces the underlying processes that govern movement execution and control. While Chapter 2 focuses on the factors that influence movement preparation, Chapter 3 explores the theoretical constructs underlying the coordination and control of human movement. Movement is then examined from a neurological perspective in Chapter 4.

Chapters 5 through 11 build on this foundational knowledge of how skilled movements are produced, examining the factors involved in their acquisition and refinement. Chapter 5 begins this discussion, introducing the changing characteristics of learners as they progress from novices to experts and the role of these characteristics in guiding the practitioner's decision making throughout the instructional process. Beginning with Chapter 6, the sequence in which concepts are introduced parallels that used by practitioners during the instructional process. Chapter 6 discusses pre-instruction considerations to facilitate learning including learning styles, transfer, and motivation to learn. Methods of presenting skills—specifically, instructions, demonstrations, and discovery learning—are then examined in Chapter 7. Next, to provide learners with ample opportunities to practice presented skills, Chapter 8 examines a number of practice variables, including sequencing and psychological strategies that a practitioner can manipulate to optimize gains in skill proficiency. This focus on practice design continues in Chapter 9, which highlights practice organization and scheduling. Once the learner begins to practice a skill, the role of the practitioner becomes one of error detection and correction. Chapter 10, unique to this text, investigates the role of motor learning and control in diagnosing errors while Chapter 11 addresses principles and guidelines regarding the provision of feedback for error correction. Finally, an epilogue contains two real-life scenarios to test readers' abilities to apply what they have learned.

## New to This Edition

This second edition continues to provide a balance between conceptual and practical material. In addition to updating all chapters to reflect current research, this edition's new and expanded topics include the use of Gentile's taxonomy in developing skill progressions, application of the constraints led approach, and expanded coverage of visual search strategies. Several topics have been reorganized to improve clarity, and new Cerebral Challenges, examples, and Research Notes will aid student understanding. A new marginal feature that will appeal to students and instructors alike directs readers to online resources, including videos, web-based activities, and additional informational sources. Finally, materials for instructors now include laboratory experiments and key talking points for selected Cerebral Challenges.

## Features

- **Accessible for all students.** The text's readability and varied applications and examples make it appealing to students pursuing careers as practitioners.
- **Theoretical coverage.** Balanced coverage is provided of movement preparation theories, motor program and dynamic interaction theories, and theoretical models of attention.
- **Broad range of examples.** Examples from sport, physical education, dance, exercise science, athletic training, rehabilitation, and "everyday life" will accommodate the great variety of majors and future professionals in this course.
- **Pretest.** The text opens with a pretest to determine students' current knowledge level with respect to motor learning and control. The test is based on Common Myths that readers will encounter marginally throughout the text, introducing and discussing common misconceptions in the field.
- **Epilogue.** The text concludes with two real-life scenarios and associated questions (and answers), allowing students to put concepts to work in an applied setting.
- **Error diagnosis and correction.** Chapter 10's unique coverage explores errors based on motor learning and control issues and their diagnosis. The chapter presents critical factors for conducting an observation, offers a categorical model for determining an error and its resolution, and discusses situational factors that should be considered before correcting an error.
- **Functional anatomy of the nervous system.** Chapter 4 helps readers to connect basic nervous system anatomy to motor learning and control concepts.
- **Introduction to learning styles.** In Chapter 6, readers are introduced to individual learning styles and their influence on the learning process, reinforcing the importance of recognizing and accommodating individual differences.

## Pedagogical Features

- **Chapter opening vignettes** introduce the key concepts to be presented in that chapter.
- Critical thinking exercises called **Cerebral Challenges,** interspersed throughout the text, require readers to engage in higher-order problem-solving activities. This feature can further serve as an instructor-directed starting point for class discussion.

- **Exploration Activities** (experiential mini-labs) enable students to use typical classroom and everyday items to explore key concepts and translate chapter content into practice. These activities can also serve as an instructor-directed starting point for class discussion, or may be completed by students outside the classroom.
- **Web links** (in text, in Exploration Activities, and in Cerebral Challenges) direct readers to relevant videos, web-based activities, and additional information sources.
- Boxed **Research Notes** provide examples of research conducted on the topics discussed in the chapter.
- **Key terms** are bolded in the text and included in a comprehensive book-end Glossary.
- End of chapter features include:

    **A Look Ahead,** previewing the coming chapter.

    **Focus Points,** concise bulleted summaries of key concepts.

    **Review Questions,** allowing students to test their comprehension of material.

## Intructor Materials

- The **Instructor's Manual** available to text adopters now includes laboratory experiments and key talking points for selected Cerebral Challenges.
- A **PowerPoint presentation** focusing on key content and art is also available.

## Acknowledgments

I would like to express my appreciation to Colette Kelly and the editorial staff of Holcomb Hathaway, Publishers, for their valuable assistance. I also wish to thank the following individuals, who reviewed this book in various stages of completion and offered constructive suggestions for its improvement: Ken Alford, Texas A&M University-Commerce; Rhonda Folio, Tennessee Technological University; Patty Hacker, South Dakota State University; Casi R. Helbig, Texas Lutheran University; Anthony P. Kontos, Humboldt State University; Kevin Lorson, Wright State University; Kay McDaniel, Lee University; Linda E. McElroy, Oklahoma Baptist University; Lisa A. Pleban, Castleton State College; Angie Smith-Nix, University of Arkansas; Maureen Walcavich, Edinboro University; and Steve Wallace, San Francisco State University.

I am indebted to my students and my colleagues, who continue to challenge me to learn and grow. I would also like to extend my gratitude to Leah Geer, not only for reading the manuscript cover to cover but also for reinforcing my faith in future generations. Last and most important, to Kim—thanks for believing in me.

# pretest

As a student of human movement, you bring to this course extensive knowledge from your past experiences. To determine your current level of knowledge with respect to motor learning and control, complete the following pretest.

## True or False?

1. Future success in a specific skill can easily be predicted.                                                    TRUE    FALSE

2. The higher the level of arousal, the better the performance.                                                    TRUE    FALSE

3. All sensory messages must go to the brain for integration.                                                      TRUE    FALSE

4. Unless the learner displays some overt changes in performance, they are no longer learning.                     TRUE    FALSE

5. All learners are motivated to learn the skills presented to them.                                               TRUE    FALSE

6. Experts are always the most effective instructors.                                                              TRUE    FALSE

7. In order for an observer to learn a movement, the demonstration must be performed correctly.                    TRUE    FALSE

8. Practice makes perfect.                                                                                         TRUE    FALSE

9. Long-term retention of a motor skill is best achieved by practicing a skill repeatedly before moving to either a different version of the task or a different task altogether.    TRUE    FALSE

10. When teaching a youngster how to catch, you should toss the ball with a high arch in order to give them enough time to follow it and get underneath it for a successful catch.    TRUE    FALSE

11. The more frequently a practitioner provides feedback to the learner, the greater the gains in learning.        TRUE    FALSE

12. A practitioner should give the learner feedback immediately following a movement/performance attempt.          TRUE    FALSE

**Answers** The answer to all of the above items is "False." You may have chosen "True" in some cases because these statements represent common myths regarding motor learning and control. Throughout the textbook, each of these statements appears as a "Common Myth" in the margin, indicating where the concept is discussed in detail. Look for them as you begin your journey through the field of motor learning and control.

# Introduction to
# Motor Learning and Control

I have come to a frightening conclusion. I am the decisive element in the classroom. It is my personal approach that creates the climate. It is my daily mood that makes the weather. As a teacher, I possess the tremendous power to make a child's life miserable or joyous. I can be the tool of torture or an instrument of inspiration. I can humiliate or humor, hurt or heal. In all situations, it is my response that decides if a crisis will be elevated or de-escalated, and a child humanized or dehumanized.

**Haim Ginott, educator**

The message of the quotation above is clear: the role of instructor is a very powerful one. The climate you create will determine the level of success that your students, patients, clients, or athletes will achieve. Fundamental to creating an effective climate is an understanding of how people learn. *Motor Learning and Control for Practitioners* focuses on the processes that govern movement acquisition and control and provides a foundation for the development of effective instructional strategies that facilitate learning and performance. By studying this book, you will learn that human movement is a complex phenomenon that is a function of the interaction of three elements, shown in Figure 1.1: the learner, the task, and the environment in which the task is performed.

When assessing performance and making instructional decisions, you must remember that none of these elements exists in isolation. Practitioners are, there-

| FIGURE **1.1** | The interaction of the learner, the task, and the environment in which the task is performed is fundamental to the understanding and facilitation of motor skill acquisition and performance. |
| --- | --- |

**LEARNER**

Does the learner possess the underlying abilities to perform the task?

Is the task developmentally appropriate?

Has he or she had any past experiences that are relevant to the task?

Is he or she motivated to learn the task?

What individual differences might influence the acquisition of this task?

**ENVIRONMENT**

In what context will the task be performed?

Is that context predictable or unpredictable?

Is there a time limitation?

**TASK**

Does the task have a high perceptual component?

Is object manipulation required?

What body movements are required?

Must the task be performed under a variety of conditions, or must the learner be able to replicate the movement pattern consistently and accurately?

fore, challenged to go beyond simply reading this text and developing a basic understanding of the theoretical constructs presented here. Instead, you are challenged to reinvent yourself as a human movement specialist by developing a working knowledge of motor learning and control, so that you can empower your learners and maximize their potential.

## MOTOR LEARNING, CONTROL, AND PERFORMANCE

**H**ow, exactly, do people acquire motor skills? What processes allow the musculoskeletal system to produce intended movements? What variables facilitate or hinder skill acquisition? Questions such as these have led to the evolution of a field of study known as motor learning. **Motor learning** is the study of the processes involved in acquiring and refining motor skills and of variables that promote or inhibit that acquisition. A related field of study, **motor control**, focuses on the neural, physical, and behavioral aspects that underlie human movement. An understanding of both motor learning and motor control is necessary to develop a complete understanding of motor skill acquisition. Such an understanding provides the human movement practitioner with foundational knowledge that not only explains why a certain behavior manifests but also provides the basis for assessing performance, providing effective instruction, and designing optimal practice, rehabilitation, and training experiences.

### What Is Learning?

The first question we should ask when we look at how people learn is *what is learning?* Before continuing, please complete Exploration Activity 1.1.

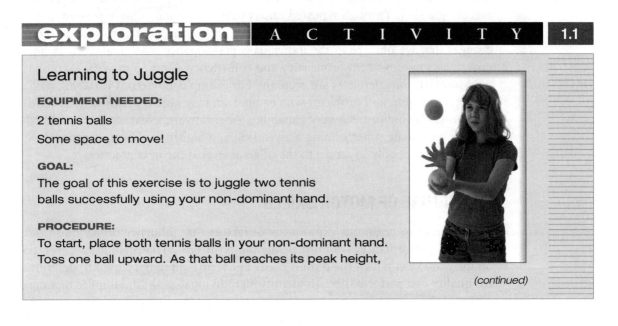

**exploration** A C T I V I T Y    1.1

### Learning to Juggle

**EQUIPMENT NEEDED:**

2 tennis balls
Some space to move!

**GOAL:**

The goal of this exercise is to juggle two tennis balls successfully using your non-dominant hand.

**PROCEDURE:**

To start, place both tennis balls in your non-dominant hand. Toss one ball upward. As that ball reaches its peak height,

*(continued)*

toss the second ball upward, leaving the hand empty to catch the first ball. Continue this pattern, attempting to achieve as many successive catches as possible. Repeat for 10 minutes, recording the number of successful catches you achieve on each trial (from the starting position to the time you drop a ball or miss a catch).

**QUESTIONS:**

1. Assuming that you were eventually able to make two or more catches, could you conclude that you had learned how to juggle two balls with your non-dominant hand? Why or why not?
2. Let's say that in your first nine minutes of juggling, you spent more time chasing balls than catching them. Up until the nine-minute mark, your record number of catches was two. All of a sudden, in the last minute, you catch six! Does this mean you have learned how to juggle?
3. Based on this juggling experience, can you formulate a definition for learning?
4. What learner, task, and environmental factors affected your performance and learning?

When used in reference to motor learning and control, **learning** is defined as a relatively permanent change in a person's capability to execute a motor skill as a result of practice or experience. To know whether you have learned how to juggle as a result of your participation in Exploration Activity 1.1, you must determine whether a persistent change in your juggling behavior has occurred.

Part of the problem we face when attempting to determine whether a motor skill has been learned is that we can't actually *see* learning, because the underlying or internal processes that result in a relatively permanent change cannot be directly observed. What we can see, however, is performance. **Performance** is the act of executing a skill. Through repeated observations of an individual's performance, we infer whether the individual has learned a skill. These inferences are based on changes that we observe in the individual's performance over time, such as improvements in movement proficiency and consistency. Caution must be exercised to ensure that the inferences are accurate. For example, numerous variables, such as fatigue, anxiety, and problems with equipment, may impair performance but do not necessarily indicate a loss of capability. Alternatively, a learner may suddenly become consistent at performing a given skill at a higher level of proficiency during one practice, only to return to the original level at the next practice.

## THE NATURE OF MOTOR SKILLS

In order to begin our exploration of factors that influence skill acquisition and performance, we must define the term *skill*. That definition depends on the context in which the term is used. The term skill may be used to describe the quality of a performance. To identify an individual as skillful implies that the person has achieved a high degree of proficiency. LeBron James, for example, is considered a highly skilled basketball player.

The term **motor skill** describes an act or task that satisfies four criteria:

1. It is goal-oriented, meaning it is performed in order to achieve some objective.
2. Body and/or limb movements are required to accomplish the goal.
3. Those movements are voluntary. Given this stipulation, reflexive actions, such as the stepping reflex in infants, are not considered to be skills, because they occur involuntarily.
4. Motor skills are developed as a result of practice. In other words, a skill must be learned or relearned.

Crutch walking would be considered a motor skill, as it satisfies these four criteria. It requires voluntary body and or limb movement to achieve a goal (e.g., move across a room), and it must be learned.

Practitioners should note the distinction between a skill and a sport. Volleyball is a sport. It consists of multiple skills, including the serve, the forearm pass, the overhead pass, and the spike, all of which have different characteristics and impose different demands on the performer.

## Skill Classifications

The nature of a skill imposes specific demands on the learner that practitioners must consider when designing learning experiences. To assist practitioners in understanding the nature of motor skills and the demands they impose, several classification systems or **taxonomies** have been developed that organize motor skills by their common elements. Knowing the relationships among diverse skills can assist the practitioner in planning learning and practice experiences, as well as provide a starting point for performance assessment.

---

C E R E B R A L **challenge**  1.2

Determine which of the following can be classified as a motor skill. Explain each classification choice.

a. Brushing your teeth

b. Tapping your pencil

c. Solving a word problem

d. Taping a wrist

e. Movement response when a hot stove is touched

f. Sewing on a button

g. Walking

h. Playing the trumpet

i. Parachute reflex of an infant

j. Performing proprioceptive neuromuscular facilitation (PNF) exercises

### *Fine versus gross motor skills*

Frequently used in adapted physical education and motor development is the classification system that distinguishes between fine and gross motor skills. This scheme is based on the precision of movements and corresponding size of the musculature required for their successful performance. Those skills involving very precise movements, which are accomplished using smaller musculature, are known as **fine motor skills.** These skills tend to be manipulative in nature; examples include sewing on a button, tying a fly (fishing), controlling dental or surgical instruments, installing memory into a desktop computer, or pulling the trigger of a biathlon rifle. Larger muscles are used in the performance of **gross motor skills,** which place less emphasis on precision and are typically the result of multi-limb movements. Examples include running, hopping, and skipping, which are generally known in physical education as fundamental motor skills.

Although this classification system categorizes skills as either gross or fine, many skills require the combined effort of both large and small muscle groups. In bowling, for instance, the large muscles of the legs propel the body forward in the approach, and those of the shoulder create the arm swing necessary to launch the ball. At the same time, a high degree of fine motor control is needed to manipulate the spin of the ball upon release. In fact, fine motor control has a significant impact on the extent to which many skills can be performed proficiently (Payne & Isaacs, 1999). Accordingly, the degree of fine motor control displayed during the performance of a skill may be used to assess skill development.

Children tend to achieve gross motor skill proficiency before they develop control over fine motor skills (Eichstaedt & Kalakian, 1993). Developmental

The precise movements required for sewing make it a fine motor skill.

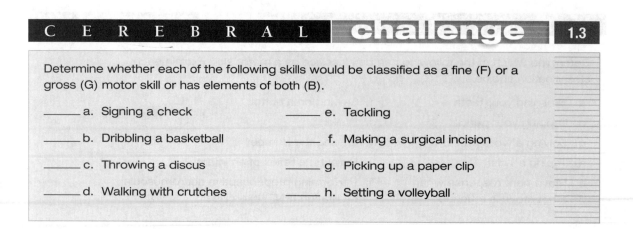

C E R E B R A L **challenge** 1.3

Determine whether each of the following skills would be classified as a fine (F) or a gross (G) motor skill or has elements of both (B).

_____ a. Signing a check

_____ b. Dribbling a basketball

_____ c. Throwing a discus

_____ d. Walking with crutches

_____ e. Tackling

_____ f. Making a surgical incision

_____ g. Picking up a paper clip

_____ h. Setting a volleyball

readiness must, therefore, be a consideration when designing teaching progressions. Skills or skill components should be introduced in a sequence moving from gross to fine.

## Nature of movement organization

A second taxonomy classifies skills into one of three categories based on the nature of their organization. A **discrete skill** is one whose beginning and end points are clearly defined. Examples are a golf swing, moving from sitting to standing, and throwing a horseshoe.

**Continuous skills** are those whose beginning and ending points are either arbitrary or determined by some environmental factor (such as a finish line) rather than by the task itself. Typically, continuous skills are repetitive in nature. They include cycling, working out on an elliptical machine, rowing, locomotion in a wheelchair, and tracing a picture.

Jumping over a puddle requires larger muscle groups and less precision, making it a gross motor skill.

Other tasks, such as a mélange in classical ballet, roping a calf, and performing a figure skating routine, are composed of a number of discrete skills whose integrated performance as serial skills is crucial for goal achievement. Because **serial skills** are collective sequences of multiple discrete skills, their complexity is greater than that of a single discrete skill. Due to their nature, however, serial skills can be simplified when necessary by practicing their components separately. The time spent practicing components in isolation, however, should be limited, as the successful performance of both serial and continuous skills depends on the performer's ability to combine movements (Rink, 2003). In basketball, for example, an outlet pass commonly follows a rebound. How the rebound is performed in a given situation will determine how the learner will have to execute the pass. Consequently, practice should emphasize the entire movement sequence, as well as other possible movement combinations (e.g., rebound, dribble, and pass). This will enable learners to discover how the skill's components interact, which will better prepare them to adjust their movements in different situations (Rink, 2003).

## C E R E B R A L  challenge  1.4

Categorize each of the following skills as either discrete (D), serial (S), or continuous (C).

_____ a. Triple jump

_____ b. Crochet shot

_____ c. Punting a football

_____ d. Lunges

_____ e. Gymnastics vault

_____ f. Transfer from wheelchair to bed

_____ g. Walking with assisted walking device

_____ h. Cross-country skiing

### *Predictability of the environment*

The predictability of the environment in which the skill is performed is the determinant of the third classification system. This classification system is based on a continuum, as the degree of predictability can vary between low and high. On one end of the continuum are skills performed in stable, predictable environments. These are called **closed skills**. With closed skills, the performer controls the performance situation, because the object being acted on or the context in which the skill is being performed does not change. For example, in bowling, regardless of how busy the bowling alley is, the pins are stationary and the performer chooses when to initiate the movement. Other examples of closed skills include chopping wood, picking up a cup of coffee, zipping up a jacket, and taping an athlete's ankle.

**Open skills** are at the other end of the continuum, as they are performed in an unpredictable, ever-changing environment. Mountain biking is a good example of an open skill, because the performer must continually adapt his or her responses to conform to the trail. Other examples of open skills include pursuing an opponent in field hockey and walking through a crowd after a concert, movie, or sporting event. The continuum is shown in Figure 1.2.

The closed/open distinction is an important one for practitioners, as the instructional goals for each differ significantly. For closed skills, consistency is the objective, and technique refinement should be emphasized. However, some closed skills, known as closed skills with inter-trial variability, are performed in a variety of contexts. For these types of skills, technique development remains important; however, learners must also be able to adapt that technique for use in a variety of situations. In bowling, for example, the learner's performance must be adjusted depending on the placement of the pins during any given trial, so potential pin combinations should be practiced. Similarly, putting practice in golf should incorporate a variety of slopes and green conditions, as well as different locations and distances from the hole.

For open skills, where the learner must constantly conform his or her movements to an unstable, unpredictable environment, successful performance becomes less dependent on mastering technique and more dependent on the learner's capability to select the appropriate response in a given situation. Con-

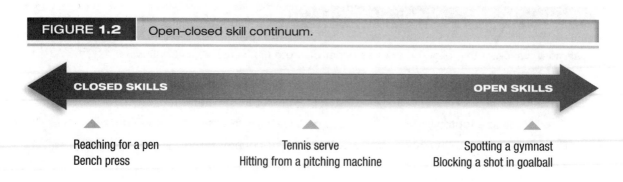

**FIGURE 1.2**   Open–closed skill continuum.

CLOSED SKILLS                                                        OPEN SKILLS

Reaching for a pen                    Tennis serve                    Spotting a gymnast
Bench press                    Hitting from a pitching machine        Blocking a shot in goalball

sequently, practice should simulate the game or context in which the skill will be performed, with an emphasis on learning to anticipate and adapt to the demands of the ever-changing performance situation.

The closed/open distinction can also assist practitioners in the regulation of task complexity. For example, throwing a football may be considered either a closed or an open skill, depending on the context. Throwing at a stationary target would be considered a closed skill. As other variables are added, such as a moving receiver or a pursuing defense, throwing a football becomes a progressively more open and, in turn, more complex task. In the early stages of skill acquisition, it is difficult for learners to focus both on the execution of the movement and on aspects of the environment (such as the position of receivers or the movements of defensive players)—traits inherent in open skills. By changing the context of a skill to make it more closed initially, the practitioner can strategically decrease attention demands and simplify the learning process.

## C E R E B R A L  challenge  1.5

1. Determine where along the closed–open continuum the following skills fall, by placing the item letters accordingly on the line.

CLOSED ←————————————————————————————————→ OPEN

_____ a. Walking with a cane through a crowded mall

_____ b. BMX racing

_____ c. Playing a video game

_____ d. Guiding a patient through PNF exercises

_____ e. Hitting a ball from a tee

_____ f. Hitting a pitched ball

_____ g. Mowing the lawn

_____ h. Snowboarding

_____ i. Balancing on a wobble board

2. Jose has driven since he was 16. Now, in college, he wants to buy a certain car, but it has a manual transmission. He has never driven a stick shift before and has asked if you will teach him. You agree. Rank order the following settings for Jose's first lesson, with 1 being the best and 3 being the worst. Explain your rankings.

_____ On a rural road

_____ In an empty parking lot

_____ In city traffic

### Multidimensional classification system

A complete understanding of the demands a task places on a performer, according to Gentile (2000), cannot be realized using a single-dimensional system. Instead, Gentile proposes a taxonomy that categorizes skills according to two general characteristics: (1) the context in which they are performed and (2) the action requirements of the skills. Combined, these two dimensions provide insight into the processes involved in skill acquisition.

**Regulatory conditions.** Skills are not performed in a vacuum. To perform a jump header in soccer, for example, the performer must conform his or her movement to the height, size, speed, and trajectory of the ball, as well as the location of the intended target. A number of environmental factors, therefore, exist for any given skill, and these factors specify the movement characteristics necessary for successful performance. These factors are known as **regulatory conditions** (Gentile, 2000), and their determination may be used to differentiate skills.

When examining the environmental context in which a task is performed, the first question of interest is whether the regulatory conditions are stable, as in shooting at a stationary target, or in motion, such as in skeet shooting. Notice that this concept parallels that of the open versus closed skill classification, in that the regulatory conditions for closed skills tend to be stable, whereas those for open skills tend to be in motion. As indicated earlier, when learners must conform to constraints imposed by the environment, they must engage in more complex processes to assess the situation and select appropriate responses.

C E R E B R A L **challenge**   1.6

1. Determine whether each of the items listed below would be considered as a regulatory (R) or non-regulatory (N) condition for dart throwing:

   _____ a. Height of the dart board

   _____ b. Crowd noise

   _____ c. Distance from the dart board

   _____ d. Sharpness of the dart tip

   _____ e. Score

2. On a separate sheet, identify regulatory conditions for each of the following:

   a. Performing a bicep curl        e. Stepping onto an escalator

   b. Hiking along a forest trail        f. Picking up your change from a counter

   c. Diving from a springboard        g. Dusting the furniture in your house

   d. Cross-country skiing        h. Retrieving your suitcase from a baggage carousel

The second question of interest is whether there is inter-trial response variability—that is, whether the regulatory conditions remain fixed or change with each successive performance attempt. A free throw, for example, has low inter-trial variability, because the context in which it is performed does not change from one shot to the next. The basket does not change, the distance from which one shoots remains constant, and defenders do not oppose the performer. A great deal of inter-trial variability is experienced by tail backs, on the other hand, as their running pattern must change each time they receive the ball in a game in order to avoid tackles and gain maximum yardage.

**Action requirements.** The other dimension proposed by Gentile (2000) pertains to the action requirements of a skill, specifically with respect to body movement and object manipulation. In this context, body movement refers to whether the performer must change locations when performing the skill. Cross-country skiing, performing the high jump, and using an assisted walking device are examples of skills that require the performer to move from one place to another. On the other end of the spectrum are skills that require body stability. Performing push-ups, lifting a coffee mug while seated, making a golf putt, and playing the drums all fall into this category.

A second determinant of action requirements is object manipulation. Some skills require the performer to manipulate objects or opponents. Wrestling, knitting, and grasping fall into this category. Other skills, including performing step patterns in aerobics and pelvic tilt exercises, do not require object manipulation.

**Application of the multidimensional classification system.** To use this classification system to understand the demands that a task imposes on a learner, practitioners must ask four questions:

1. Are the regulatory conditions stable or in motion?
2. Do the regulatory conditions remain fixed (no inter-trial variability), or do they change (inter-trial variability) with each successive performance attempt?
3. Is the performer required to change locations or maintain body position when performing the skill?
4. Does the task require the performer to manipulate an object or opponent?

Once the answer to each question is determined, the skill can be classified into one of 16 resulting categories, as shown in Table 1.1.

For example, in the forearm pass in volleyball, the performer must track a moving ball, move to a position to intercept it, and then control its deflection to propel it in the desired direction. Consequently, the regulatory conditions are moving and change from trial to trial, and the performer is required to change

**TABLE 1.1**    Gentile's multidimensional classification system, with task examples.

| | ACTION REQUIREMENTS | | | |
| --- | --- | --- | --- | --- |
| | Neither body transport nor object manipulation | Object manipulation only | Body transport only | Both body transport and object manipulation |
| Stationary and fixed | Doing a sit-up **1** | Moving a chess piece **2** | Climbing a ladder **3** | Shot put **4** |
| Stationary and variable | Writing ABCs with foot for ankle rehabilitation **5** | "Round the clock" in darts **6** | Following a dance pattern that has been placed on the floor **7** | With a partner, following a dance pattern that has been placed on the floor **8** |
| Moving and fixed | Floating on a river in an inner tube **9** | Playing with a yo-yo **10** | Running down a hill **11** | Walking on crutches in a clear hallway **12** |
| Moving and variable | Riding in a tube pulled by a speedboat **13** | Playing Fooze Ball **14** | Skating on a crowded ice rink **15** | A forearm pass in volleyball **16** |

(REGULATORY CONDITIONS)

locations and manipulate an object. Given this assessment, the forearm pass falls into category 16.

The human movement practitioner may use Gentile's multidimensional classification system in several ways. First, as you move diagonally from the top left box to the bottom right box, task complexity increases, with a corresponding increase in the demands placed on the performer. Accordingly, the simplest skill is one that is stationary, involves no inter-trial variability or body transport, and does not require object manipulation. On the other end of the spectrum, the most complex skill is one performed in an environmental context that is in motion, involving high inter-trial variability, and requiring both body transport and object manipulation. To perform such a skill successfully, the performer must be

Using the chart below, assess the regulatory conditions and action requirements of each skill. Based on your assessment, determine into which of the 16 categories in Gentile's multidimensional classification system (Table 1.1) the skill would be classified.

| Skill | Regulatory Conditions (environment) | | Regulatory Conditions (inter-trial variability) | | Body Transport (changing locations) | | Object Manipulation | | Category Number |
|---|---|---|---|---|---|---|---|---|---|
| | stable | in motion | fixed | change | yes | no | yes | no | |
| Putting a golf ball | X | | | X | | X | X | | 6 |
| Propelling a wheelchair through a crowd of people at a concert | | | | | | | | | |
| Performing a lunge on a BOSU ball | | | | | | | | | |
| Texting on your cell phone | | | | | | | | | |
| Short track speed skating | | | | | | | | | |
| Wii Fit Game shown at www.youtube.com/watch?v=fmHRVjAlt_c | | | | | | | | | |

able to scan the environment to identify and process relevant information, decide how to respond, and allocate attentional resources to control body transport and object manipulation concurrently. By understanding the level of complexity of a skill, the practitioner can better design challenging yet realistic learning experiences. A logical progression that moves from simple to complex ultimately leads to simulations of the actual context in which the skill will be performed. Refer to Figure 1.3 for an example of a simple-to-complex progression.

| FIGURE **1.3** | Sample simple-to-complex progression for the forearm pass. |
|---|---|

**SKILL:** Volleyball Forearm Pass

**VARIABLES THAT CAN BE MANIPULATED:**

1. Stability of regulatory conditions
2. Inter-trial variability
3. Body transport

| Activity | Gentile's Taxonomy |
|---|---|
| 1. Partner tosses the ball at a constant trajectory and location. | 1. Regulatory conditions are relatively stable<br>2. No inter-trial variability<br>3. No body transport<br>4. Object manipulation |
| 2. Partner tosses the ball at a constant location but changes the trajectory each time. | 1. Regulatory conditions are moving<br>2. Inter-trial variability<br>3. No body transport<br>4. Object manipulation |
| 3. Partner tosses the ball to different locations and with different trajectories but indicates where the ball will go prior to tossing it. | 1. Regulatory conditions are relatively stable<br>2. Inter-trial variability<br>3. Body transport<br>4. Object manipulation |
| 4. Partner randomly tosses the ball to different locations and with different trajectories without giving prior notification as to where it is going. | 1. Regulatory conditions are moving<br>2. Inter-trial variability<br>3. Body transport<br>4. Object manipulation |

Practitioners may also use Gentile's model to systematically evaluate a learner's movement capabilities and limitations. This assessment affords a better understanding of the degree of complexity that a learner is able to handle and insight into what performance demands (e.g. scanning the environment, processing information, allocating attention) are problematic.

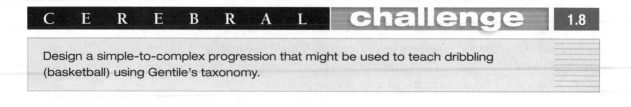

C E R E B R A L challenge 1.8

Design a simple-to-complex progression that might be used to teach dribbling (basketball) using Gentile's taxonomy.

# INDIVIDUAL DIFFERENCES

**O**ne challenge that practitioners face is the fact that all learners are unique. Each person's uniqueness is a function of relatively stable and enduring characteristics known as **individual differences.** Factors such as height, body type, physiological makeup (e.g., number of white twitch fibers), learning styles, type and amount of previous movement experience, motivation, developmental level, cultural background, psychological makeup, attitude, and confidence all affect the rate of and potential for developing skill proficiency. Because of individual differences, teaching strategies will not be equally effective for all learners, and practitioners must identify the best strategies to employ based on diverse learner needs and qualities.

## Motor Abilities

Of interest to human movement practitioners are individual differences in motor abilities. **Abilities** are genetic traits that are prerequisite for skilled performance. Accordingly, the degree to which a learner could potentially develop proficiency in a particular motor skill depends on whether he or she possesses the necessary underlying abilities.

Although many different abilities have been identified to date, researchers initially hypothesized that there existed a single general motor ability (Brace, 1927; McCloy, 1934). The impetus behind this notion was the observation that accomplished athletes often were able to pick up new skills quickly and excel at numerous other skills without much practice. Therefore, it seemed reasonable to surmise that there existed a high correlation between one's level of general ability and one's potential for skill proficiency at a variety of tasks. In other words, if you had inherited a high level of general motor ability, you should be able to achieve a high level of proficiency in all motor skills, from golf to bobsledding to kayaking.

Challenging the existence of a general motor ability, the specificity hypothesis proposed that not only do individuals inherit a large number of motor abilities but also those abilities are independent of one another (Henry, 1968). In addition, each skill requires a particular set of abilities for successful performance. Consequently, an individual who obtains a high degree of proficiency in archery will not necessarily achieve that same degree of proficiency in wrestling, as these two skills have different underlying ability requirements.

Research examining the strength of interrelationships between motor abilities silenced the debate between proponents of general motor ability and the specificity hypothesis. In general, researchers found low correlations between an individual's performances of two different tasks (including those that appeared to be closely related), which supported the specificity hypothesis (Drowatzky & Zucatto, 1967; Henry, 1968; Robertson et al., 1999; Zelaznik, Spencer & Doffin, 2000). However, because low correlations were found, instead of no correlation at all, it remained possible that some of the same underlying abilities

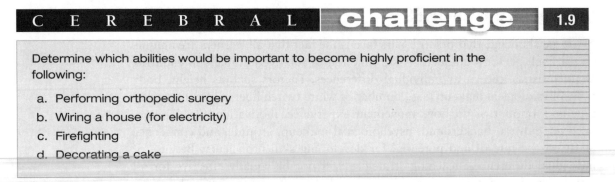

Determine which abilities would be important to become highly proficient in the following:

a. Performing orthopedic surgery
b. Wiring a house (for electricity)
c. Firefighting
d. Decorating a cake

were required by different tasks. Recognizing this, Fleishman (1962) set out not only to identify underlying motor abilities that were predictive of high skill proficiency levels, but also to create a taxonomy by which skills could be classified.

## Categorizing Motor Abilities

Fleishman's taxonomy groups motor abilities in two categories: (1) perceptual motor abilities and (2) physical proficiency abilities. The 11 perceptual motor abilities and nine physical abilities are identified in Table 1.2, along with an example of a skill for which the ability is elemental. It should be noted that this list is not all-inclusive, nor is it likely that all abilities have yet been identified.

## Practical Implications

All of us have different abilities that enhance or limit our capability to become skilled at a particular task. But even if we possess the prerequisite abilities for accomplishing a task, there is no guarantee that we will become skillful. We only have the *potential* to become skillful. Practice and experience play a role in realizing that potential. Consequently, children should be provided with as many varied movement experiences as possible. Those experiences should be developmentally appropriate. Learners will modify skills according to their current

C E R E B R A L   **challenge**   1.10

1. Which of the following statements is/are true? Justify your answer.
   a. An individual can have abilities but not be skilled.
   b. An individual can be skilled without ability.
2. Khalilah is strong in control precision, rate control, and finger dexterity but weak in arm–hand steadiness and response orientation. What is her potential for fulfilling her dream of becoming a famous tattoo artist? Fully explain your response.

| | Fleishman's taxonomy of motor abilities. | TABLE **1.2** |
|---|---|---|
| **ABILITIES** | **DEFINITION** | **ILLUSTRATION** |
| **PERCEPTUAL MOTOR ABILITIES** | | |
| Control precision | Ability for highly controlled movement adjustments, especially those involving larger muscle groups | Dribbling a soccer ball |
| Multi-limb coordination | Ability to coordinate numerous limb movements simultaneously | Volleyball spike |
| Response orientation | Ability to select a response rapidly from a number of alternatives, as in choice reaction time situations | Tail back trying to find an opening |
| Reaction time | Ability to initiate rapidly a response to an unexpected stimulus | Sprint start in swimming |
| Speed of limb movement | Ability to make gross rapid limb movement without regard for reaction time | Hockey slap shot |
| Rate control | Ability to make continuous speed and direction adjustments with precision when tracking | Mountain biking |
| Manual dexterity | Ability to control manipulations of large objects using arms and hands | Water polo |
| Finger dexterity | Ability to control manipulations of small objects primarily through use of fingers | Dialing a number on a cell phone |
| Arm–hand steadiness | Ability to make precise arm–hand positioning movements where involvement of strength and speed are minimal | Dentistry |
| Wrist finger speed | Ability to move the wrist and fingers rapidly | Blackjack dealing |
| Aiming | Ability to direct hand movements quickly and accurately at a small object in space | Marksmanship |
| **PHYSICAL PROFICIENCY ABILITIES** | | |
| Static strength | Ability to generate maximum force against weighty external object | Pushing car out of snowbank |
| Dynamic strength | Muscular endurance or ability to exert force repeatedly | Rock climbing |
| Explosive strength | Muscular power or ability to create maximum effort by combining force and velocity | Throwing javelin |
| Trunk strength | Dynamic strength of trunk muscles | Pole vault |
| Extent flexibility | Ability to move trunk and back muscles through large range of motion | Circus contortionist |
| Dynamic flexibility | Ability to make repeated, rapid flexing movements | Diving, aerial ski jumping |
| Gross body coordination | Ability to coordinate numerous movements simultaneously while the body is in motion | Slalom skiing, synchronized swimming |
| Gross body equilibrium | Ability to maintain balance without visual cues | Tightrope walking while blindfolded |
| Stamina | Cardiovascular endurance or ability to sustain effort | Climbing Everest |

Used and adapted with permission of Robert Glaser, Ph.D., from *Training Research and Education* (pp. 137–175), University of Pittsburgh Press.

level of ability. For example, successful performance of a regulation free throw requires a prerequisite level of strength. A young learner who has not yet developed strength to that point will modify his or her performance accordingly in an attempt to achieve the goal of the task, making a basket. Rather than employing correct technique, the learner may instead execute the free throw using more of a "shot put" type movement in order to generate enough force to project the ball high enough and far enough. Rather than reinforce this type of movement, practitioners should lower the baskets to a more suitable height. As learners continue to develop, their level of skill will increase. However, it should be noted that learners will not all progress at the same rate and that there exists a genetic ceiling for each learner's level of skill regardless of practice.

The concept of abilities is also useful for skill classification. Through a method known as **task analysis**, we can determine the underlying abilities im-

**common** *myth*

Future success in a specific skill can easily be predicted.

portant to the successful performance of a specific skill. Skills can then be grouped accordingly. To perform a task analysis, a skill is first broken down into its key elements or component parts. Once the key components have been identified, the important abilities necessary to meet their requirements can be more readily determined. By conducting a task analysis, the practitioner can develop a greater understanding of the requirements of the skill. Figure 1.4 illustrates a task analysis and subsequent examples of ability prerequisites for a volleyball spike.

| **FIGURE 1.4** | Task analysis of a volleyball spike. |

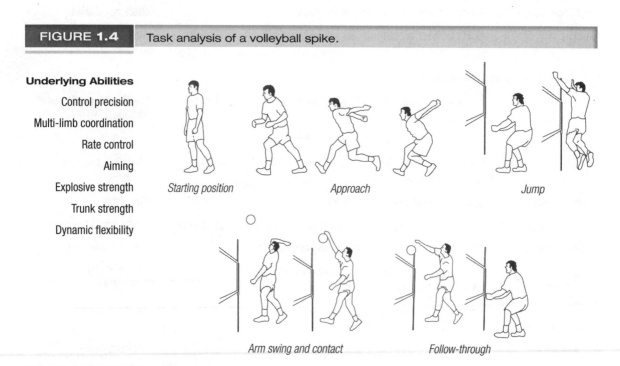

**Underlying Abilities**

Control precision
Multi-limb coordination
Rate control
Aiming
Explosive strength
Trunk strength
Dynamic flexibility

*Starting position*    *Approach*    *Jump*

*Arm swing and contact*    *Follow-through*

1. For a skill of your choice, perform a task analysis to determine its component parts and the underlying abilities required to achieve a high degree of proficiency.
2. Think about activities that you tend to participate in versus activities you tend to avoid. Speculate as to why you make these choices by comparing the underlying abilities needed to accomplish these activities.

If underlying abilities are important to the successful performance of a specific skill, it would stand to reason that an individual who possesses those abilities would be predisposed to achieving a high level of proficiency. Imagine the impact this would have on sports programs, as we could predict future performance simply by screening individuals for certain abilities. In fact, talent identification programs have existed for decades. They screen children and adolescents using a battery of tests constructed to determine the extent to which the individuals possess certain abilities. The test results are then used to select those individuals who appear to have the potential to succeed in a given sport. Other test batteries screen candidates for professions such as firefighting. Visit the links provided on the next page to view an example of a physical agility test used for law enforcement and to see if you meet the minimum standards set by the Washington State Criminal Justice Training Commission for the Basic Law Enforcement Academy.

How successful have these programs been in predicting a person's potential for success in a specific skill? And what can we learn from them to help us identify future stars in, for example, T-ball? Results of talent identification programs have been mixed. To understand why, we must consider three limitations of these programs. First, as was indicated earlier, it is likely that all of the abilities that contribute to skilled performance have yet to be identified. Second, a high level of performance in the early stages of learning does not always correlate to advanced performance, owing to changes in the requirements of the skill. For example, a child may be an outstanding hitter in T-ball when the ball remains stationary, but the results may be different when he or she moves to the next level, when the ball is pitched. Third, abilities alone cannot predict performance; other individual differences must be considered. Because of differences in reaching physical maturity, for example, players who possess the underlying abilities to excel in a sport may get cut from a team. A great example is Michael Jordan, who was cut from his high school basketball

Can future success in a skill be predicted?

## RESEARCH NOTES

Hoare and Warr (2000) conducted a study to examine the effectiveness of applying an Australian talent identification model that is traditionally used with individual sports to the team sport of women's soccer. Subjects (ages 15–19) with a background in team sports or track and field were recruited to participate in the program. Following two days of testing, which included the assessment of physiological (vertical jump, acceleration, speed, agility, and aerobic power), anthropometric (height, mass), and skill (juggling, dribbling, ball control, passing and receiving) attributes, 17 of the original 71 athletes were chosen, based on their abilities, to take part in a 12-month training program. At the conclusion of the program, which included 25 competitions, 10 players (59 percent) were selected for regional teams, with two being selected for the state team within six months. Based on their results, the authors recommended that speed and acceleration should be weighed more heavily in the future and suggested that selection procedures would benefit from the development of an objective test of "game sense" (technical and tactical competence).

## www.

### Talent Identification

Video example of a police physical ability test:

www.youtube.com/watch?v=8d5e3Enny98

Example of a physical ability test used for law enforcement:

https://fortress.wa.gov/cjtc/www/blea/PAT_Website_Info_030905.pdf

team when he was a sophomore, yet went on to become one of the greatest basketball players ever to play the game!

While it is apparent that individual differences must be taken into account for the development of a successful talent identification program, the impact of these differences on learning should be the practitioner's primary concern. Practitioners must remember that all learners are unique in what they bring to the learning environment. Consequently, a particular teaching strategy will not work for everyone. Practitioners should develop a large repertoire of instructional strategies so they can accommodate the needs of all learners. Furthermore, practitioners should take the time to get to know each learner. What types of past experiences do they have? What motivates them? What situations lead to increased anxiety? Because of the influence of individual differences, this will be time well spent.

## ▶ a look ahead

Human movement is a complex phenomenon that is a function of the interaction of three elements: the learner, the task, and the environment in which the task is performed. Because this concept is foundational to the development of optimal learning experiences, practitioners must develop a working knowledge of this interaction in order to help learners realize their potential. Further development of this working knowledge requires an understanding of the underlying processes that govern movement execution and control. The following chapter begins this discussion, focusing on the factors that influence movement preparation.

# focus points

After reading this chapter, you should know . . .

- The interaction of the learner, the task, and the environment in which the task is performed is fundamental to the understanding and facilitation of motor skill acquisition and performance.
- The field of motor learning examines the processes and variables that influence the acquisition and refinement of motor skills, while the field of motor control focuses on the neural, physical, and behavioral aspects that underlie movement.
- Learning and performance are not synonymous. Learning is a relatively permanent change in the capability to execute a motor skill as a result of practice or experience, while performance is simply the act of executing a skill.
- Motor skills are categorized by several classification systems:
  - The gross–fine motor skills classification is based on the precision of the movement.
  - Skill may be classified as discrete, serial, or continuous according to the nature of their movement organization.
  - The open–closed motor skills continuum is based on the predictability of the environment.
  - Gentile's multidimensional classification system categorizes skills according to the context in which they are performed and the action requirements of the skill.
- All teaching strategies will not be equally effective for all learners, owing to individual differences.
- Each of us possesses different levels of abilities, which are genetically determined traits that enhance or limit our potential to become skilled at a particular task.
- By conducting a task analysis, one can identify the underlying abilities important to the successful performance of a specific skill.
- Talent identification programs have shown mixed results when athletes are screened using a battery of tests to predict future success based on whether they possess certain abilities.

# review questions

1. Compare and contrast motor learning and motor control.
2. Define learning. What is the relationship between learning and performance?

3. What four criteria must a task meet if it is to be classified as a skill?

4. How are skills and abilities different?

5. Explain why most of the classification systems discussed involve a continuum.

6. Briefly summarize each classification system.

7. Explain how Gentile's taxonomy differs from the other classification types. Why is this significant?

8. Explain the controversy over general versus specific motor abilities.

9. Explain why predictions of future performance success are not always accurate.

10. What is the relevance of the interaction of the learner, the task, and the environment in human movement?

# REFERENCES

Brace, D.K. (1927). *Measuring motor ability.* New York: A.S. Barnes.

Drowatzky, J.N. & Zucatto, F.C. (1967). Interrelationships between selected measures of static and dynamic balance. *Research Quarterly, 38,* 509–10.

Eichstaedt, C.B. & Kalakian, L.H. (1993). *Developmental/adapted physical education: making ability count* (3rd ed.). New York: MacMillan.

Fleishman, E.A. (1962). The description and prediction of perceptual motor skill learning. In R. Glasser (Ed.), *Training research and education* (pp. 137–75). Pittsburgh, PA: University of Pittsburgh.

Gentile, A.M. (2000). Skill acquisition: action, movement, and the neuromotor processes. In J.H. Carr and R.B. Shepard (Eds.), *Movement science: foundations for physical therapy in rehabilitation* (pp. 111–80). Rockville, MD: Aspen.

Henry, F.M. (1968). Specificity vs. generality in learning motor skills. In R.C. Brown and G.S. Kenyon (Eds.), *Classical studies on physical activity* (pp. 331–40). Englewood Cliffs, NJ: Prentice-Hall.

Hoare, D.G. & Warr, C.R. (2000). Talent identification and women's soccer: an Australian experience. *Journal of Sports Sciences, 18,* 751–58.

McCloy, C.H. (1934). The measurement of general motor capacity and general motor ability. *Research Quarterly, 5* (Suppl. 5), 45–61.

Payne, V.G. & Isaacs, L.D. (1999). *Human motor development: a lifespan approach* (4th ed.). Mountain View, CA: Mayfield.

Rink, J.E. (2003). Motor learning. In B.S. Mohnsen (Ed.), *Concepts and principles of physical education: what every student needs to know* (pp. 15–37). Reston, VA: NASPE.

Robertson, S.D., Zelaznik, H.N., Lantero, D.A., Bojczyk, K.G., Spencer, R.M., Doffin, J.G. & Schneidt, T. (1999). Correlations for timing consistency among tapping and drawing tasks: evidence against a single timing process for motor control. *Journal of Experimental Psychology: Human Perception and Performance, 25*(5), 1316–1330.

Zelaznik, H.N., Spencer, R.M. & Doffin, J.G. (2000). Temporal precision in tapping and circle movements at preferred rates is not correlated: further evidence against timing as a general-purpose ability. *Journal of Motor Behavior, 32,* 193–99.

2

# Understanding Movement Preparation

**A** fter 90 grueling minutes of regulation and 30 minutes of overtime, the score was tied: USA 0, China 0. The 1999 Womens' Soccer World Cup would be decided by penalty kicks. China shot first and Xie Huilin found her mark in the top left corner of the goal. U.S. co-captain Carla Overbek answered back. Next, China's Haiyan Qui and the United States' Joy Fawcett were equally successful, tying it up at 2–2. This brought up Liu Ying. As her kick shot toward the left side of the goal, the U.S. goalkeeper, Briana Scurry, dove with outstretched arms, making an amazing save that sent a record crowd of 90,185 fans into a frenzy. The United States then went ahead 3–2 after Kristine Lily easily scored. Ouying Zhang beat Scurry with China's fourth penalty shot, and Mia Hamm answered, putting the United States ahead once again. The final kicker for China, Sun Wen—the tournament's top scorer—put her shot far left of Scurry, tying the game at 4–4. The hopes of the U.S. team rested on the fifth and final kicker, Brandi Chastain. The packed stadium was silent as all watched her approach the ball. She drilled it off her left foot, and the Chinese goalkeeper, Gao Hong, responded, but she was too late. The ball soared past her and history was made. The United States won its first-ever World Cup title: USA 5, China 4.

The interaction of the performer, the task, and the environment in the generation of a goal-directed action suggests that some form of movement preparation precedes the execution of a motor response. Faced with the task of blocking a penalty kick, for example, the goalkeeper must somehow assess the situation to determine both where the ball will go and what movement will intercept it. The task is further complicated by a time constraint, as she has a fraction of a second to make these decisions and to organize and execute the motor response before the ball reaches the goal line. So why was Scurry able to make a save, while Hong responded too late?

## THEORETICAL APPROACHES TO MOVEMENT PREPARATION

**O** ur senses are constantly being bombarded with information from both internal and external sources (sensory information or input). Before any of that information can potentially be used to assist a learner in selecting an appropriate response for a given situation, it must first be interpreted. The recognition and interpretation of sensory stimuli, or, said another way, the process by which meaning is attached to sensory information, is known as **perception**. Two approaches explaining the nature of perception are prevalent today.

### Information Processing Model

The first explanation, a product of cognitive psychology, maintains that perceptual processes lead to the creation of some form of symbolic representation of environmental and task information. This information traverses a series of mental processes, including a comparison with existing memory stores, and results in a decision as to which action, if any, is needed in response to the situation. Because there is a "need for sensory input to be processed or elaborated to pro-

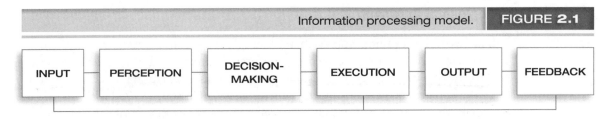

Information processing model.    FIGURE 2.1

INPUT — PERCEPTION — DECISION-MAKING — EXECUTION — OUTPUT — FEEDBACK

vide the perceiver a meaningful description of the world," perception in this paradigm is considered to be indirect (Burton, 1987, p. 258).

This view of perception has generally been associated with a model for movement preparation known as **information processing,** shown in Figure 2.1. In this model, a performer, such as a goalkeeper, will receive an abundance of information, including, in this instance, the foot used to kick the ball; characteristics of the ball itself, including velocity, trajectory, spin, and direction; the score; the feel of sweat on her skin; the sight and sound of the crowd; the sound of a plane flying overhead; the smell and color of the grass; memories of prior success or failure in similar situations; and an assessment of the area of the net to be covered. Some of this information is relevant or useful in assessing the demands of the task, such as the velocity, trajectory, and direction of the ball, while other information, such as the plane flying overhead, is not and should be ignored. By focusing on pertinent **stimuli,** the goalkeeper will receive information crucial to the production of a response that will intercept the shot. Once the information has been gathered, it is transformed into afferent or sensory nerve signals and conducted to the brain, where it is integrated or compared to similar past experiences that are stored in long-term memory. Based on this comparison, a response is selected (dive right, catch, jump), organized, and executed through efferent (motor nerve) commands. This paradigm further suggests that as the movement is initiated, information regarding its progress is fed back to the performer. This information, referred to as **intrinsic feedback,** may be used to make adjustments to the movement, if there is a discrepancy in what was intended and what is actually occurring (time permitting), and it enables the performer to evaluate the outcome of the response.

## CEREBRAL challenge    2.1

1. Generate a list of stimuli, both relevant and irrelevant, that may be available to a goalkeeper when facing a penalty kick.
2. In addition to deciding what response to make, the performer must determine details regarding that response, such as when to initiate it. Generate a list of possible responses and response details for the above situation.
3. For a skill and situation of your choice, repeat items 1 and 2.
4. Speculate as to the differences in processing demands for open versus closed skills. Give examples to support your response.

## Ecological Approach

The second prevailing approach regarding perception suggests that the environment and task are perceived or interpreted directly in terms of affordances. Affordances are the action possibilities of the environment and task in relation to the perceiver's own capabilities (Burton, 1987; Gibson, 1977, 1979). In other words, the environment or task is perceived in terms of the actions the perceiver can potentially exert on it (Burton, 1987). Because of individual differences, several learners could be faced with the exact same situation and perceive entirely different affordances. For example, while walking through a clothing store, the affordances perceived by an adult will be very different from those of a small child because of differences in height. The actions afforded by a cell phone for a college student differ from those for a toddler. Typically, college students use a cell phone to talk with or text their friends, whereas toddlers typically use it for hitting, banging, or chewing. Since affordances are directly perceived, this perspective, known as the **ecological approach** to perception, argues against the need to refer to stored representations, and it views the relationship between perception and action as circular, as illustrated in Figure 2.2 (Summers, 1988).

Under this paradigm, the goalkeeper needs to decide whether she will catch the ball or dive to block the shot. Rather than making a decision based on an elaboration of the ball's characteristics and memory stores of similar experiences, as suggested by the indirect approach to perception, the goalkeeper directly perceives the ball in terms of its "catchableness" in relation to her own body scaling and capabilities (Burton, 1987). If the goalkeeper perceives herself as being quick enough to position herself in front of the ball to make the catch, this action will be selected. If she doesn't think she can make it, or doubts her catching ability, she may instead choose to block it. Try Exploration Activity 2.2 to gain a better understanding of how affordances influence movement decisions.

**FIGURE 2.2**  The ecological approach to perception suggests a direct relationship between perception and action.

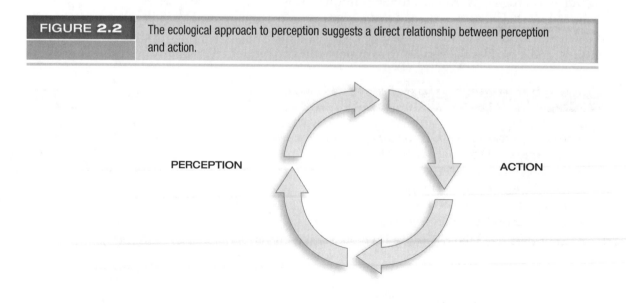

PERCEPTION                          ACTION

## exploration    A C T I V I T Y    2.2

### Affordances

**EQUIPMENT NEEDED:**

Sliding glass door          Backpack stuffed with clothes          3 friends

**PROCEDURE:**

*Task A*

Fully open the sliding glass door. Ask each of your friends to walk through it. (Participants may choose the manner in which they go through the door—e.g., they may turn to the side—provided they do not change the width of the opening.) Reduce the opening by 4 inches and repeat the procedure. Continue reducing the opening and repeating the procedure until all three friends have indicated that they cannot go through the door. Record your observations for each friend on each trial.

*Task B*

Repeat Task A, but have each friend wear the backpack on each trial. Record your observations.

**QUESTION:**

Explain your observations in terms of affordances.

## PREPARING A RESPONSE

T he conceivability of both theoretical approaches to movement preparation, in addition to the possible integration of the two, continues to be debated and explored by scientists. But regardless of the paradigm used to explain the internal processes that occur, research has clearly shown that a brief time lag occurs between the moment when a stimulus is presented and the initiation of a response. This time interval, known as **reaction time (RT)**, is a measure of the time needed to prepare a response.

## exploration    A C T I V I T Y    2.3

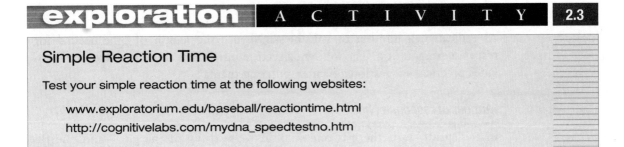

### Simple Reaction Time

Test your simple reaction time at the following websites:

www.exploratorium.edu/baseball/reactiontime.html

http://cognitivelabs.com/mydna_speedtestno.htm

Oudejans, Michaels, Bakker, and Dolné (1996) examined the relevance of action in perceiving affordances. The purpose of their study was to determine whether perceptual information about the perceiver's own actions has to be available in order to determine the catchableness of a fly ball. Because catchableness depends on both spatial (distance to be covered) and temporal (time available to cover that distance) aspects, the researchers speculated that judgments regarding catchableness would be more accurate when information about the catcher's action was available. Six non-experts and six expert outfielders were tested in two conditions. The first condition, the perceiving-only condition, required subjects, who remained stationary, to determine as quickly as possible whether a ball could be caught if they were permitted to make an attempt at catching it. The second condition was an actual catching condition. The results revealed that when compared to actual catching, perceivers who are stationary, regardless of experience, make poor judgments as to the catchableness of a ball. These results suggest that stationary perceivers, who

were prevented from receiving current information about their running capabilities, did not rely on other information, such as information stored in memory, to determine the catchableness of a ball. A follow-up study was conducted to determine whether judgments of catchableness improved when observers were moving. Twelve non-experts were tested in three conditions. In the first two conditions, participants were to indicate verbally whether the projected ball would have been catchable. Condition 1 required that participants remain stationary, and vision of the projected ball occurred 1 second after its release. Condition 2 differed in that participants started to run in an attempt to catch the ball. Vision was also occluded for this condition for 1 second after the ball was projected. The task of participants in the third condition was actually to catch the projected ball. The results indicated that judgments made when moving were superior to ones made when stationary. The authors concluded that when running is permitted, information that is available regarding the performer's actions makes more accurate judgments of catchableness possible.

Reaction time is not constant; it depends on the processing demands imposed by a given situation. As those demands increase, reaction time also increases, indicating the need for more time to prepare a response. The result, however, is a delay that can be detrimental to avoiding a collision, catching an item that has fallen from the kitchen counter, or stopping a penalty kick in soccer. Understanding the variables that cause such delays is, therefore, paramount in developing strategies for reducing them and, in some cases, eliminating them during the performance of open skills. Of equal interest to coaches and athletes is how to cause delays in an opponent's responses in order to gain an advantage.

## Factors Influencing Reaction Time

As indicated, a number of variables influence the length of time needed for response preparation. The following section introduces those variables and provides practical suggestions for manipulating them.

### Number of response choices

In the sprint start, there is one stimulus—the firing of the gun—and one response choice—exploding out of the blocks. Because there is only one choice

# exploration A C T I V I T Y 2.4

## Choice Reaction Time

To examine the influence of number of response choices on reaction time, go to www.ryerson.ca/dmp/portfolio/teachtech/reactionTime/demoassignment.html#.

in this situation, uncertainty as to how to respond is essentially eliminated. In contrast, a shortstop faces a number of response choices, as he or she may have to catch a fly ball or a line drive or field a ground ball hit directly at, to the right, or to the left of his or her position. Similarly, in a penalty kick, a number of possible shots that can be taken, leading to a corresponding increase in the number of the response choices available to the goalkeeper. Because of the uncertainty of the impending hit or shot, the shortstop or goalie needs additional processing time to prepare a response. This increase in processing demands is reflected by an increase in RT.

The relationship between the number of choices and the time to prepare a response was found to be so stable that it has become known as **Hick's Law** (Hick, 1952), named for its discoverer. Hick's Law states that <u>**choice RT**,</u> the reaction time resulting from a situation that involves a choice as to how to respond, is logarithmically <u>related to the number of response choice alternatives.</u> This relationship is illustrated in Figure 2.3.

Predicted relationship between number of stimulus–response choices and reaction time (Hick's Law).    **FIGURE 2.3**

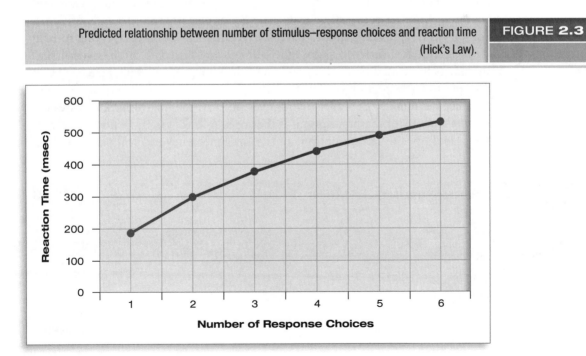

Notice that in a situation requiring one definitive response, such as the sprint start discussed earlier, RT is approximately <u>190 ms</u>, but in the situation faced by the shortstop, RT may be two to three times that long. This increase in RT has important implications when the movement situation demands a quick and accurate response.

**Response time** is measured from the moment that a stimulus is presented to when a response is completed and includes both RT and movement time, as shown in Figure 2.4. **Movement time (MT)** is the interval between the initiation of the movement and its completion. Both RT and MT must be considered when analyzing a goalkeeper's task of intercepting the ball. For example, suppose that because of ball placement and speed, a goalkeeper has approximately 360 ms from the time the ball leaves the kicker's foot to decide how to respond and execute that movement (RT + MT) before the ball crosses the plane of the goal. Assuming that she has only two response choices, according to Hick's Law, RT will be approximately 300 ms. This leaves only 60 ms to execute the response. When examined from this perspective, it is not surprising that blocking a shot on goal in soccer is such a difficult task.

**Controlling levels of uncertainty.** Since, according to Hick's Law, increased uncertainty leads to delayed or even inaccurate responses, practitioners should be aware of strategies that can increase or reduce this uncertainty to facilitate learning and performance. The goal of many competitive situations is to gain an advantage over an opponent. By having a large repertoire of proficient serves, plays, moves, pitches, and the like, the player can increase the uncertainty of which response will be required and diminish the ability of the opponent to respond quickly and accurately. In other competitive tasks, successful performance depends on quick decision making. When a quarterback is executing an option play, trying to read all of the stimuli in order to choose the best option to execute can be overwhelming and, as illustrated by Hick's Law, time consuming. As a result, coaches teach their quarterbacks to look systematically for key defensive characteristics in order to reduce the number of choice alternatives. In play, the quarterback assesses the potential success of the first option. If that option looks good, he takes it; if not, he will look for the second option, and so on. Emergency medical personnel em-

| FIGURE **2.4** | Components of response time. |

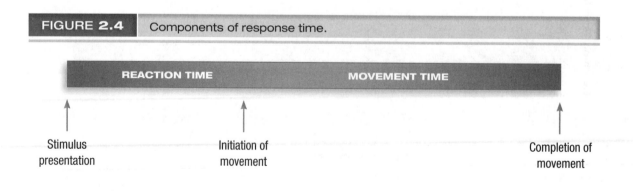

REACTION TIME | MOVEMENT TIME

Stimulus presentation | Initiation of movement | Completion of movement

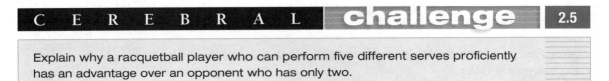

Explain why a racquetball player who can perform five different serves proficiently has an advantage over an opponent who has only two.

ploy this same strategy when they arrive at the scene of an accident. Using what's known as the ABCs (airway, breathing, and circulation), they systematically assess the situation, reducing their response preparation time.

The technique of reducing uncertainty by systematically reducing the number of possible response alternatives may be used to facilitate skill learning. When teaching the forearm pass in volleyball, instructors often organize practice so that learners are working in pairs. In each pair, one person tosses the ball and the other passes it back. At first, the tosses are thrown directly to the learner. Once the learner has developed some proficiency, the tosses may be directed to the right or left, in front of, or behind the learner, forcing her to move into the correct position and perform the skill. The first step of a normal progression for this drill is for the tosser to tell the passer in which direction the toss will be made. Because the learner knows in advance where the ball will go, the number of response alternatives is reduced, which reduces the processing demands of the task. The next step is to eliminate the pre-toss information, forcing the passer to be prepared for any of the four possible response alternatives.

## Anticipation

When the performer is given advance information about not only what event will occur but also when it will occur, movement preparation is optimized and response delays are reduced. Although situations exist where the performer is directly told in advance what to expect (for example, a car's turn signals communicate intent, and highway signs tell drivers about driving and road conditions),

1. The goal of some "shooting" video games is to shoot the bad characters but not the good characters. The challenge is that the characters literally jump out of nowhere and the player must quickly decide whether they are "good" or "bad." If you were playing such a video game, what strategies might you use to decrease uncertainty and response time and increase accuracy?
2. What might you suggest to police officers who face this same situation?
3. For a skill of your choice, explain how you would increase or decrease uncertainty, depending on your objective.

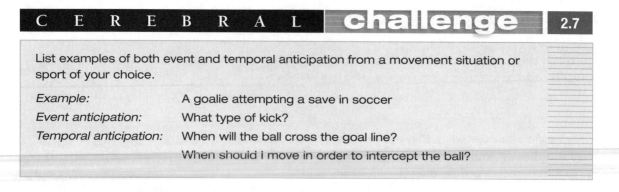

List examples of both event and temporal anticipation from a movement situation or sport of your choice.

*Example:*                    A goalie attempting a save in soccer
*Event anticipation:*         What type of kick?
*Temporal anticipation:*      When will the ball cross the goal line?
                              When should I move in order to intercept the ball?

this is obviously not always the case. Performers typically must learn how to reduce temporal and event uncertainty through **anticipation.**

Anticipation involves predicting what event will occur (**event anticipation**) and/or when an event will occur (**temporal anticipation**). The more predictable a stimulus, the more quickly and accurately a learner can respond. This concept is closely related to the technique of reducing the number of response choices, as the learner essentially narrows down the possible options through anticipation.

Prediction depends on the performer's ability to detect clues, or **precues,** that are often present in the environment. Therapists, for example, may watch for subtle changes in a patient's posture to anticipate when they should intervene. Similarly, parents use precues to anticipate when to catch a toddler who is learning to walk. In athletic contests, players scrutinize their opponents to identify tendencies that can serve as precues. For example, an offense may always use the same play in a given situation, or a pitcher may tend to use a certain pitch depending on the count. Perhaps right before making a pass, a basketball player always looks at the player he is going to pass to. A racquetball player might change her back swing depending on the serve she is about to perform.

C E R E B R A L  **challenge**  2.8

"Briana Scurry looked at the Chinese midfielder, Liu Ying, as she walked to the penalty spot. Liu's head was down and her shoulders drooped, and it seemed to Scurry that Liu did not want the burden of the kick. 'This is the one,' Scurry said to herself. Liu set the ball down, backed up at a sharp angle, and began her approach with a tentative jog. Her intention became obvious, and her hips rotated in a way that gave the shot away. Scurry lunged with an explosive step, then planted her feet wide and dived to her left."

Longman, J. (2000). The Girls of Summer. *Women's Sports and Fitness,* July/August, p. 72

Liu's hips served as a precue for Scurry that allowed her to anticipate what response she would have to make to block the shot. For a skill of your choice, list precues that increase the predictability of a certain response.

Research has shown that as the probability of a particular response increases (at a level of approximately 80 percent), the performer will likely bias response preparation in its direction (Larish & Stelmach, 1982). The result is that the action can be prepared in advance, decreasing RT. For example, in racquetball, if, based on the opponent's positioning and swing motion, a player anticipates that the shot will go to the right, she may start moving in that direction before the opponent has contacted the ball.

Anticipation is not without risks. If the response required is anything other than that which the performer was preparing, the consequence will be a RT that is even slower than if the response had not been biased at all (Larish & Stelmach, 1982).

**Practical applications for anticipation.** Through practice, learners' capability to recognize cues, idiosyncrasies, and tendencies of opponents will improve, resulting in better anticipation of predictable events and the capacity to prepare required actions in advance. By identifying potential precues, focusing learners' attention to where in the environment they might find precues, and designing drills in which precues are incorporated, practitioners can facilitate this development. Learners must also be taught to avoid presenting the same cues or making the same responses in a competition, which could help the opponent anticipate the impending action.

## Foreperiod consistency

The extent to which a learner is prepared to respond in a given situation can also influence response preparation time. The provision of a warning signal, for example, leads to significantly faster reaction times, as it alerts the performer to the approach of a stimulus (Brebner & Welford, 1980). The "set" command issued prior to the firing of the starting gun, the toss of the ball in the tennis serve, and the turn signal on a car all serve as warning signals. However, the mere presence of a warning signal is not enough for a performer to achieve and maintain optimal preparedness. Ideally, the interval of time that transpires between the presentation of the warning signal and the stimulus, called the **foreperiod,** should range from 1 to 4 seconds. Foreperiod durations that fall short of this range do not permit adequate time to prepare, while expectancy levels fall when durations are too long.

The consistency of the foreperiod influences the performer's ability to capitalize on anticipation. When foreperiod lengths are constant or predictable, temporal anticipation becomes possible (Queseda & Schmidt, 1970). Provided that the response to the signal is predetermined, such as in a sprint or swimming start, reaction time will be significantly reduced. Good starters prevent this effect by continually varying the foreperiod length prior to firing the starting gun. Foreperiod consistency considerations are not solely restricted to racing events. To avoid anticipation and quick responses from the defense, for example, a

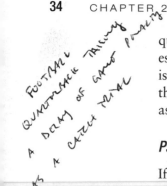

*(handwritten margin note)* FOOTBALL QUARTERBACK TALKING A DELAY OF GAME PENALTY AS A CRITICAL PERIOD

quarterback varies the snap count. Randomizing foreperiod length is, therefore, essential in preventing an opponent from gaining an advantage. Situations do exist where a constant foreperiod is desirable. Successful performance in music and the performing arts, for example, is highly dependent on temporal anticipation, as performers must be able to initiate their movements at a precise moment.

### Psychological refractory period

If you have ever been faked out, you have experienced what happens when two stimuli, each of which requires a different response, are presented in succession within a short period of time. Those who haven't directly experienced this phenomenon have probably seen it occur: when a performer buys into a head fake to the right, for example, he will prepare and initiate the corresponding response, but if the opponent then quickly moves in the other direction, there is a momentary delay in response to this second stimulus. This delay, known as the **psychological refractory period (PRP)**, is reflected in a RT that is slower than the RT for the first stimulus (the fake). Figure 2.5 illustrates the PRP.

A successful fake depends on two performance factors. First, the fake must be realistic. For example, when volleyball players want to draw a block in order to tip the ball around it, they have to execute a convincing spike approach, or the defense will read their actual intentions. Second, timing is critical. If the fake and the actual move are executed too closely in time, the opponent will not have enough time to buy into the fake and will ignore it. On the other hand, if the faker allows too much time to elapse between the fake and the actual move, the opponent will have enough time to respond effectively to both. This timing comes with practice.

Through practice, performers can also learn how to read a fake, and they will be fooled less often. Focusing on an opponent's center of gravity, for ex-

---

**FIGURE 2.5**   The psychological refractory period (PRP).

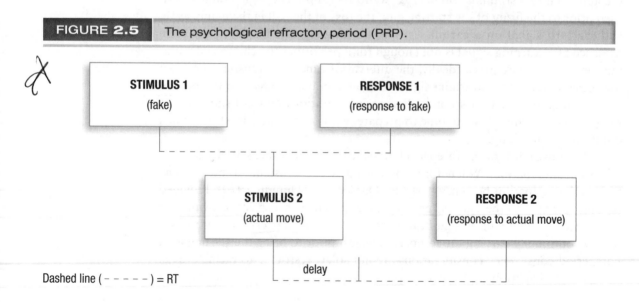

Dashed line ( - - - - - ) = RT

ample, provides clues as to the impending motion, because the center of gravity must be shifted in the desired direction of movement prior to a change in course.

Fakes clearly illustrate the psychological refractory period, but a performer who anticipates incorrectly also experiences a PRP. An excellent example is the batter who, having anticipated a fastball (because the pitcher was behind in the count), suddenly realizes that the pitch is a change-up (Shea, Shebilske & Worchel, 1993). Similarly, goalies often fall victim to PRP delays when the puck or ball is deflected in front of the net, as do players of tennis, table tennis, badminton, and volleyball when the ball's direction suddenly changes when it clips the net on the way over.

Goalies experience delays due to the psychological refractory period when the ball or puck is deflected in front of the net.

## Stimulus–response compatibility

When a number of stimulus–response (S–R) choices are available, another factor found to affect movement preparation time is **stimulus–response compatibility**, which refers to the extent to which a stimulus and its required response are naturally related. When stimulus–response compatibility is low, additional time is needed to prepare a response, and this is reflected in increased reaction times. A classic example involves the arrangement of stovetop burners and their controls. Traditionally, the burners are arranged in a rectangular pattern and the controls are positioned horizontally. The spatial discrepancy in arrangement creates confusion and results in response delays. A more compatible organization would be to arrange the knobs in the same pattern as their corresponding burners.

To further illustrate the concept, let's say the government issues a mandate that all vehicle brake lights must be white in color instead of red. What will be the likely outcome when this law goes into effect? In our society, red is strongly associated with "stop" or danger. In other words, there is a high compatibility between the illumination of red brake lights (stimulus) and stopping (response). If the brake lights were changed to white, the stimulus–response compatibility would be lower, resulting in an increase in the reaction times of drivers to the lights. Fortunately, with practice, responses become more compatible and reaction times improve.

Aerobics instructors pay attention to S–R compatibility when conducting classes. Because of the imitative nature of an aerobics class, the instructor must remember to mirror each move. This means that when facing the group, if the instructor wants the participants to raise their right hands, the instructor must raise her left hand. Mirroring increases the compatibility of the stimulus–response

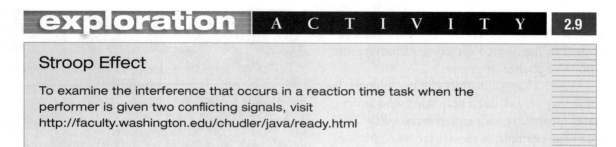

## Stroop Effect

To examine the interference that occurs in a reaction time task when the performer is given two conflicting signals, visit
http://faculty.washington.edu/chudler/java/ready.html

choice and reduces response delays and incorrect movements, facilitating participants' ability to perform the routine.

Finally, equipment manufacturers in the therapeutic modality and fitness industries have not ignored the issue of compatibility. Start and stop buttons on ultrasound machines and treadmills are colored the green and red that we are accustomed to. In addition, the buttons and switches used to manipulate intensity levels are often accompanied by + and − signs, which indicate increase and decrease, respectively.

### Reducing Response Time: Beyond Movement Preparation

Strategies targeted at reducing movement preparation delays can be effective in decreasing response time, but they are not always sufficient to lead to successful performance. Recall that response time is the combination of both reaction time and movement time. Consequently, slow responses may result from prolonged movement time (see Figure 2.4). Therefore, one strategy for decreasing response time is to increase the speed at which the movement is executed. Increased bat speed, for example, is the result of improved swing mechanics and conditioning. Another strategy is to reduce the length of the movement. This technique is used frequently in self-defense classes, where learners are taught not to cock back their arm fully prior to striking. In hockey, players use little or no backswing for shots in front of the net, in order to get the shot off as quickly as possible.

Rather than changing the speed or distance of the movement, an alternative approach is to increase the distance between the performer and the opponent. Tennis provides an excellent example of this strategy: the player will stand behind the baseline to receive the serve, allowing more time for decision-making and movement execution.

## ATTENTION

**B** efore strategies for the reduction of response delays can be successfully implemented, another factor must be considered. There is a limit to how many activities an individual can pay attention to or process at any given time. When this limit is exceeded, a competition for attentional resources occurs, the consequences of which may include a reduction in the speed or quality of the performance of one or more activities or even a complete disregard for one of the activities.

## Theoretical Models of Attention

Two important theoretical models of attention are the bottleneck theory and attentional resource theories.

### Bottleneck theory

In early theories of attention, scientists speculated that when we are subjected to a continuous flow of information, that flow is impeded at some point by an attentional filter that separates the information that will be processed further and that which will not (Broadbent, 1958; Deutsch & Deutsch, 1963; Norman, 1968; Welford, 1952). Stimuli selected for further processing then pass (via processing) through the filter in a serial fashion (one at a time). Because the filter essentially creates a bottleneck in the flow of information traffic, this theory is often referred to as the bottleneck theory. It is illustrated in Figure 2.6.

Bottleneck theory of attention: information flow is impeded by an attentional filter that allows through only the information that will be processed further.    **FIGURE 2.6**

Sensory input

"Filter"

Information attended to

### Attentional resource theories

The bottleneck theory accounts for phenomena such as the psychological refractory period, but it lacks flexibility and cannot explain situations such as walking on a treadmill and reading a magazine, where an individual can successfully attend to more than one stimulus at a time. More contemporary theories suggest the existence of limited attentional resources or space (Kahneman, 1973; Wickens, 1984). According to this view, two tasks can be successfully performed simultaneously provided that, combined, they do not exceed the attentional resources available. In other words, if walking on a treadmill requires 25 percent of the total available attentional space and reading a magazine requires 50 percent, the combined total of 75 percent falls within the amount available (Figure 2.7a). However, if another task were introduced, such as watching a news report on the TV across from the treadmill, that, combined with walking on the treadmill and reading a magazine, would require more attentional space than is available. In this situation, interference occurs, and either the level of performance on one or more tasks declines or a task may even be totally ignored (Figure 2.7b).

## Factors Influencing Attentional Demands

Complicating the issue of limited attentional capacity is the fact that the attentional demands of a given task are not constant. Practitioners should be aware that environmental, task, and learner characteristics all influence the attentional demands placed on the performer. These characteristics have important implications with regard to designing instructional experiences.

**FIGURE 2.7**  Representation of attentional demands on available attentional resources.

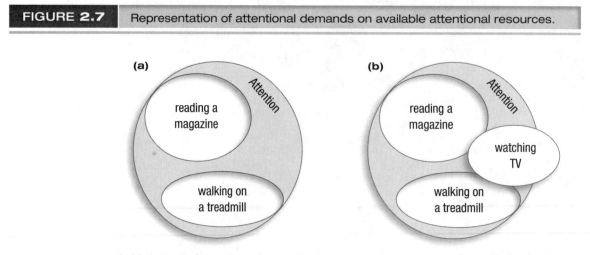

In (a), the two tasks can be performed simultaneously, as they do not exceed the attentional capacity.

In (b), the combination of these tasks requires more attentional space than is available. The level of performance on one or more tasks will decline, or a task may be ignored.

## R E S E A R C H   N O T E S

On any given day, as you make your way to work or school, you probably notice drivers engaging in activities that can divert their attention from driving. One such activity is cell phone use. Wanting to gain a clearer understanding of the effects of conversing on a cell phone while driving, Strayer, Drews, and Crouch (2006) conducted a study to compare the driving performance of a cell phone–using driver to that of a drunk driver. The study was conducted in a controlled laboratory setting using a driving simulator. Variables such as driving speed, following distance, time to collision, and braking time were examined, using a car-following paradigm, where participants drove on a multilane freeway following a pace car that would randomly brake. The results indicated that drivers using cell phones, regardless of whether they were conversing on a handheld or hands-free phone, exhibited delayed braking reactions and were involved in more traffic accidents than when they were not talking on the phone. The drivers who were intoxicated, on the other hand, were more aggressive in their driving, followed the vehicle in front of them more closely, and applied more force when braking. The authors of the study concluded that the impairments resulting from cell phone use while driving are as profound as those associated with drunk driving.

### Environmental and task complexity

As the environment or task increases in complexity, the attentional demands will undergo a corresponding increase, reducing the amount of attentional space available for additional tasks. For instance, sufficient processing space appeared to be available in the example of reading a magazine while walking on a treadmill. However, these same two tasks would likely interfere with one another if, rather than a treadmill, the performer were walking on a crowded sidewalk. Practitioners may want to decrease the complexity of the environment or task so that attentional limits will not be exceeded, enabling learners to allocate the necessary attentional resources toward the task being learned. For example, an optimal environment for a first-time driver would be a large, empty parking lot instead of a city street during rush hour. Similarly, by removing defenders as individuals are learning skills such as layups, dribbling, and offensive plays, a coach can ensure that attentional capacity is not likely to be exceeded.

Consideration should be given to attentional limits in gait training. Research has shown that the attentional demands on an individual can vary according to

## C E R E B R A L  challenge  2.10

1. Observe an individual performing a closed skill and another individual performing an open skill. Describe your observations. How do the attentional demands differ for the two performers?
2. For teaching a skill of your choice, explain how you might design the instructional environment in order to reduce the attentional demands imposed on the learner.

**R E S E A R C H   N O T E S**

Using the volleyball set, Sibley and Etnier (2004) examined the effect of decision-making on attention demands and task performance. Twenty intermediate volleyball players participated in the study, which employed a dual task paradigm, whereby participants complete a primary and secondary task both individually and simultaneously.

The primary task in this investigation was the volleyball set, received from an underhand toss. Set direction was dictated by ball color, with a blue-and-white striped ball indicating a back set and a white ball indicating a front set. Sets were scored according to their accuracy in dropping through a hoop that was placed parallel to the ground, 12 feet from the participant and at net height. A point value of 3 was assigned if the ball went through the hoop, 2 if it hit the hoop, 1 if it missed within one ball diameter (near misses), or 0 if it missed completely.

The secondary task required participants to respond to an auditory tone by yelling "ball" as fast as possible. Reaction time was measured from the time the tone was sounded to the participant's first auditory response. To examine attentional demands at various points in the ball's flight, tones were sounded: (a) as the ball was tossed, (b) just before the tossed ball reached its peak, (c) just after the tossed ball reached its peak, and (d) just before ball contact by the participant. Catch trials were also administered where no tone was given in order to eliminate anticipation.

All participants were given time to warm up and practice setting to the targets. Baseline measures for both the primary and secondary tasks were then obtained. Following a 5-minute rest period, the two tasks were performed simultaneously in a block of 20 front sets, a block of 20 back sets, and two blocks of 20 choice sets. Four tones at each of the four points of the ball's flight (probe positions) and four catch trials were administered randomly within each block of 20. Blocks were presented in random order.

Results indicated that attentional demand was higher on the choice sets at the first two probe positions, suggesting that "choosing the direction to set the ball and preprogramming the motor portion of the task affected attention during the first half of the ball's flight" (Sibley & Etnier, 2004, p. 105). In addition, when participants were forced to choose set direction, a small but significant decrease in setting performance was found. Results also revealed an increase in attentional demand for the first and last portions of ball flight and a lowered attentional demand mid-flight. This is consistent with the literature, in that visual selective attention is thought to be required to gather information on flight characteristics during the initial portion of a ball's flight in order to intercept it, while visual tracking does not appear to be necessary during the middle phase. As the participant prepares to contact and contacts the ball, greater attention is likely required in order to process proprioceptive information and make necessary positioning adjustments during contact.

the type of assistive device being used and the patient's familiarity with that device (O'Sullivan, 1988). It appears that both a standard pick-up walker and a rolling walker are attention demanding, whereas a roller walker requires less attention to use.

### Skill level of performer

Beginners, characteristically, have difficulty attending to more than one thing at a time when learning a new skill. Remember your juggling experience from Chapter 1? Imagine having to carry on a conversation while you were attempting to juggle. You probably needed all your attentional resources to focus on the task at hand. The addition of a conversation would have overloaded your attentional space, and the two tasks would have interfered with one another. A skilled circus performer, on the other hand, can not only juggle and carry on a conversation but do so while riding a unicycle. When teaching beginners new skills, be sure that they have been given sufficient practice on the first task before you teach them additional tasks. Also, highly complex skills with many components are often overwhelming for beginners. Breaking such skills into parts for initial practice may facilitate learning. This strategy will be discussed in Chapter 8.

### Numbers of cues

Attentional limitations are exceeded when a performer tries to think about too many things at one time when learning or refining a motor skill. This can be remedied with a few simple teaching strategies. First, when teaching a new skill, focus on only a small number of meaningful cues. Second, when correcting performance by providing feedback, avoid overloading the learner with information. Again, provide only one or two cues for the learner to think about. Finally, most performance situations present an abundance of information. Some of this information is relevant to the skill (relevant cues) and some is not (irrelevant cues). Teaching learners to attend selectively to relevant cues and ignore irrelevant ones will reduce the competition for attentional space.

## Selective Attention

The performance environment is teeming with information, some of it relevant and some of it irrelevant to the impending response. Because attentional capacity appears to be limited, successful performance depends on the performer's ability to attend to meaningful information. Fortunately, we have the capacity to do this through **selective attention.**

The classic example demonstrating our ability to attend to or focus on one specific item selectively in the midst of countless stimuli is what is known as the cocktail party phenomenon (Cherry, 1953). Let's say that you are at a large tailgate party in the midst of many other tailgate parties. Although countless conversations are taking place around you, you are able to attend selectively to the conversation in which you are engaged. Of further interest is the fact that if you hear your name mentioned in another conversation, this will divert your attention to the individual who said your name. For another example of selective attention, try Exploration Activity 2.11.

## Attentional Focus

The process of selectively attending to or concentrating on specific environmental information is known as **attentional focus.** Attentional focus may be subdivided along two intersecting dimensions, width and direction (Nideffer, 1993). The width of focus refers to the amount of information and size of the perceptual field to

# exploration ACTIVITY 2.11

## Selective Attention

Read the bold print in the following paragraph:

Somewhere **Among** hidden **the** in **most** the **spectacular** Rocky Mountains **cognitive** near **abilities** Central City **is** Colorado **the** an **ability** old **to** miner **select** hid **one** a **message** box **from** of **another.** gold. **We** Although **do** several **this** hundred **by** people **focusing** have **our** looked **attention** for **on** it, **certain** they **cues** have **such** not **as** found **type** it **style.**

What conclusions can you draw regarding selective attention? Include what you remembered about the regularly printed text in your response.

From www.mtsu.edu/~sschmidt/Cognitive/attention/attention.html#Broadbent. Accessed Sept. 8, 2000.

which a performer attends (Roberts, Spink & Pemberton, 1999). It ranges from a broad focus, where the performer attends to a large quantity of information, to a narrow focus, where attention is directed to only one or two cues. An Ultimate Frisbee player needs a broad focus to scan the field for an open teammate, but once one is located, the passer must focus her attention on that individual (narrow focus) to execute the pass (Roberts, Spink & Pemberton, 1999). Direction of focus may be either external or internal. When adopting an external focus, the performer attends to information in the environment, such as the opponent. When a performer focuses on his thoughts or feelings, this is an internal focus. As Figure 2.8 shows, width and direction interact to create four types or styles of attentional focus: broad–external, broad–internal, narrow–external, and narrow–internal.

Different performance situations place different attentional demands on the performer. Success is often contingent on the performer's ability to employ the appropriate attentional focus for a given situation. For instance, situations requiring proficient environmental awareness and assessment, such as a bicycle courier maneuvering through New York City traffic, necessitate the use of a broad–external attentional focus. On the other hand, the employment of a broad–internal focus would be necessary in situations where strategic analysis is required, such as when a billiards player plans the next shot. Mentally rehearsing the impending action, such as visualizing one's performance in the high jump prior to actually performing it, requires a narrow–internal focus, while a volleyball player executing a set is an example of the use of a narrow–external focus.

It is important to understand that many situations require performers to shift their attentional focus continually throughout the performance. For example, a soccer player performing a penalty kick will likely use all four attentional focus styles. She must assess the environment (goalie position, wind, etc.) through a

| Four attentional styles based on the interaction of two dimensions: direction and width. | **FIGURE 2.8** |
|---|---|

**EXTERNAL**

**Broad External**

Used to **assess** the external environment/situation, e.g., a bicycle courier maneuvering in traffic

**Narrow External**

Used to focus exclusively on one or two external cues to **perform** the motor response, e.g., a volleyball player executing a set

**BROAD** ←—————————————————————→ **NARROW**

**Broad Internal**

Used to **analyze** and **plan** strategy or the impending motor response, e.g., a billiards player taking a shot

**Narrow Internal**

Used to monitor internal cues and mentally **rehearse** an upcoming performance, e.g., a high jumper visualizing her performance prior to performance

**INTERNAL**

broad–external focus. Once this information is gathered, her focus will shift to broad–internal as she decides what shot to take. A narrow–internal focus will be necessary as she mentally rehearses the shot to be executed. During its execution, she will adopt a narrow–external focus (Nideffer & Sagal, 2001).

The example just given may seem to indicate that attentional switching follows a certain pattern or sequence, but this assumption is inaccurate. In the performance of open skills, for example, performers must be able to shift their attentional focus quickly and accurately according to the demands of the situation. If, rather than a penalty kick, the soccer player were executing a pass and a defender suddenly appeared in the vicinity of her open teammate, she would have to revert quickly back to a broad–external focus.

## *Tips for practitioners*

Performers who know where, when, and how to focus their attention are able to disregard irrelevant information that would cause response delays. Practitioners should not assume that learners will inherently be able to do this (Wilson, Peper & Schmid, 2001). By teaching them to recognize the attentional demands of their sport or movement, as well as by providing ample practice opportunities, practitioners can help learners sharpen their attentional switching skills.

Practitioners should also be aware that they can inadvertently cause learners to shift their attentional focus in the wrong direction (Ziegler, 2002). For example, a physical therapist might tell a patient who is undergoing gait training to learn to walk with a new prosthesis, "Don't think about falling." The thought of falling has now been planted in the patient's mind, changing his attentional style

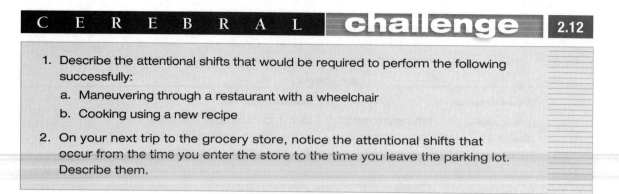

from the desired narrow–external focus to a narrow–internal one, which will likely disrupt performance (Ziegler, 2002). Similarly, a coach who tells a hurdler not to worry about hitting the hurdles will trigger a disruptive attentional response. To maximize performance, practitioners must be careful to use language that elicits positive attentional responses.

In some instances, it may be advantageous to disrupt attentional focus. A coach may call time out before an opponent's free throw or pivotal field goal attempt in the hopes of creating a distraction that will negatively influence the opponent's performance (Ziegler, 2002). Fans try to disrupt an opponent's attentional focus by yelling, heckling, waving, and calling out players' names.

## AROUSAL

rousal is "a general physiological and psychological activation of the organism that varies on a continuum from deep sleep to intense excitement" (Gould & Krane, 1992, pp. 120–121). It should not be confused with **anxiety**, which is an emotion resulting from an individual's perception of a situation as threatening—although changes in anxiety levels do lead to changes in arousal levels. A performer's level of arousal does influence her performance, but the manner in which it affects performance is not as simple as the common myth implies.

**common** *myth*

The higher the level of arousal, the better the performance.

### Relationship Between Arousal and Performance

The relationship between arousal and performance is captured by the **inverted-U principle**, also known as the Yerkes–Dodson Law (1908). According to the inverted-U principle, illustrated in Figure 2.9, there is an optimal level of arousal for peak performance.

That optimal level is not a constant, however; it depends on both task and performer characteristics. As a task increases in complexity due to increased

Inverted-U principle.    **FIGURE 2.9**

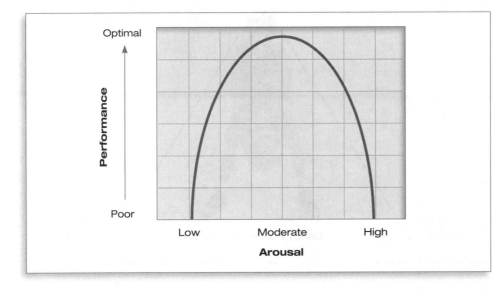

fine motor control, decision-making, and attentional requirements, lower levels of arousal will be optimal. On the other hand, higher arousal levels are appropriate for tasks involving gross movements, minimal decision-making, and low attentional demands. The optimal level of arousal for maximum performance is quite different for performing a delicate surgical procedure versus executing a power clean.

A second factor is the performer. Individual differences exist with respect to arousal and anxiety. The natural arousal level for one individual may be significantly higher than that of another individual (known as **trait anxiety,** an individual's propensity to perceive situations as threatening or non-threatening). In addition, if an individual perceives a situation as threatening, given the relationship between arousal and anxiety mentioned earlier, the person's arousal level will rise. These factors—a naturally high level of arousal and perception of the situation as threatening (e.g., possible performance failure)—both make an individual more susceptible to exceeding an optimal level of arousal.

A higher arousal level is optimal for peak performance of a power clean.

## Arousal and Movement Preparation

The **cue utilization hypothesis** (Easterbrook, 1959) provides an explanation for the relationship between arousal and performance. According to this hypothesis, changes in attentional focus occur according to arousal levels (Figure 2.10). Under low

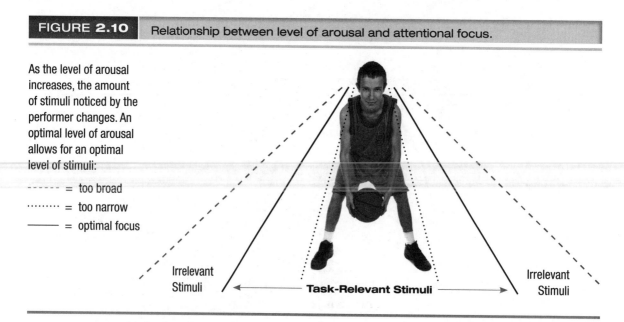

FIGURE **2.10** | Relationship between level of arousal and attentional focus.

As the level of arousal increases, the amount of stimuli noticed by the performer changes. An optimal level of arousal allows for an optimal level of stimuli:

- - - - - = too broad
·········· = too narrow
———— = optimal focus

Irrelevant Stimuli ← **Task-Relevant Stimuli** → Irrelevant Stimuli

arousal conditions, a performer's attentional focus is relatively broad. If attentional focus becomes too broad, both task-relevant and irrelevant cues become available to the performer. Because of our limited attentional capacity, as we saw earlier, a competition for attentional resources will occur, resulting in response delays and a corresponding decrement in performance. In other words, performers are more likely to become distracted by irrelevant environmental cues such as a taunting fan, the actions of players on the sideline, or even the appearance of the playing facility, and the consequence will be failure to attend to relevant performance information, such as a shift in the opponent's defensive formation (Wrisberg, 2007).

As arousal approaches optimal levels, attentional focus narrows, enabling the performer to concentrate on task-relevant cues while ignoring irrelevant ones. These are the conditions necessary for maximum performance, and here the individual is considered to be in the **zone of optimal functioning** (Hanin, 1980), the range of arousal levels that leads to optimal functioning. As arousal continues to increase, **perceptual narrowing**—the narrowing of attentional focus with increasing levels of arousal—continues, and at some point attentional focus becomes so narrow that the performer may no longer be capable of effectively scanning the environment, so that potentially significant stimuli are left undetected. This phenomenon is frequently seen in the opening minutes of a major championship. Often players become overaroused, and their attentional focus becomes so narrow that they are not able to detect the cues needed for appropriate decision-making. Fans are often baffled by how a quarterback, for example, fails to spot a wide-open receiver.

Perceptual narrowing has greater implications than simply missing a scoring opportunity. For lifeguards, medical personnel, firefighters, police officers, air traffic controllers, and military personnel, learning to control arousal levels is paramount.

C  E  R  E  B  R  A  L  **challenge**  2.13

1. The focus of a performer whose arousal levels are too low may become too broad. As a result, he will direct some attention to irrelevant stimuli. One example of such irrelevant stimuli is a heckler in the crowd. From your own experience, list other examples of irrelevant stimuli that might draw the attention of an individual with low arousal and affect overall performance.

2. An emergency-room physician who is overly excited may experience perceptual narrowing to the degree that she becomes susceptible to making poor decisions. List other professions or situations that may lend themselves to perceptual narrowing and resultant poor decision making. Fully explain your answer, using specific examples.

C  E  R  E  B  R  A  L  **challenge**  2.14

Are team pep talks before a game beneficial for performance? Fully explain your answer.

## *Tips for practitioners*

Numerous techniques are available to assist students, athletes, clients, and patients in managing their arousal levels. Strategies to increase arousal include increasing the rhythm and rate of breathing, listening to upbeat music prior to play, and increasing physical activity. Practice and rehabilitation sessions should be designed to include a wide variety of activities to keep learners motivated (Martens, 2004).

To decrease arousal, encourage slow and controlled breathing, progressive muscular relaxation (which involves alternately contracting and relaxing various muscle groups), positive self-talk (where negative thoughts are replaced with constructive ones), visualization, and focusing on performance rather than outcome. For a more comprehensive review, see Weinberg and Gould (2007).

## ▶ a look ahead

In this chapter, we have examined many variables that influence the time it takes to gather information and make a decision before a movement can be organized and an overt response can be made. The following chapter will add to your knowledge of movement production. It discusses theoretical information regarding how responses are organized, executed, and controlled once the decision has been made as to how to respond.

# focus points

After reading this chapter, you should know . . .

- The process by which meaning is attached to sensory information is known as perception.

- Two prevailing theoretical approaches to perception are: the direct approach, where the environment and task are perceived in terms of affordances, and the indirect approach, which is generally associated with information processing.

- A time lag occurs between the moment when a stimulus is presented and when a response is initiated. This interval of time is known as reaction time and is indicative of the time needed to prepare a response before it can be executed.

- Reaction time is not constant; it depends on the processing demands imposed by a given situation.

- Numerous variables influence the time needed to prepare a response, including the number of response choices available, temporal and/or event anticipation, the psychological refractory period, stimulus–response compatibility, and amount of practice.

- There is a limit to how many things an individual can pay attention to or process at any given time. When that limit is exceeded, those items compete for attentional resources and interfere with one another, and performance declines.

- Selective attention is the ability to attend to or focus on specific aspects of the environment while ignoring others.

- Successful performance is often contingent on whether the learner can employ the appropriate attentional focus (attend to relevant information while ignoring what is irrelevant) for the situation. The performers must also be able to shift that focus according to the changing demands of the task, to avoid response delays.

- An optimal level of arousal exists for each performer. When that level is too low, attentional focus is too broad, and the learner attends to both relevant and irrelevant cues. When arousal is too high, the learner may no longer be capable of effectively scanning the environment due to perceptual narrowing, which may cause him to miss potentially significant cues.

# review questions

1. Compare and contrast direct and indirect perception.
2. What are affordances?

3. What is the relationship between reaction time and movement preparation?

4. Give an example of a situation where your goal would be to reduce response delays.

5. In WWII, pilots were given a deck of cards, with a different picture of an enemy aircraft on each card. What might have been the purpose of these cards? Support your answer.

6. According to an ABC News report (June 18, 2000), there is a 400 percent greater chance of being involved in an accident when talking on a cell phone while driving. In addition, the report stated that 87 percent of the drivers who use computer maps (global positioning maps) while driving veer out of their lane while watching the map. Discuss these data with respect to attention. Provide suggestions for reducing these statistics.

7. Explain the cost–benefit trade-off associated with anticipation.

8. You are driving along a road when a deer-crossing sign catches your eye. When you look back to the road, you notice the illuminated brake lights of the vehicle in front of you. A car is approaching in the opposite lane, and there is a ditch on your right.

   a. What objects in this scenario served as warning signals?

   b. List the relevant and irrelevant stimuli that might be available in this situation.

   c. How is Hick's Law a factor in this situation?

   d. Identify an example of stimulus–response compatibility in this situation.

   e. The car in front of you swerves to the right. As you begin your response, it suddenly changes direction back to the left. What impact will this sudden change in direction have on your performance? Fully explain your answer.

   f. What attentional style(s) are necessary to avoid a collision?

   g. Discuss how arousal may be a factor in this situation.

   h. Explain the 2-second safe following distance driving rule, based on what you have learned in this chapter.

*[handwritten margin notes: Diagram info processing; Diagram exmb of RT; Hick's Law]*

## R E F E R E N C E S

Brebner, J.T. & Welford, A.T. (1980). Introduction: an historical background sketch. In A.T. Welford (Ed.), *Reaction times* (pp. 1–23). New York: Academic Press.

Broadbent, D.E. (1958). *Perception and communication*. London: Pergamon Press.

Burton, A.W. (1987). Confronting the interaction between perception and movement in adapted physical education. *Adapted Physical Education Quarterly, 4*, 257–67.

Cherry, E.C. (1953). Some experiments on the recognition of speech, with one and two ears. *Journal of the Acoustical Society of America, 25*, 975–79.

Deutsch, J.A. & Deutsch, D. (1963). Attention: some theoretical considerations. *Psychological Review, 70*, 80–90.

Easterbrook, J.A. (1959). The effect of emotion on cue utilization and the organization of behavior. *Psychological Review, 66*, 183–201.

Gibson, J.J. (1977). The theory of affordances. In R. Shaw & J. Bransford (Eds.), *Perceiving, acting and knowing: toward an ecological psychology*. Hillsdale, NJ: Erlbaum.

Gibson, J.J. (1979). *The ecological approach to visual perception*. Boston: Houghton Mifflin.

Gould, D. & Krane, V. (1992). The arousal-performance relationship: current status and future directions. In T.S. Horn (Ed.), *Advances in sport psychology* (pp. 119–42). Champaign, Il: Human Kinetics.

Hanin, Y.L. (1980). A study of anxiety in sports. In W.F. Straub (Ed.), *Sport psychology: An analysis of athlete behavior* (pp. 236–49). Ithaca, NY: Mouvement.

Hick, W.E. (1952). On the rate of gain of information. *Quarterly Journal of Experimental Psychology, 4*, 11–26.

Kahneman, D. (1973). *Attention and effort*. Englewood Cliffs, NJ: Prentice-Hall.

Larish, D.D. & Stelmach, G.E. (1982). Preprogramming, programming and reprogramming of aimed hand movements as a function of age. *Journal of Motor Behavior, 14*, 322–40.

Martens, R. (2004). *Successful coaching*. Champaign, IL: Human Kinetics.

Nideffer, R.M. (1993). Attention control training. In R.N. Singer, M. Murphy, and L.K. Tennant (Eds.), *Handbook of research on sport psychology* (pp. 542–56). New York: MacMillan.

Nideffer, R.M. & Sagal, M.S. (2001). Concentration and attention control training. In J.M. Williams (Ed.), *Applied sport psychology: personal growth to peak performance* (pp. 312–32). Mountain View, CA: Mayfield Publishing.

Norman, D.A. (1968). Toward a theory of memory and attention. *Psychological Review, 75*, 522–36.

O'Sullivan, S. (1988). Clinical decision making: planning effective treatments. In S. O'Sullivan & T. Schmitz (Eds.), *Physical rehabilitation: assessment and treatment*. Philadelphia: FA Davis.

Oudejans, R.D., Michaels, C.F., Bakker, F.C. & Dolné, M.A. (1996). The relevance of action in perceiving affordances: perception of catchableness of fly balls. *Journal of Experimental Psychology: Human Perception and Performance. 22*(4), 879–91.

Queseda, D.C. & Schmidt, R.A. (1970). A test of Adam-Creamer decay hypothesis for the timing of motor responses. *Journal of Motor Behavior, 2*, 273–83.

Roberts, G.C., Spink, K.S. & Pemberton, C.L. (1999). *Learning experiences in sport psychology: a practical guide to help students understand important concepts in sport psychology*. Champaign, IL: Human Kinetics.

Shea, C.H., Shebilske, W.L. & Worchel, S. (1993). *Motor learning and control*. Englewood Cliffs, NJ: Prentice-Hall.

Sibley, B.A. & Etnier, J. (2004). Time course of attention and decision making during a volleyball set. *Research Quarterly for Exercise and Sport, 75*, 102–106.

Strayer, D.L., Drews, F.A. & Crouch, D.J. (2006). A comparison of the cell phone driver and the drunk driver. *Human Factors, 48*, 381–91.

Summers, J.J. (1988). Has ecological psychology delivered what it promised? In J.P. Piek (Ed.), *Motor behavior and human skill: a multidisciplinary approach* (pp. 385–402). Champaign, IL: Human Kinetics.

Weinberg, R.S. & Gould, D. (2007). *Foundations of sport and exercise psychology*. Champaign, IL: Human Kinetics.

Welford, A.T. (1952). The psychological refractory period and the timing of high-speed performance: a review and a theory. *British Journal of Psychology, 43*, 2–19.

Wickens, C.D. (1984). Processing resources in attention. In R. Parasuraman & D.R. Davies (Eds.), *Varieties of attention* (pp. 63–102). New York: Academic Press.

Wilson, V.E., Peper, E. & Schmid, A. (2001). Strategies for training concentration. In J. Williams (Ed.), *Applied sport psychology* (5th ed., pp. 404–22). New York: McGraw-Hill.

Wrisberg, C.A. (2007). *Sport skill instruction for coaches*. Champaign, IL: Human Kinetics.

Yerkes, R.M. & Dodson, J.D. (1908). The relation of strength of stimulus to rapidity of habit-formation. *Journal of Comparative Neurology and Psychology, 18*, 459–82.

Ziegler, S.G. (2002). Attentional training: our best kept secret. *Journal of Physical Education, Recreation and Dance, 73*, 26–30.

# 3

## Behavioral Theories
## of Motor Control

**W**e watch in awe as elite athletes perform incredible feats: the pole-vaulter who becomes one with the pole while being projected into the sky, the trapeze artist who completes a flip and is caught at just the right moment, and the swimmer with an above-the-knee amputation completing the race in record time. We look with equal wonder at the Parkinson's patient who has difficulty raising a glass to take a drink, or the car accident victim who must relearn how to walk. Indeed, the human body and its ability to perform both simple and complex movements is truly fascinating. How the nervous system organizes the muscles to perform skilled movements is a complex puzzle that continues to challenge movement scientists.

In this chapter, we will examine theories of the organization and execution of skilled movements. Understanding theory is important for practitioners, as it is the foundation on which all instructional decisions should be made. After all, how can we design and implement effective instruction if we don't understand how people learn?

## COORDINATION AND CONTROL

**T**he human body has numerous joints, each of which is capable of moving in various directions. Hence, due to its anatomical structure, the human body has numerous independent elements or **degrees of freedom** that afford abundant action possibilities. To produce a specific, coordinated movement, all of these independent elements must be controlled.

To illustrate this concept, highlight the word "coordination" in the heading above. To accomplish this task, you must somehow manipulate your highlighter and produce a limb movement that corresponds with the dimensions and location of the word on the page. The process of organizing a system's available degrees of freedom (in this case the arm and highlighter) into an efficient movement pattern to achieve a specific goal effectively is known as **coordination** (Sparrow, 1992; Turvey, 1990). But this alone does not solve the movement problem.

**www.**
**Robot Development**
*http://world.honda.com/HDTV/ASIMO/*

What if you were asked instead to highlight only the first five letters, or what if your highlighter was running low on ink? Variables within the movement pattern, such as how hard to push, where to start and finish, and how fast to complete the movement, must also be resolved to achieve the goal of the task. The manipulation of variables within a movement to meet the demands of a given situation is known as **control**. The performance of skilled movement, therefore, requires the learner not only to coordinate the available degrees of freedom but also to control the resulting movement. How we coordinate and control the available degrees of freedom to produce a particular movement is known as the **degrees of freedom problem** (Bernstein, 1967)—a problem that has plagued not only human movement scientists but also robotic engineers, whose work in humanoid development is limited by the gaps in our understanding of human movement. Check out ASIMO, Honda's latest advancement in humanoid technology, to see how closely a humanoid can replicate purposeful human movement.

# SKILLED MOVEMENT: COMMAND CENTER OR DYNAMIC INTERACTION?

**C**urrently, two predominant theoretical approaches offer explanations of how skilled movement is coordinated and controlled. Motor program theories suggest the existence of a command center in the brain that is thought to make all decisions regarding the movement. When a decision to act is made, an appropriate movement plan is retrieved from memory, and instructions are sent to the rest of the body to carry out the action. Dynamic interaction theories, on the other hand, contend that a plan created by a command center couldn't possibly account for all variations and adjustments in skilled movement, and that the load on memory would be too great. Instead, skilled movement results or "emerges" from a dynamic interaction of numerous variables in the body, the environment, and the skill.

# MOTOR PROGRAM THEORIES

**T**he mechanism at the core of the command center–based construct is the **motor program**. A motor program is an abstract representation of a movement plan, stored in memory, that contains all of the motor commands required to carry out the intended action.

## Early Theories

Early motor program theories proposed that, for each movement to be made, a separate motor program existed and was stored in memory. When a specific action was required, the appropriate program was simply retrieved from memory and executed. However, as the idea of motor programs was examined more closely, two inherent problems were found. The first involved storage. If a motor program existed for each and every possible movement and movement variation, there would have to be limitless storage space in memory. The second problem lies in the production of novel responses. If a movement or variation of a movement has never been performed before, where does the program for that specific action come from?

## Generalized Motor Program

Unlike the authors of earlier motor program theories, Schmidt (1975) proposed that every movement does not require a separate motor program for its execution and that the motor program is more general in nature. This **generalized**

**motor program** represents a class of actions or pattern of movement that can be modified to yield various response outcomes. Some elements of the generalized motor program (called **invariant features**) are thought to be relatively fixed from trial to trial, defining the motor program itself, while others (called **parameters**) are more flexible and define the program's execution (Schmidt, 1985). See if you can identify some of these features in Exploration Activity 3.1.

### Invariant features

Regardless of how you were instructed to write your name in Exploration Activity 3.1, some underlying features of your signature remained constant. These underlying features, or invariant features, are similar to fingerprints. Just as our fingerprints can identify each of us, each motor program can be identified by its invariant features. To date, researchers have identified three possible invariant features: the sequence of actions or components, relative timing, and relative force.

**Sequence of actions.** In Exploration Activity 3.1, regardless of the directions given, you spelled your name the same way each time. For example, if your name is Kim, the "i" always follows the "K" and precedes the "m." Any disruption of

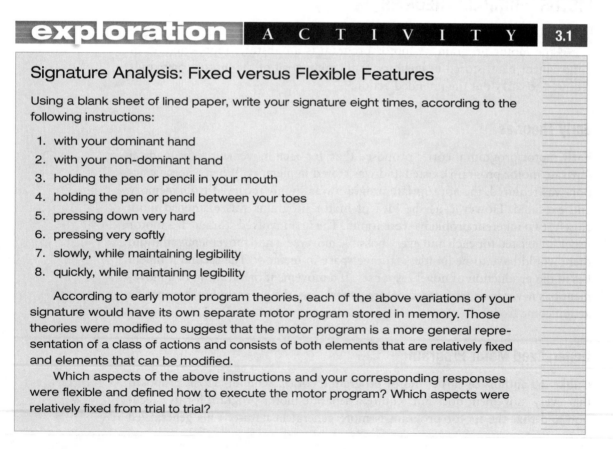

## exploration   A C T I V I T Y   3.1

### Signature Analysis: Fixed versus Flexible Features

Using a blank sheet of lined paper, write your signature eight times, according to the following instructions:

1.  with your dominant hand
2.  with your non-dominant hand
3.  holding the pen or pencil in your mouth
4.  holding the pen or pencil between your toes
5.  pressing down very hard
6.  pressing very softly
7.  slowly, while maintaining legibility
8.  quickly, while maintaining legibility

According to early motor program theories, each of the above variations of your signature would have its own separate motor program stored in memory. Those theories were modified to suggest that the motor program is a more general representation of a class of actions and consists of both elements that are relatively fixed and elements that can be modified.

Which aspects of the above instructions and your corresponding responses were flexible and defined how to execute the motor program? Which aspects were relatively fixed from trial to trial?

that specific order would result in both an error in your signature and the creation of a different name. Similarly, in a volleyball spike, regardless of where the ball has been set, the approach, the jump, the arm swing, and ball contact must be sequentially executed. The sequence of actions, or the order of components, is an invariant characteristic.

**Relative timing.** Relative timing has been suggested as another invariant feature of the generalized motor program, with supporting evidence offered from a variety of activities, including walking (Shapiro, Zernicke, Gregor & Diestal, 1981), throwing (Roth, 1988), hurdling (Hay & Schoebel, 1990), and gait initiation (Brunt et al., 1991). In essence, relative timing refers to the internal rhythm of the skill. The arm movement in the freestyle stroke, for example, can be broken down into five components. Of the total time needed to complete one cycle, let's say that 35 percent is accounted for by the entry, 13 percent by the catch, 8 percent by the mid-pull, 12 percent by the finish, and 32 percent by the recovery. Because relative timing is considered invariant, these percentages will remain the same regardless of whether the athlete is swimming fast or slowly. See Figure 3.1 for an illustration.

**Relative force.** A relationship has also been proposed with respect to ratios of force. When the overall force used to execute a movement changes, as would occur when a patient performed a leg lift with different amounts of weight, the actual force characteristic of each component should change proportionately. In other words, the tension created in each muscle throughout the movement

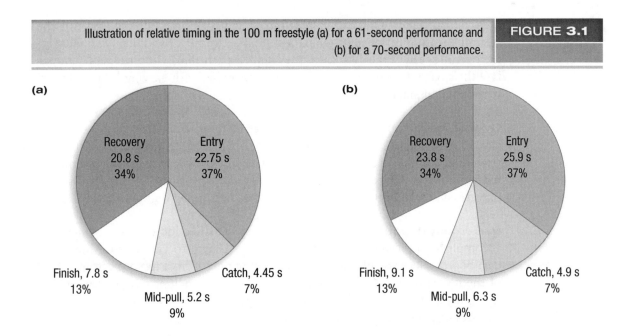

Illustration of relative timing in the 100 m freestyle (a) for a 61-second performance and (b) for a 70-second performance.

FIGURE **3.1**

(a)

Recovery
20.8 s
34%

Entry
22.75 s
37%

Finish, 7.8 s
13%

Mid-pull, 5.2 s
9%

Catch, 4.45 s
7%

(b)

Recovery
23.8 s
34%

Entry
25.9 s
37%

Finish, 9.1 s
13%

Mid-pull, 6.3 s
9%

Catch, 4.9 s
7%

R E S E A R C H        N O T E S

Shapiro, Zernicke, Gregor, and Diestal (1981) tested the notion of relative timing by having subjects walk on a treadmill at different speeds. Hypothetically, the relative timing of the components of the walking cycle should not change as the overall speed of the treadmill increases. The results showed that for speeds up to 6 km/hr, the relative timing of the step cycle components did indeed remain intact. However, as the speed increased to 8 km/hr and beyond, the relative timing changed. Since members of a class of actions share similar characteristics in relative timing, we can infer that above 8 km/hr, a different motor program is controlling the action. The shift in relative timing characteristics corresponded to the participants' shift from walking to running.

should remain proportionate. This concept is known as **relative force** and has received some attention as an invariant feature.

### Parameters

The features of a motor program that are flexible and define how to execute the program are termed parameters. Parameters are easily modified from one performance to another to produce variations of a motor response without altering the fundamental movement pattern. This "adaptability" of parameters enables a center fielder to throw to third base from different areas of the field and allows an individual to walk up and down steps of varying heights. Four parameters have been proposed: overall duration, overall force, movement direction, and muscle selection (Schmidt, 1985; Schmidt & Wrisberg, 2008).

**Overall duration.** One aspect of a movement that can be easily varied is the overall duration or speed at which a skill is performed. Swimmers can increase the overall speed of their stroke as they approach the finish line, runners manipulate their pace during a race, and hitters can swing with varying bat speeds, all without changing the underlying pattern of the movement.

**Overall force.** Similarly, the overall force or amplitude (size) of a movement can be modified. Patients can learn to lift off plastic container lids of various sizes (e.g., the lid on a margarine container and the lid on a yogurt container), individuals can perform sit-to-stand motions from varying heights, and soccer players can make both long and short passes, depending on the situation.

**Movement direction.** Variations in movement direction can also be made to accomplish a movement goal. A dart can be thrown to various locations on a dart board, a lacrosse player can propel a shot on goal to a top or bottom corner of the net, and a shopper can reach for a can on a shelf at a supermarket that is slightly to the right or left of his position, all without altering the invariant features of the motor program (Schmidt & Wrisberg, 2008).

**Muscle selection.** Different limbs or muscles may be used to perform movements. This was demonstrated in Exploration Activity 3.1, where you used your hand, foot, and mouth to write your name. Additionally, many bilateral skills exist—skills in which the performer may execute the task with either the dominant or the non-dominant side. Examples include dribbling in basketball and soccer, movement patterns in dance, and manipulating buttons and zippers. In each instance, the underlying movement pattern remains intact.

## Schema

According to the generalized motor program theory, a shortstop is able to throw to different bases from various positions on the field by assigning appropriate parameter values, such as throwing speed, to the program. How does the performer know exactly how fast the ball should be thrown in each situation? The answer lies in another aspect of Schmidt's theory (1975, 1985), the development of a schema.

Basically, a **schema** is or a rule or relationship that directs decision-making when a learner is faced with a movement problem. It develops as the result of accumulated experiences within a class of actions. Each movement attempt provides the learner with information about the movement, which is translated into a relationship that will be used to guide future attempts. The more movements a performer has executed, the more developed the rule will become.

A swimmer can increase overall stroke speed without changing the invariant features of the motor program.

Let's say you go to the fair and come across a ball toss game whose prize is a stuffed animal. The objective of the game is to toss a softball into a peach basket in such a way that it does not bounce out. Feeling confident that you can accom-

C E R E B R A L  **challenge**  **3.2**

1. The use of over-weight implements is a common training method for conditioning in many sports. Throwers use heavier shots, discuses, and javelins than are normally used in competition; pitchers throw heavier baseballs; and hitters swing heavier-than-normal bats. Does this technique involve a manipulation of invariant features or parameters? Can you think of a situation or condition where the use of over-weight implements could hinder the development of correct technique? What signs might a practitioner look for to avoid this problem?

2. Another training technique is to practice when the athlete is fatigued. Based on your understanding of invariant features and parameters, is this a good idea? Why or why not?

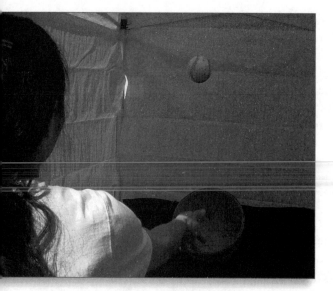

With practice and subconscious abstraction of information regarding the initial conditions, the response specifications, the sensory consequences, and the response outcome on each attempt, you develop a schema for the skill.

plish this goal, you purchase three chances. Having assessed some of the previous players, you decide that the best approach will be an underhand toss. On your first toss, the ball ricochets off the bottom of the basket. On your second attempt, you decide to lean over the barrier and adjust the toss, decreasing the height of the arch and aiming more toward the front of the basket. Again, the ball bounces out of the basket, but this time with less force. On your final attempt, you lean over the barrier as far as possible and throw the same low arched toss, but with a little less force. Unfortunately, the ball bounces out of the basket again, just barely.

According to the schema concept, on each attempt you subconsciously abstract four pieces of information:

1. *Initial conditions* are the conditions that are present at the start of the movement, including limb and body position and the environmental conditions when the movement was begun. Leaning over the barrier as far as possible is an example of initial condition information.

2. *Response specifications* are the parameter values used in the execution of the movement, such as the speed and force of your throw.

3. *Sensory consequences* include the response-produced sensory information or sensory feedback of the movement. What the throw felt like is an example.

4. *Response outcome* is the success of the response obtained, in relation to the originally intended goal or outcome. Although none of the three attempts stayed in the basket, the response outcome for each of the three tosses was different. In the first attempt, the ball ricocheted out of the basket, suggesting that it had a great deal of force. In subsequent attempts, the magnitude of that force was reduced, indicating that the movement was approaching that which was necessary to achieve the goal.

These four sources of information are briefly stored in memory after a movement attempt, allowing the performer to abstract some relationship among them. For example, in the first ball toss, the initial conditions (e.g., starting position), the response specifications (whatever parameter values were assigned to the program), the sensory consequences (what the performer's sensory system perceived), and the response outcome (the ball ricocheting out of the basket)—

and their relationship with one another—are all assessed, leading to an inference about how to perform the task successfully. The schema has begun to develop. Not only does this process occur for each additional attempt, but the resulting relationship from each attempt becomes incorporated with the relationship already developed in the existing schema. Hence, the strength of the overall relationship increases with practice. The result is the development of the motor response schema, which is thought to be composed of two relationships, the recall schema and the recognition schema (Schmidt, 1985).

**Recall schema.** The recall schema is responsible for organizing the motor program that initiates and controls the desired movement. When an individual attempts to perform a movement, she considers the desired outcome for that movement and the initial conditions. A recall schema is then subconsciously selected, based on the relationship between actual outcomes and response specifications that has been developed through experiences with similar movements. From this relationship, the performer determines the specifications that will be required to achieve the intended outcome. She then executes the motor program according to these movement parameter values.

**Recognition schema.** The recognition schema is responsible for the evaluation of a movement attempt. It is formulated based on the relationship between the initial conditions, past actual outcomes, and past sensory consequences. A set of expected sensory consequences that represent the best estimate of the sensory consequences of the correct movement is generated, based on the relationship between actual outcomes and sensory consequences. By comparing the actual sensory feedback from the initiated movement with the expected sensory feedback, the performer assesses the correctness of the movement. When a mismatch occurs between feedback and the reference of correctness, an error signal is generated. Error signals provide the performer with information that is used to update the recall schema. Additional information provided by the teacher or coach also serves to update the recall schema.

By continually revising its estimates of the expected sensory consequences and response specifications, the recall schema updates the instructions to the muscles, which leads to more accurate responses on subsequent attempts. Through this process, the schema becomes more established, and the performer can more accurately select appropriate response specifications or parameter values to accomplish a movement goal.

### Executing the motor program

Once a learner decides what movement to execute in a given situation, he subconsciously retrieves the appropriate generalized motor program from memory, based on the existing schema, and adds to it the estimated parameter values that will achieve the desired outcome. The details of the desired movement are, there-

A hockey coach uses the following teaching strategy. Having taught the slapshot and given the athletes an opportunity to develop a basic understanding of the movement, Coach X gives her players these instructions:

"Using the slapshot technique that we have been learning, perform the actions listed below from each of these four locations:

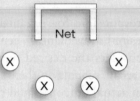

First, shoot the puck so that it misses the net to the right.

Second, shoot the puck so that it misses the net to the left.

Third, shoot the puck so that it goes in the net."

Will this experience help or hinder the athletes' technique development for the slapshot? Why or why not? Use the schema theory to support your answers.

fore, organized in advance by the motor program and sent to the rest of the body to be carried out. How is the movement controlled once the motor program initiates it? Does the motor program contain all of the information needed to carry out the action from start to finish, or are continuous adjustments made to the movement based on response-produced feedback? The answer to this question lies in the details of the initial movement commands.

Before you can start your workout on a stair-climbing fitness machine, you have to select from a number of program options, such as the hill profile or interval training. Once you select the desired program, that program will be executed for the amount of time you specify. It cannot sense whether you don't like the program you have selected or whether the program is too easy or too difficult for you. It simply runs its course. E-mail operates in a similar fashion. Once the message leaves your "out" box, it is automatically sent. You cannot change it; it will be sent exactly as it was when it left the out box. These two examples illustrate the notion of *open-loop control*.

**Open-loop control** mechanisms function through a two-level hierarchy, as seen in Figure 3.2. An executive level or command center generates action plans that contain all of the information necessary to complete a response. These action plans are carried out at the second level—the effector level—by the limbs and muscles (the effectors) without modification. Applying this to human movement, input is perceived via processes in the brain. A decision as to how to respond is made, instructions to execute that response are sent to the muscles via the nervous system, and the response is performed. Feedback is constantly present during movement, but it comes too late to adjust the ongoing movement. Once the pre-structured commands are initiated (sent to the nervous system), the action has to run as planned. The feedback received regarding this trial can be used to modify the next trial.

A second kind of control mechanism allows adjustments to be made after a program has been initiated. This is known as **closed-loop control.** A thermostat that regulates room temperature is a good example of a closed-loop system. The heating system, once set, continuously monitors the actual room temperature and compares it to the desired temperature. If a discrepancy is detected (the room becomes too hot or too cold), the system makes the corresponding adjustments automatically by turning the heater on or off.

Like open-loop systems, closed-loop systems function in a hierarchical fashion, with one important distinction—they involve feedback. Instead of having to generate all of the information needed to complete the response, the command center must only generate an action plan that initiates the movement. Sensory information resulting from the movement's progress (response-produced feedback) is then continually compared to the desired movement, and any discrepancies detected are sent to the command center for correction. This cycle continues until the response is completed. The distinction between open- and closed-loop systems, then, is that the feedback that accompanies a movement can be used to modify an ongoing action in a closed-loop system, but it cannot be used until the next response in an open-loop system.

(a) An open-loop control system model and (b) a closed-loop control system model.    FIGURE **3.2**

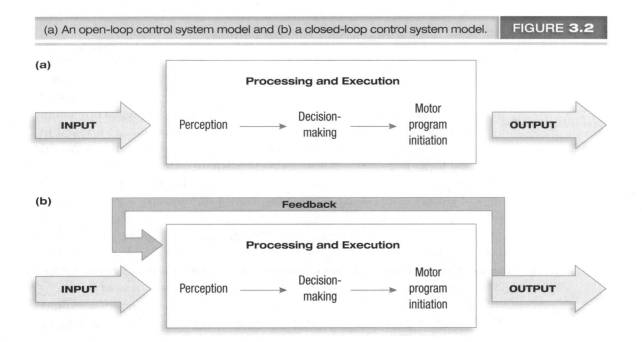

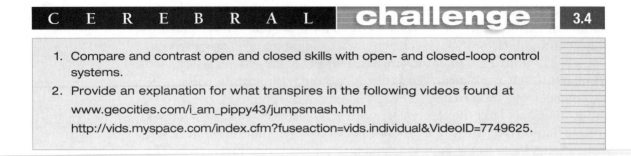

C  E  R  E  B  R  A  L    **challenge**    3.4

1. Compare and contrast open and closed skills with open- and closed-loop control systems.

2. Provide an explanation for what transpires in the following videos found at
   www.geocities.com/i_am_pippy43/jumpsmash.html
   http://vids.myspace.com/index.cfm?fuseaction=vids.individual&VideoID=7749625.

Open- and closed-loop systems served as precursors to current motor program–based theory. Present-day theories consider motor control as a function of both open- and closed-loop mechanisms, with motor programs operating in an open-loop fashion. Basically, skilled movements are believed to be planned in advance, initiated, and carried out with limited modification, unless time permits the incorporation of response-produced feedback. Consequently, in rapid movements, the pre-structured motor program will control the movement from start to finish, as there is insufficient time to process response-produced feedback and make the corresponding adjustments. For movements where there is sufficient time to process feedback, the initiation of the skill is controlled by open-loop mechanisms, but closed-loop control is used to continue the movement to its completion. It should be noted that initial skill acquisition is governed predominantly by closed-loop control. As skill proficiency increases, a shift occurs to more automatic open-loop control processes characteristic of skilled performance.

## Evidence Supporting Motor Program Control

Three lines of evidence support the notion of motor program control. First, if the motor program organizes the details of the desired movement in advance, it seems logical that as a task increases in complexity, the amount of time needed to organize the motor program must also increase. Henry and Rogers (1960) tested this notion by measuring the reaction time of subjects performing three tasks that varied in complexity. The tasks, moving from lowest level of complexity to highest, were: (a) lifting the finger from a switch being pressed down, (b) lifting the finger from the switch and then reaching and grasping a tennis ball that hung 30 cm away, and (c) lifting the finger from the key, striking the tennis ball, reversing direction to push a button, and finishing by reversing direction again to grasp another tennis ball. Results showed that as the complexity of the movement increased, reaction time increased (165 msec, 199 msec, and 212 msec, respectively). Since reaction time measures the time from the onset of a stimulus to the initiation of a response (Chapter 2), these findings support the idea that movements are planned in advance.

A second experimental approach used to test the notion of motor programs involved deafferentation. Deafferentation is a technique where the sensory nerves of a limb, for example, are surgically severed so that response-produced feedback cannot reach the central nervous system. Early studies of this type examined the motor behaviors of monkeys before and after deafferentation (Polit & Bizzi, 1978; Taub & Berman, 1968). In the Polit and Bizzi study, three monkeys were trained in a pointing task prior to undergoing deafferentation of the arm. After deafferentation, they were retested on the same pointing task. Results revealed that after deafferentation and the loss of sensory feedback from the limb, the monkeys were still able to move their arm and point to the target accurately, further supporting the notion of motor program control.

Experiments exploring the effects of a limb being unexpectedly blocked during movement are the basis of the third line of research supporting motor program control. Using electromyography (EMG), researchers compared the electrical activity in muscles during limb movements to the electrical activity in those same muscles when the limb movements were suddenly and unexpectedly blocked (Wadman, Dernier van der Gon, Geuze & Mol, 1979). Researchers inferred that if a motor program does indeed organize all of the instructions for carrying out a movement prior to the movement's initiation, without regard for feedback, then the EMG of the blocked muscle should temporarily display a similar pattern to that of the muscle that was not blocked. Comparisons of the two limb movement conditions (unblocked and blocked) revealed that this was in fact the case.

Many baseball and softball players, much to their dismay, have probably experienced a real-world example of this concept. The change-up has left many accomplished hitters looking foolish at the plate. An effective change-up is designed to look like a regular-speed pitch but is manipulated just prior to release, so that the ball leaves the pitcher's hand much more slowly than the hitter is anticipating from the windup. In this situation, the hitter selects the motor program

C  E  R  E  B  R  A  L  **challenge**    3.5

A good illustration of the difficulty we have in stopping a planned movement was provided by Slater-Hammel (1960). Subjects were asked to lift their finger from a response key at the same instant that the sweep hand of a clock they were watching passed over the number 8. However, if the sweep hand stopped prior to reaching the 8, subjects were instructed to continue to press down on the response key. Results showed that when the sweep hand was stopped less than 140 msec before reaching the target, subjects had a difficult time not lifting their finger. In most cases, subjects could not stop the action of lifting their finger in trials where the sweep hand stopped 50 to 100 msec before reaching the 8.

Can you think of other real-life examples where you start a movement and then recognize that you shouldn't do the movement you started, but have difficulty stopping? Describe one example.

for the swing, assigning to it the parameter values that will successfully contact a regular-speed pitch. Once that program is organized and initiated, it will run its course even if the hitter recognizes that the pitcher has thrown a change-up. According to motor program–based theory, to change the tempo of the swing, the hitter must not only recognize that an error has been made in parameter selection but also has to re-organize and initiate the corrected program in order to meet the demands of the task. Because hitting is a rapid movement, there is often not enough time to do this, and the hitter swings prematurely.

## Summary of Generalized Motor Program Theory

Schmidt's "schema" theory (1975, 1985) is an open-loop theory of motor control that combines the basic idea of a schema (an abstract representation of rules governing movement) and the idea of a generalized motor program. The theory proposes that, for a given class of actions, such as the overhand throw, we abstract different pieces of information from every throwing experience we've ever had that involved an overhand pattern (Magill, 1993). We then construct schemas that will enable us to use the overhand throw in a number of situations and circumstances.

The schema theory proposes that movements are generalized and are run by complex rules that are revised with each movement experience. The stronger the rule (schema), the more skilled the performance. The task of the instructor, once the fundamental movement pattern has been achieved, is to provide the learner with appropriate activities designed to strengthen the schema.

C E R E B R A L  **challenge**  3.6

Answer the following questions according to Schmidt's schema theory:

1. You are coaching an athlete who has a major competition in three weeks. You have noticed a flaw in her performance. Should you correct the flaw? Why or why not? What questions must you ask to help you make your decision?

2. You are coaching an eighth-grade volleyball team and are receiving complaints about the soreness in the players' forearms from bumping the ball. To help the athletes, you decide to let them wear wristbands on their forearms in practice. Is this a good idea? Why or why not?

3. You are teaching a unit on basketball in middle school, specifically the free throw. Unfortunately, there are 28 students in your class and only four baskets in your gymnasium. In addition to the lack of baskets, there are only 10 functional basketballs. You remember reading an article in college that encouraged you to be creative and use substitute equipment to increase time on task. You come up with the idea to use playground balls in addition to the basketballs, and to tape targets on the wall at the height of a normal basket. Are these good ideas? Why or why not?

# DYNAMIC INTERACTION THEORIES

**P**roponents of dynamic interaction theories argue that motor program–based theories fall short in accounting for the control of complex movements. They contend that a plan created by a command center couldn't possibly account for all variations and adjustments in skilled movement. They further note that the fact that movements occur in response to a dynamic interaction of the person and the environment is not accounted for.

## Dynamic System Theory

The Dynamic System Theory (also termed the Dynamic Pattern Theory) suggests that, rather than functioning in a hierarchical manner, with a command center issuing instructions that are carried out by the limbs and muscles, movement patterns emerge or **self-organize** as a function of the interacting, ever-changing organismic (learner), environmental, and task constraints. In other words, the arrangement of a movement pattern will emerge from the dynamic interaction of the learner, the environment, and the task, rather than being generated by a motor program (see Figure 3.3).

### Constraints

The optimal pattern of any movement is determined by the interaction of internal constraints placed on the performer by the state of the body's subsystems and external constraints imposed by the movement that is to be executed and by the environment within which that movement will take place (Caldwell & Clark, 1990). **Constraints**

## exploration A C T I V I T Y 3.7

### Self-Organization

To demonstrate the concept of self-organization, perform the following activities over a 10 m distance and then observe another person performing the same activities.

  a. Walk at a normal pace wearing running shoes.
  b. Walk at a normal pace wearing the running shoes on the opposite feet.
  c. Walk at a normal pace wearing a pair of running shoes that are at least two sizes too large.
  d. Walk at a normal pace wearing a pair of running shoes that are at least two sizes too small.

1. Based on your experience and observations, discuss the concept of self-organization.
2. Speculate as to what changes you might see in someone's gait pattern when the person is (a) walking on ice, (b) walking on a sandy beach, and (c) walking across a log. Include the concept of self-organization in your response.

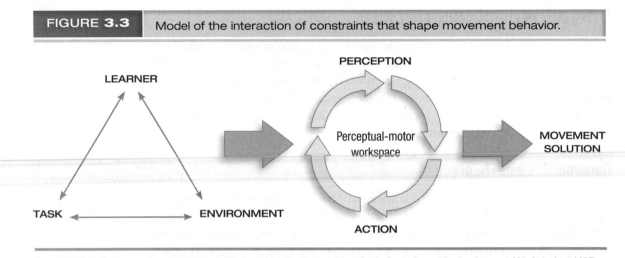

FIGURE **3.3**  Model of the interaction of constraints that shape movement behavior.

are, then, defined as the boundaries that have a bearing on the movement capabilities of an individual (Clark, 1995; Newell, 1986). Although the term seems to imply a limiting or negative factor, this is not always the case. Constraints should instead be thought of as all of the factors, both limiting and enabling, within the practice environment that influence skill acquisition and performance (Araújo et al., 2004).

**Organismic constraints.** Organismic constraints include a person's biological and functional characteristics (Newell, 1986). Examples include body attributes (shape, height, weight, and body composition), personality characteristics (e.g., high or low trait anxiety, motivation, confidence), fitness variables (e.g., flexibility, power, strength, speed, endurance, aerobic capacity, agility), and perceptual and decision-making skills (e.g., spatial and temporal anticipation capability). In Exploration Activity 3.8 you will explore organismic constraints.

**Environmental constraints.** Gravity, temperature, and natural light are examples of physical environmental constraints. In the javelin throw, for example, the wind is an important factor. The force and direction of the wind, therefore, place an environmental constraint on the performer, and failure to take them into account will negatively influence the throw.

Social environmental factors also serve as constraints. These include societal expectations, cultural norms, and the presence and characteristics of spectators, as well as family and peer networks (Haywood & Getchell, 2005). Exploration Activity 3.8 explores environmental constraints.

**Task constraints.** The task itself imposes constraints on motor skill acquisition and performance. Three categories of task constraints have been proposed (Newell, 1986):

# exploration | A C T I V I T Y | 3.8

## Organismic, Environmental, and Task Constraints

Perform the following activities to develop a greater understanding of the role of constraints.

### Organismic Constraints

Try to jump up and touch the ceiling. Were you able to do it? What organismic constraints enabled you to accomplish this task or prevented you from doing so?

Can you do the splits? What organismic constraints enable you to perform the splits or prevent you from doing so?

### Environmental Constraints

**EQUIPMENT NEEDED:**

2 pieces of paper                    A small fan

With the pieces of paper, make two identical paper air-planes. Mark a starting point on the ground to ensure the same starting position for each trial. Place the fan perpendicular to the direction of throw, on your throwing side, and approximately 3 meters in front of the starting line, as depicted at right.

Turn on the fan and throw your first plane straight ahead, so that it must pass through the stream of air created by the fan. Note the resulting flight path. Now, turn off the fan and throw your second plane using the same throwing motion you used to throw the first plane. Again, note the resulting flight path.

What influence did the airstream produced by the fan have on the flight path of the first airplane? The second? What adjustments would have to be made to get the plane to land directly in front of you when the fan is turned on?

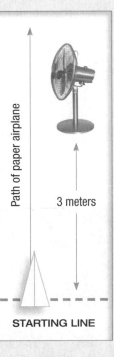

Path of paper airplane

3 meters

**STARTING LINE**

### Task Constraints

**EQUIPMENT NEEDED:**

1 tennis ball or baseball            1 partially deflated volleyball

1 basketball                          1 large playground ball

Large open field or area

Using a mature overhand throwing pattern, throw each ball as far as possible into the open area. If possible, have a friend videotape each attempt.

Compare and contrast the attempts. How did each ball influence the distance of the throw? Did you use the same techniques to throw each ball? What compensations did you make, and why? Did any organismic constraints influence the task?

1. *Goal.* All tasks are governed by goals that relate to the product or outcome of the action. For example, the goal of the long jump is to maximize horizontal displacement, and the goal of a tennis serve is to gain an advantage over one's opponent.

2. *Rules.* Sport skills typically have rules that dictate the specific coordination pattern that must be produced. For example, in collegiate fastpitch softball, the pitcher's feet must remain in contact with the pitching rubber throughout the initiation of the pitch (until her weight is transferred forward). This rule prevents the pitcher from taking a step backward prior to the pitch, which would allow the pitcher to generate added momentum and create an unfair advantage. If the pitcher breaks contact with the rubber at any time during the onset of the pitch, the base umpire will charge her with an illegal pitch. The performer must carry out the specific pattern of coordination for the movement to be called a legal pitch.

Other motor tasks do not have rules that specify a pattern of coordination, but the rules of the sporting event constrain the movement that can be performed to achieve a desired outcome. For example, in a volleyball serve, the ball must pass over the net with or without touching it, and it must land within the boundaries of the court. However, the performer may choose to serve underhand or overhand or use a jump serve.

In other cases, the optimal pattern of coordination for a given individual becomes the prominent issue (Newell, 1986). Since interactions of internal and external constraints determine the optimal movement coordination and control, individual differences must be considered—there is no "one size fits all" strategy. Because individuals often interpret the constraints differently, one individual may generate one type of response while another will produce a different movement for the same set of task constraints. Thus, two people may be placed in a situation with identical environmental and task constraints but produce entirely different movement patterns because of the internal constraints of the body.

Fitness equipment constrains movement possibilities.

3. *Implements or machines.* The third category of task constraints results from the interaction of the individual with an implement or a machine. Examples include stepping on a Stairmaster, walking on a treadmill, using crutches, skiing, kayaking, opening a can with a can opener, and performing core stability exercises on a therapeutic ball. The size, dynamics, and weight of sporting equipment relative to the body size of the individual constrains the optimal coordinated movement. For example, if a client sets the seat for a stationary bike too high, not only will this reduce the efficiency of the exercise, but also, over time, it could lead to an injury. Exploration Activity 3.8 will help you gain a better understanding of how an implement can affect the resulting movement pattern.

## RESEARCH NOTES

The Balanus Multi Chair (BMC) is designed with a forward-tilted seat and a padded rest for the lower legs, enabling the user to assume a semi-kneeling position. To examine the resulting postural control induced by this design, Shenoy and Aruin (2007) compared the electrical activity of muscles (using EMG) of the trunk and legs when subjects were seated on a standard stool (identified as REG) and the BMC. Nine participants were seated with arms extended toward a wooden horizontal piece mounted at shoulder level. A force sensor was attached to the palm of the hand. When an auditory tone was sounded, participants were to produce a brief pulse of force against the wooden piece with both hands, creating a self-initiated perturbation (body disturbance). Six force applications against the wooden frame were performed, in four directions: (a) horizontal forward push, (b) horizontal pull, (c) upward vertical push,

and (d) downward vertical push. EMG data were recorded before and during perturbations. Results indicated that sitting on both types of chairs was associated with utilizing anticipatory activation of postural muscles and that the magnitude of activation depended on the direction of the self-initiated perturbation. In addition, anticipatory activation of distal muscles was found for sitting in the REG chair but not for sitting in the BMC chair, suggesting that the body position induced by the BMC's design may not allow for effective activation of the lower leg muscles to preserve body stability. Shenoy and Aruin (2007) conclude that "these findings stress the important role of chair designs in the control of sitting posture" (p. 309).

*Question:* Relate the concept of constraints to the findings of this study.

## Constraints-Led Approach

The notion that interacting constraints shape movement behavior has led to the development of another theoretical framework for understanding and facilitating skill acquisition, the **constraints-led approach.** According to this view, the learner searches through a range of potential movement solutions for the optimal movement strategy that will satisfy the imposed constraints (Davids, Araújo & Shuttleworth, 2005; Davids, Button & Bennett, 2008; Newell, 1991).

**WWW.**

**Balanus Multi Chair**

www.officechairadvice.com/ergonomic/kneeling/reviews/balans-ergonomic-chair.html

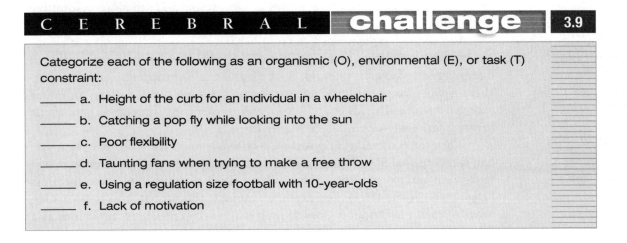

## CEREBRAL challenge 3.9

Categorize each of the following as an organismic (O), environmental (E), or task (T) constraint:

_____ a. Height of the curb for an individual in a wheelchair

_____ b. Catching a pop fly while looking into the sun

_____ c. Poor flexibility

_____ d. Taunting fans when trying to make a free throw

_____ e. Using a regulation size football with 10-year-olds

_____ f. Lack of motivation

### Perceptual-motor workspace

Critical to this search process is the exploration of what is known as the **perceptual-motor workspace** (Shumway-Cook & Woollacott, 2007). According to Davids (2006), "The perceptual-motor workspace represents the practice context for the learner" (p. 1004). When an individual explores perceptual information sources and the range of movement possibilities to discover task solutions unique to that individual, she is involved in exploring her perceptual-motor workspace.

Shumway-Cook and Woollacott (2007) offer an excellent illustration of this concept. A patient who is relearning how to reach for and lift a glass of milk must match relevant *perceptual cues,* such as the location of the glass in relation to the body, the size and texture of the glass, and how full the glass is, to the available *movement possibilities* to determine the optimal *movement solution* to accomplish the goal. This movement solution will differ according to the constraints imposed by the situation. For example, when the glass is perceived as full, the optimal movement solution will differ in speed and trajectory from the optimal solution were it half full.

### Movement pattern stability

According to the constraints-led approach, skill acquisition is the result of an ongoing search for and stabilization of specific, functional movement patterns. A **functional movement pattern** is one that will accomplish a specific task goal. Initially, through continued exploration of the perceptual-motor workspace, the individual arrives at an approximate task solution (Davids et al., 2008). As practice progresses, that movement pattern gains increasing stability, and less successful patterns are discarded because they are no longer as functional.

The state of a movement pattern's stability is called an **attractor.** Ennis (1992) suggested that attractors function much like basins or wells, the depth of which indicates the amount of stability of the system. As Figure 3.4 illustrates, deep attractor basins are characteristic of stable systems and are difficult to change. Conversely, shallow basins are less stable and are more susceptible to change.

As indicated earlier, constraints on behavior are ever-changing. For example, the perceptual cues that are selectively attended to depend on the learner's interpretation of what is relevant. As the learner gains experience, her attentional focus will change. Accordingly, movement solutions are not static but rather evolve over time (Davids et al., 2008), and movement variability is part of the learning process (Newell, Liu & Mayer-Kress, 2001).

When the constraints imposed on a system change, the stability of that system is endangered. If the magnitude of the change is high enough, the system will reorganize into a new form within the boundaries established by the constraints (Thelen & Ulrich, 1991). For example, initially, the patient who is relearning how to reach for and lift a glass of milk may have experienced difficulties as a

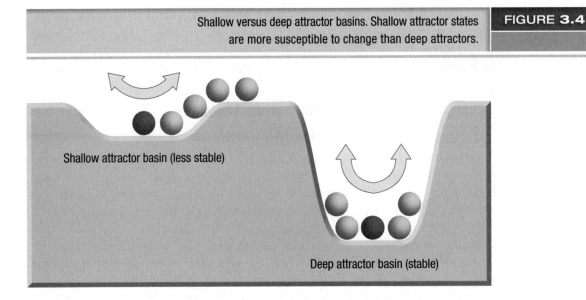

**FIGURE 3.4**

Shallow versus deep attractor basins. Shallow attractor states are more susceptible to change than deep attractors.

Shallow attractor basin (less stable)

Deep attractor basin (stable)

result of a strength deficiency. Through an appropriate rehabilitation program, his grip strength levels can be increased. With these increased strength levels (a change in constraints), there is a decrease in the stability of the current attractor state. The result is the self-organization of a new movement solution that accounts for the improved grasping capabilities of the individual.

### Hands-off practitioners

The constraints-led perspective views the learner as an active problem-solver. Accordingly, this approach emphasizes discovery learning (see Chapter 7) and advocates the concept of the *hands-off practitioner* (Davids et al., 2008; Handford, Davids, Bennett & Button, 1997). This concept redefines the role of the practitioner as a facilitator—rather than an information provider who, through verbal instructions, practice structure, and feedback, dictates the correct movement response. Specifically, the role of the practitioner as facilitator is one of identifying and manipulating key constraints to guide the learner's search for optimal movement solutions (Araújo et al., 2004; Davids, Araújo, Shuttleworth & Button, 2003).

Strategies for creating effective learning environments are limited only by the practitioner's imagination. Challenges can be developed that encourage learners to adapt movement behaviors to meet task requirements. Task constraints, including rules, equipment, playing area, and situational factors (e.g., relative positioning of players, the number of attackers and defenders) may be manipulated to facilitate learners' discovery of functional movement solutions. Questioning strategies may be used to guide learners in their search process. Teaching Games for Understanding, a pedagogical method utilized in physical education, reflects the constructs outlined under the constraints-led approach (see Griffin & Butler [2005] for a comprehensive review of this methodology). Finally, practitioners should emphasize game-related and context-related skills so that learners can explore potentially important sources of information to hone their decision-making capability and develop functional movement patterns.

## Evidence Supporting Dynamic System Theory and the Constraints-Led Approach

Kelso and Schöner (1988) demonstrated that spontaneous movement patterns could self-organize as a consequence of a change in a constraint. In their study, participants were asked to place their hands on a table, as illustrated in Figure 3.5a. They were then asked to move their index fingers, keeping in beat with a metronome, so that both fingers pointed to the left or right at the same time. This movement pattern was labeled as an anti-phase pattern, because the two fingers were actually performing opposite movements (one in adduction and the other in abduction), as illustrated in Figure 3.5b. As the speed of the metronome was gradually increased, a sudden phase shift occurred, and the fingers spontaneously began to perform the same movement pattern (in-phase pattern), illustrated in Figure 3.5c. Because a motor program should have been trying to keep the fingers moving out of phase, the motor program theory falls short in explaining the spontaneous shift to in-phase behavior. From a dynamic system perspective, the change in speed caused the system to self-organize, and a new behavior emerged.

More recently, Nakayama (2008) examined the effect of playing area size (a task constraint) on the passing skills of young soccer players. In the task, three attackers attempted to retain possession of the ball while one defender tried to take it away (3 v. 1). Play was conducted in three playing areas of different sizes:

---

**FIGURE 3.5**  Finger movement in Kelso and Schöner's (1988) experiment demonstrating spontaneous phase shifts: (a) starting position; (b) anti-phase finger movement; (c) in-phase finger movement.

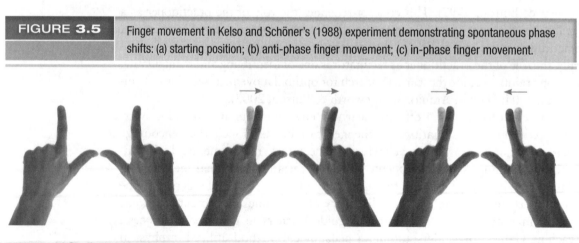

(a) Starting position          (b) Anti-phase          (c) In-phase

Following a stroke, patients often stop using their affected limb because they are discouraged by the initial difficulties and failures they experience. To encourage affected limb use, Dr. Edward Taub of the University of Alabama recently developed constraint-induced movement therapy (CIMT). This rehabilitative technique constrains the less impaired limb in an effort to increase the use of the limb affected by the stroke. In a study examining the effectiveness of this strategy, 226 stroke patients participated in a two-week program where they received either CIMT or usual and customary care. Under the CIMT protocol, they engaged in repetitive task practice (including training tasks such as opening a lock, turning a doorknob, or pouring a drink) with their affected hand while wearing a restraining mitt on the less affected hand (Wolf et al., 2006). The researchers found that those patients who received the CIMT showed significantly greater improvements in hand function that persisted for at least one year than those receiving customary care.

8 m × 8 m, 10 m × 10 m, and 12 m × 12 m. Results indicated clear differences in play as a result of play area size. The 12 m area permitted greater distance between the attacker and the defenders and yielded the highest percentage of pass success. The 10 m and 8 m areas had similar play aspects, but the 8 m area required speedier play. The author concluded that a wide area would reinforce player success, while a narrow area would reinforce skill development and enhance decision-making.

## Summary of Dynamic System Theory and the Constraints-Led Approach

The complexity of human behavior has led to the development of the dynamic system approach, which emphasizes the dynamic interaction of the learner and the environment. The notion that interacting constraints shape movement behavior has further led to the development of a theoretical framework for understanding and facilitating skill acquisition, known as the constraint-led approach. Human behavior is seen as complex and representing a compression of degrees of freedom. This compression of degrees of freedom allows behavior to emerge in a self-organizing fashion that accounts for the cooperation of the many subsystems in a task context. New movements self-organize, and movement variability—where patterns stabilize and destabilize as a function of the changing constraints on the system—is an integral part of the learning process. A patient who is re-learning to walk after sustaining an injury, for example, will display a given gait pattern as a result of the constraints imposed upon her system. If her leg strength reaches a critical level, a new movement solution (gait pattern) will emerge. The task of the instructor in this process is to identify and manipulate constraints in a manner that facilitates the learner's discovery of functional movement patterns.

# CEREBRAL challenge 3.10

1. Fear often serves as a rate limiter (a constraint that hinders the ability of the system to change). In hurdling, for example, beginning learners are often afraid that they will not clear the hurdle and will be injured. If you were teaching hurdles, what strategies would you use to overcome this rate limiter? What other rate limiters might be involved? Discuss your answer in terms of the dynamic system theory.

2. Explain how orthotics function from a constraints perspective.

3. Given what you have learned about dynamic systems, can the speed at which a sit-to-stand transfer is executed influence performance? Fully explain your answer.

# ▶ a look ahead

In this and previous chapters, we have explored theoretical constructs underlying the coordination and control of human movement from a behavioral perspective. In the remaining chapters we will revisit these theories, as practitioners must consider them in order to make effective instructional decisions. In the next chapter, we will examine movement from a neurological perspective. We will consider the role the nervous system plays in movement and the clues it offers movement scientists about the human movement puzzle.

# ● focus points

After reading this chapter, you should know . . .

- Skilled movement requires the learner not only to condense the available degrees of freedom (coordination) but also to control the resulting movement.

- Two prominent theories, motor program theory and the dynamic system theory, offer explanations of how movement is coordinated and controlled.

- A generalized motor program is an abstract representation of a class of actions that can be modified to yield various response outcomes.

- Some elements of the generalized motor program (invariant features) are thought to be relatively fixed from trial to trial, defining the motor program itself, and others (parameters) are more flexible, defining the program's execution.

- Parameters for a given situation are specified according to one's schema, which is a rule or relationship that is developed through practice and directs decision-making.

- Motor control is thought to be a function of both open- and closed-loop mechanisms, where movements are planned in advance, initiated, and carried out with limited modification, unless time permits the incorporation of response-produced feedback.

- The dynamic system theory argues against the notion of a central command center and suggests instead that movement emerges or self-organizes as a function of the constraints imposed on the system at any given time.

- Three categories of constraints have been identified: organismic, environmental, and task.

- According to the constraints-led approach, the learner searches through a range of potential movement solutions for the optimal movement strategy that will satisfy the imposed constraints.

- The role of the practitioner is one of identifying and manipulating key constraints to guide the learner's search for optimal movement solutions.

## ? review questions

1. Define the terms *coordination* and *control*. Explain their relationship.

2. Explain the degrees of freedom problem.

3. What two major flaws were identified in early motor program theories? How does Schmidt's schema theory solve these problems? How does the dynamic system theory solve them?

4. What is a schema? How do the recall schema and recognition schema work together?

5. What is the relationship between parameters and schema?

6. How could you determine whether snow skiing and waterskiing share the same motor program? Explain your answer, using motor learning terminology and providing specific examples.

7. What three lines of evidence suggest the existence of motor program control?

8. Compare and contrast open- and closed-loop systems.

9. What is a constraint? List the three types of constraints and provide an example of each.

10. Discovery learning is emphasized in the constraints-led approach. What is discovery learning, and how can the practitioner design practice to create it?

# REFERENCES

Araújo, D., Davids, K., Bennett, S.J., Button, C. & Chapman, G. (2004). Emergence of sport skills under constraints. In A.M. Williams and N.J. Hodges (Eds.), *Skill acquisition in sport: research, theory and practice* (pp. 409–33). London: Routledge, Taylor and Francis.

Bernstein, N. (1967). *The coordination and regulation of movements*. Oxford, England: Pergamon Press.

Brunt, D., Lafferty, M.J., Mckeon, A., Goode, B., Mulhausen, C. & Polk, P. (1991). Invariant characteristics of gait initiation. *American Journal of Physical and Medical Rehabilitation, 70*(4), 206–12.

Caldwell, G. & Clark, J.E. (1990). The measurement and evaluation of skill within the dynamical systems perspective. In J.E. Clark and J.H. Humphrey (Eds.), *Advances in motor development research* (pp. 165–99). New York: AMS Press.

Clark, J.E. (1995). On becoming skillful: patterns and constraints. *Research Quarterly for Exercise and Sport, 66*(3), 173–83.

Davids, K. (2006). Perceptual-motor workspace. In R. Bartlett, C. Grafton and C. Rolf (Eds.), *Encyclopedia of international sports studies* (p. 1004). London: Taylor and Francis.

Davids, K., Araújo, D. & Shuttleworth, R. (2005). Applications of dynamical systems theory to football. In T. Reilly, J. Cabri and D. Araújo (Eds.), *Science and football: the proceedings of the 5th world congress on sports science and football* (pp. 537–50). London: Routledge, Taylor and Francis.

Davids, K., Araújo, D., Shuttleworth, R. & Button, C. (2003). Acquiring skill in sport: a constraints-led perspective. *International Journal of Computer Sciences in Sport, 2*, 31–39.

Davids, K., Button, C. & Bennett, S. (2008). *Dynamics of skill acquisition: a constraints-led approach*. Champaign, IL: Human Kinetics.

Ennis, C. (1992). Reconceptualizing learning as a dynamical system. *Journal of Curriculum and Supervision, 7*(2), 115–30.

Griffin, L.L. & Butler, J.I. (Eds.). (2005). *Teaching games for understanding: theory, research, and practice*. Champaign, IL: Human Kinetics.

Handford, C., Davids, K., Bennett, S. & Button, C. (1997). Skill acquisition in sport: some applications of an evolving practice ecology. *Journal of Sports Sciences, 15*, 621–40.

Hay, L. & Schoebel, P. (1990). Spatio-temporal invariants in hurdle racing patterns. *Human Movement Science, 9*, 37–54.

Haywood, K.M. & Getchell, N. (2005). *Life span motor development*. Champaign, IL: Human Kinetics.

Henry, F.M. & Rogers, D.E. (1960). Increased response latency for complicated movements and the "memory drum" theory of neuromotor reaction. *Research Quarterly, 31*, 448–58.

Kelso, J.A.S. & Schöner, G. (1988). Self-organization of coordinative movement patterns. *Human Movement Science, 7*, 27–46.

Magill, R. (1993). *Motor learning: concepts and applications*. Dubuque, IA: Wm. C. Brown.

Nakayama, M. (2008). The effects of play area size as task constraints on soccer pass skills. *Football Science, 5*, 1–6.

Newell, K.M. (1986). Constraints on the development of coordination. In M.G. Wade and H.T.A. Whiting (Eds.), *Motor development in children: aspects of coordination and control* (pp. 341–60). Dordrecht: Martinus Nighoff.

Newell, K.M. (1991). Motor skill acquisition. *Annual Review of Psychology, 42*, 213–37.

Newell, K.M. (1996). Changes in movement and skill: learning, retention and transfer. In M.L. Latash and M.T. Turvey (Eds.), *Dexterity and its development*. Mahwah, NJ: Lawrence Erlbaum.

Newell, K.M., Liu, Y.T. & Mayer-Kress, G. (2001). Time scales in motor learning and development. *Psychological Review, 108*(1), 57–82.

Polit, A. & Bizzi, E. (1978). Processes controlling arm movements in monkeys. *Science, 201*, 1235–1237.

Roth, K. (1988). Investigations on the basis of the generalized motor programme hypothesis. In O.G. Meijer and K. Roth (Eds.), *Complex movement behavior: the motor action controversy* (pp. 261–88). Amsterdam: North-Holland.

Schmidt, R.A. (1975). A schema theory of discrete motor skill learning. *Psychological Review, 82*(4), 225–60.

Schmidt, R.A. (1985). The search for invariance in skilled movement behavior. *Research Quarterly for Exercise and Sport, 56*(2), 188–200.

Schmidt, R.A. & Wrisberg, C.A. (2008). *Motor learning and performance: a situation based learning approach*. Champaign, IL: Human Kinetics.

Shapiro, D.C., Zernicke, R.F., Gregor, R.J. & Diestal, J.D. (1981). Evidence for generalized motor programs using gait pattern analysis. *Journal of Motor Behavior, 13,* 33–47.

Shenoy, S. & Aruin, A.S. (2007). Effect of chair design on feed-forward postural control in sitting. *Motor Control, 11,* 309–21.

Shumway-Cook, A. & Woollacott, M.H. (2007). *Motor control: translating research into clinical practice.* Philadelphia: Lippincott, Williams & Wilkins.

Slater-Hammel, A.T. (1960). Reliability, accuracy and refractoriness of a transit reaction. *Research Quarterly, 31,* 217–28.

Sparrow, W.A. (1992). Measuring changes in coordination and control. In J.J. Summers (Ed.), *Approaches to the study of motor control and learning* (pp. 147–62). North Holland: Elsevier Science Publishers.

Taub, E. & Berman, A.J. (1968). Movement and learning in the absence of sensory feedback. In S.J. Freedman (Ed.), *The neuropsychology of spatially oriented behavior* (pp. 173–92). Homewood, IL: Dorsey Press.

Thelen, E. & Ulrich, B.D. (1991). Hidden skills: a dynamical systems analysis of treadmill walking in infants. *Monographs of the Society for Research in Child Development, 56,* serial #223.

Turvey, M.T. (1990). Coordination. *American Psychologist, 45,* 938–53.

Wadman, W.J., Dernier van der Gon, J.J., Geuze, R.H. & Mol, C.R. (1979). Control of fast goal-directed arm movements. *Journal of Human Movement Studies, 5,* 3–17.

Wolf, S.L., Winstein, C.J., Miller, J.P., Taub, E., Uswatte, G., Morris, D., Giuliani, C., Light, K.E. & Nichols-Larsen, D. (2006). Effect of constraint-induced movement therapy on upper extremity function 3 to 9 months after stroke. *Journal of the American Medical Association, 296,* 2095–2104.

# CHAPTER 4

# Neural Mechanisms:
# Contributions and Control

I t was a seemingly normal play in the Buffalo Bills' season opener. But a player was still down. Medical teams rushed out onto the field. The news was not good. Tight end Kevin Everett was rushed to the hospital. It was later reported that he had sustained a fracture and dislocation of his cervical spine while trying to make a tackle. Initial reports indicated that it was unlikely he would walk again. But on December 23, 2007, four months after the accident, Everett walked again in public for the first time, at Ralph Wilson Stadium before the Bills' final home game against the New York Giants. While he will never be 100 percent, Kevin Everett never gave up on his recovery. In July, at the 2008 ESPY awards, he received a standing ovation as he walked onto the stage and accepted the Jimmy V award for perseverance.

## THE NERVOUS SYSTEM

T he nervous system is responsible for the processes that underlie movement preparation, execution, and control. It may be subdivided into two primary components, the central nervous system (CNS) and the peripheral nervous system (PNS). The CNS consists of the brain and the spinal cord. It is within the CNS that sensory information is integrated, decisions are made, and signals are generated and sent to the effectors (muscles and glands) to carry out responses. The PNS consists primarily of nerves that extend from the brain and spinal cord, linking the body and the CNS. The PNS may be further subdivided into a sensory or **afferent** division, which detects changes in the environment and conducts nerve impulses from the various sensory receptors toward the CNS, and a motor or **efferent** division, which transmits impulses away from the CNS to the effectors.

### Sensory Receptors

We are constantly being bombarded with stimuli. These stimuli are detected through components of the nervous system known as sensory receptors. There are numerous forms of stimuli, and a variety of sensory receptors exist, each of which is sensitive to a particular stimulus. A useful method of classifying these various receptors is by location or, more specifically, by the location of the stimuli to which they respond. **Exteroceptors** detect stimuli outside the body and provide information about the environment. They are located at or near the body's surface and include receptors for pressure, pain, touch, temperature, vibrations, hearing, vision, smell, and taste. **Interoceptors** detect stimuli from the internal viscera and provide information about the internal environment, leading to feelings such as hunger and nausea. Finally, **proprioceptors,** which are located in the muscles, tendons, joints, and internal ear, provide information regarding body position and movement by detecting changes in muscle tension, joint position, and equilibrium.

## Sensory Contributions to Movement

The information that sensory receptors relay to the CNS for processing and interpretation allows us to interact with our environment. Of particular importance in the acquisition and performance of skilled movement are vision and proprioception. We will see how these two sources of information contribute to the selection of a movement, its regulation, and even its correction when necessary.

# VISION

**A**mong our numerous sensory receptors, the visual system predominates. In fact, as is demonstrated in Exploration Activity 4.1, our dependence on vision is so strong that information from other sensory receptors may even be ignored in its favor (Lee & Aronson, 1974). This dominance of the visual system is also reflected in estimates that 70 percent of all the body's sensory receptors are located in the eyes. Furthermore, 40 percent of the cerebral cortex is thought to be involved in some aspect of processing visual information (Marieb, Mallatt & Wilhelm, 2008). It is not surprising, then, that interest in the role of vision in the production of skilled movement has not only increased but has also led to the development of a sub-discipline known as sport vision, which focuses on investigating visual contributions to performance, with an emphasis on visual correction, enhancement, and injury (Kluka, 1999).

## exploration  A  C  T  I  V  I  T  Y    4.1

### Visual Dominance

**Activity #1**

**EQUIPMENT NEEDED:**

Pencil

Mirror                              1 piece of cardboard (20 x 20 cm or 8" x 8")

**PROCEDURE:**

Sit in front of a mirror with your textbook in front of you on a flat surface so that the diagram on the next page is visible in the mirror. Now, place the tip of your pencil in between the two lines. You may start anywhere. Using the cardboard, cover the hand using the pencil so that you can see your hand and its movements only through the mirror in front of you. Using only the image in the mirror, trace the diagram by moving the pencil around the shape while staying between the lines. You may move in either direction.

*(continued)*

How did you do? Were you able to stay in the lines and move around the shape efficiently?

*Activity #2*

You will need a partner for this activity. Hold your arms straight out in front of you so that they are parallel with the floor. Now, cross your arms over one another. From this position, turn your palms so that they are facing one another, and interlock your fingers. Pull your hands down and toward your chest. Continue this rotation until your knuckles are facing the sky. Once you are in position, ask your partner to point to one of your fingers. It is important that the person only point to it and not touch it. Your task is simply to move the finger that your partner pointed to.

Do you think the result would have been different if your partner had touched the finger to be moved while your eyes were closed? Try it.

In both of these activities, a sensory conflict between vision and proprioception is created. Our vision is so dominant that even when we know the visual information we are receiving is not accurate, such as when the image is reversed in a mirror, we will often rely on it anyway. The consequence is poorer performance. Lee and Aronson (1974) demonstrated visual dominance in their moving wall study. Subjects stood in a special room where the walls could be moved but the floor remained stationary. The study found that the subjects adjusted their posture to compensate for changes in visual information even though proprioceptive information did not change. The results of this study not only support the notion of visual dominance but also provide insight into the role vision plays in the maintenance of posture.

Our capacity to see objects clearly, at variable distances and under various conditions of light, depends on the actions of a complex arrangement of structures in and around our eyes, shown in Figure 4.1. Light rays enter the eye, where they are manipulated and focused onto the retina, forming an image that is converted into nerve impulses by light-sensitive cells called **photoreceptors.**

There are two types of photoreceptors, rods and cones. Rods are more numerous and are specialized for vision in dim light. They enable us to see shapes and movements, and they discriminate between different shades of light and dark, making them the primary receptor used in night vision. Cones, on the other hand, operate best in bright light and are specialized for color vision and visual acuity (sharpness of vision). Cones are most densely concentrated in the fovea, the area of maximal visual acuity. Given the location of the fovea, our vision is most clear and sharp when we look directly at an object.

The electrical signals generated by the photoreceptors are sent to the brain via the optic nerve. At one point, known as the optic chiasm, some fibers from each of the optic nerves cross, as illustrated in Figure 4.2. Because of this crossing, visual sensations from the left side of the visual field are sent to the right side of the brain for processing, while those from the right are sent to the left side.

Basic structures of the eye. | FIGURE **4.1**

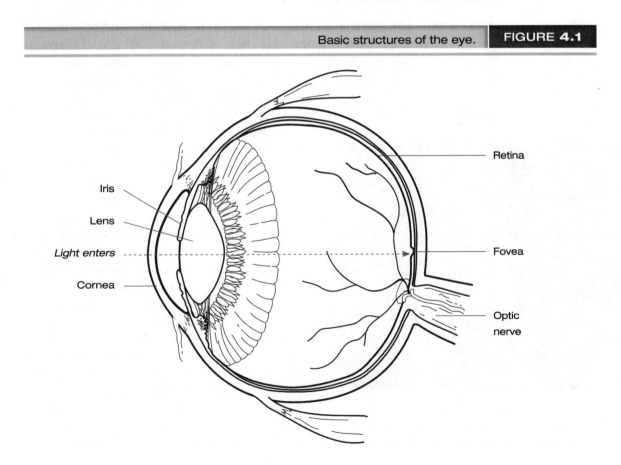

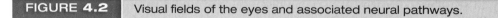

FIGURE **4.2**    Visual fields of the eyes and associated neural pathways.

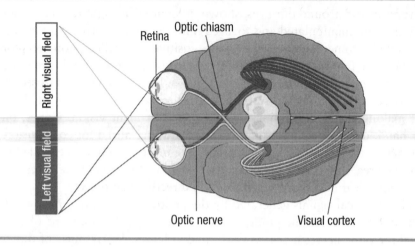

FIGURE **4.2**    Visual fields of the eyes and associated neural pathways.

## Focal versus Ambient Vision

The existence of two separate visual pathways to the brain has led to the belief that two separate but parallel-functioning visual systems exist. The **focal system,** which involves the fovea, functions to identify objects primarily located in the central region of the visual field. Focal vision is strongly linked to consciousness and, therefore, operates under voluntary control. Its function is hampered in low light conditions. In contrast, the **ambient system,** which functions at a subconscious level, is thought to be responsible for spatial localization and orientation. Unlike focal vision, it involves the entire retina, serves both the central and peripheral visual fields, and is not affected by changes in light level.

During movement, parallel processing of information obtained through each system likely occurs. While mountain biking through a forest, for example, a rider rarely identifies the trees that are on the side of the trail, but he does need to be aware of where those trees are so he can avoid collisions and successfully follow the trail. Ambient vision serves the rider in this task. At the same time, the rider is using focal vision to identify changes in the trail, such as a fallen tree across it or a rider in front of him. The rider's ability to identify such objects will be hampered when the forest is very dense or if the tint of his sunglasses

A mountain biker uses focal vision to identify changes in the trail, while awareness of the trees off to the side is acquired through ambient vision.

is too dark, because of a decrease in focal sensitivity. Try Exploration Activity 4.2 to experience the use of ambient versus focal vision.

## exploration  A C T I V I T Y  4.2

### Ambient versus Focal Vision

*Activity 1*

Try walking around the room while reading this book. You should be able to accomplish this without running into furniture because of the combined efforts of focal and ambient vision. You used focal vision to read, while ambient vision allowed you to locate obstacles and successfully move about the room.

*Activity 2*

Now perform the task again with a pair of sunglasses on. What influence did the sunglasses have on your performance? How can these results be explained?

*Activity 3*

For the final activity, you will need a piece of three-hole paper. Hold the paper horizontally about one inch from your face so that you can see through the middle hole. Wrap the rest of the paper around to touch the sides of your head. Now walk around the room again. Explain the results.

Source: Shea, Shebliske & Worchel, 1993.

## Vision and Performance

Vision is used throughout all aspects of performance. Not only do we use it to detect environmental stimuli, which are subsequently used to make movement decisions, but it also provides important feedback that we use to guide our resulting action. Therefore, the role of various visual abilities in performance warrants exploration.

### Eye dominance

Information is not processed and transmitted to the brain by both eyes equally. One of your eyes, the dominant eye, carries out these actions a few milliseconds faster. Those individuals whose dominant eye is on the same side of the body as their dominant hand are considered same-side dominant, while those whose dominant eye is opposite that of their dominant hand are considered cross-dominant. Exploration Activity 4.3 provides a simple method for discovering which eye is dominant.

Eye dominance has received attention with respect to hitting performance in baseball and softball. It has been suggested that cross-dominant hitters have an

## exploration ACTIVITY 4.3

### Eye Dominance

Find a small object, such as a clock, on a wall. Stand directly in front of it, approximately 10 feet away. Once you are in this position, create a small triangular window with your hands by overlapping your thumbs and fingers. Stretch your arms in the direction of the wall so that you can see the object through your triangular window, as in the illustration. Now, close one eye, and then open it. Repeat with the other eye. Your dominant eye is the one where the object remained in the triangular window.

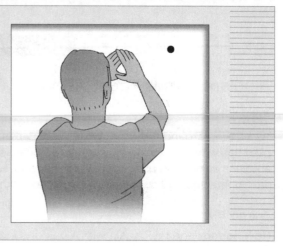

advantage because their dominant eye is closer and more in line with the pitcher. Although research has not substantiated this claim (Milne, Buckholz & Cardenas, 1995), turning the head to give both eyes a clear view of the pitch has been advocated (Kluka & Knudson, 1997).

### Spotting

**Spotting** is a technique used in the performance of rotational skills (e.g., dance, diving, gymnastics, and figure skating) to reduce the dizziness associated with spinning and keep the performer oriented. In spotting, the rotation of the head is delayed relative to the body's rotation. This is accomplished by focusing or **fixating** one's visual attention on a specific spot. Once the body has turned to where the individual begins to lose sight of the mark, the head quickly turns to the opposite side to re-focus on the target spot. The BallroomDancers.com link offers more information and a demonstration of spotting.

**www.**

**Spotting demonstration**

www.ballroomdancers.com/Learning_
Center/Lesson/2/Default.asp?page=5

### Visual search

In some skills, successful performance depends on the **visual search** strategies or gaze behavior employed by the performer to scan the environment to locate critical regulatory cues. During this active scan, numerous fixations may occur. By observing the characteristics of those fixations, such as their order, location, and duration, we can infer how and to what information the performer attends (Kluka, 1999). One variable in particular, called the *quiet eye* (Vickers, 1996), has enhanced our understanding of how performers use vision to control their movements.

The **quiet eye** is defined as the final fixation located on a specific target or object before the initiation of movement. Research has shown that the quiet eye of elite performers is significantly longer, has an earlier onset, and is of more optimal duration for the task at hand relative to that of near-elite or lower-skilled performers (e.g., Martell & Vickers, 2004; Panchuk & Vickers, 2006; Vickers, 1992, 1996, 2004; Vickers & Adolphe, 1997; Williams, Singer & Frehlich, 2002). What this means is that higher-level performers are not only able to see critical regulatory cues sooner, but they also have more time to process the information.

**Targeting skills.** Targeting skills typically involves accurately propelling an object toward a target (Vickers, 2007). Examples are archery, rifle shooting, golf putt, basketball free throw, volleyball serve, and throwing or kicking a ball to a receiver. According to Vickers (2007), targets may be fixed, abstract, or moving, and they present different gaze control constraints.

**Fixed targets,** such as a basketball hoop, are stable and predictable in position and require a performer to fixate on a specific location prior to executing a response. An example of an **abstract targeting task** is the golf putt. In putting, the performer must account for the slope of the green when aiming. Although the target itself (the hole) is fixed in space the optimal aiming location is more difficult to detect. The final category, **moving target tasks,** requires the performer to anticipate the target's impending location. Examples include passing or kicking an object to a receiver or attempting to strike an opponent in elusive sports such as fencing, boxing, and martial arts (Vickers, 2007).

Systematic differences in visual search behavior for targeting tasks have been found between skilled performers and their less skilled counterparts. In basketball, for example, not only did expert shooters turn their head toward the basket sooner, but they had longer fixations on the target (hoop region) than did novices (Ripoll, Bard & Paillard, 1986). Vickers (1996) further noted that the duration of final fixation prior to the initiation of the free throw was significantly longer for experts.

Similar findings have been demonstrated in abstract targeting tasks. In putting, high-skilled golfers were found to fixate for a longer duration on the hole, had a more precise scan path, and displayed longer quiet eye durations than poor putters (Vickers, 1992). In addition, the unskilled putters often tracked the movement of the clubhead on the backswing, whereas the high-skilled golfers maintained their gaze on the top or back of the ball. Quiet eye durations were also found to be longer for expert pool players, who fixated on the cue and target ball longer than novices (Williams et al., 2002).

**Interceptive skills.** Interceptive skills are complex in nature, as they require the performer to track a moving stimulus, decide when and/or where the stimulus will arrive, and determine and execute the appropriate limb movement to intercept it. Examples are skills involving striking, catching, creating or avoiding a collision, and landing. One variable critical to successful performance of interceptive skills is the prediction of time to contact. Time-to-contact information is determined via a single optic variable, *tau,* which is determined by taking the size of the retina image at any position of an object's approach and dividing it by the rate of change of the image (Lee, 1976, 1980). As an object approaches, its retinal image enlarges. The rate at which this enlargement occurs is directly related to the speed of the object's approach and is, therefore, indicative of time to contact. In other words, the faster the enlargement occurs, the faster the object is approaching.

A question of interest in interceptive skills is whether the performer must visually track a moving object in order to contact it. Several studies indicate that continuous tracking to contact is unlikely. For example, Bahill and LaRitz (1984) studied skilled baseball hitters tracking a pitch. Their findings suggested that the athletes did not "keep their eyes on the ball" until contact and that they were unable to track the ball closer than 5 feet from the plate. Vickers and Adolphe (1997) also found that elite and near-elite volleyball players tracked the ball until contact during the forearm pass on only 7 percent to 8 percent of the trials, respectively. The researchers concluded that although tracking to contact was possible, it was not favored. The more prevalent response during ball reception and passing was to leave the gaze in front. For elite table tennis players, Ripoll and Fleurance (1988) also found that players did not track the ball throughout its entire trajectory. More recently, Land and McLeod (2000) demonstrated that cricket batters tracked the ball for the initial 100 to 200 ms and then quickly moved their eyes to the point where they anticipated that the ball would bounce on the ground. These anticipatory saccades, where a performer's gaze jumps to an anticipated location, have also been reported in baseball (Bahill & LaRitz, 1984), table tennis (Ripoll, Fleurance & Cazeneuve, 1987; Rodrigues, Vickers & Williams, 2002), and catching a self-tossed wall-bounced ball (Mennie, Hayhoe, Stupak & Sullivan, 2005). To learn more about the influence of visual tracking in baseball, visit the adjoining link.

**www.**

**There's More Than Meets the Eye**

www.sciencedaily.com/releases/2006/04/060411223044.htm

Although continuous tracking does not appear to be necessary, evidence does suggest that the object's flight must be monitored initially to determine key flight characteristics. However, marked differences exist in the visual search strategies used by experts and novices in interceptive tasks. For example, when waiting to receive a serve, beginning tennis players spend more time looking at the server's head region than do experts (Singer et al., 1994). Shank and Haywood (1987) found that expert hitters fixated on a pitcher's release point, while novices tended to move their eyes before the release of the ball, alternating their fixations between the release point and the pitcher's head, which resulted in poorer pitch identification. In badminton and squash, Abernethy (1991) found that experts were better than novices at using earlier-occurring cues from the opponent's arm to predict the speed and direction of the forthcoming shot. Finally, in soccer, as a kicker approached the ball, the

Baseball players who are hitting well often say that the ball appears much bigger than it really is. To investigate this phenomenon, Witt and Proffitt (2005) set up a table at local softball fields and recruited intramural and city league players who had just finished playing to participate in the experiment. Players were shown a poster displaying eight black circles varying in size from 9 cm to 11.8 cm in diameter and were asked to select the one that best matched

the size of a softball. Next, they were asked how many times they had been at bat, how many hits and walks they had in the game, and how many times they had been on base because of an error. These data were used to compute each individual's batting average. The results indicated that players who had just been successful at hitting during their game did in fact recall the ball to be bigger than those players who were less successful.

focus of experienced goalkeepers progressed from the kicker's head to the nonkicking foot, to the kicking foot, and finally to the ball, whereas novices focused more on the trunk, arms, and hips (Savelsbergh, Williams, van der Kamp & Ward, 2002).

**Tactical skills.** Tactical skills require quick and accurate situational decision-making, selective attention to relevant environmental cues, and pattern recognition. Expert–novice differences in gaze behavior again shed light on the role of vision in the performance of sport skills. Experts have been shown to be faster and more accurate at decision-making than their non-elite counterparts (Helsen & Pauwels, 1992; Williams & Davids, 1998; Williams, Davids, Burwitz & Williams, 1994). Differences in the location and duration of fixations have also been found. For example, inexperienced soccer players tend to focus more frequently on the ball and the player passing the ball rather than on the positions and movements of the other players, which was found to be the focus of experienced players (Williams et al., 1994). Expert soccer players were also shown to fixate more often on the knee and hip regions of their opponents, suggesting that the information in these areas is important in anticipating an opponent's next move (Nagano, Kato & Fukuda, 2004). Also, in soccer, successful goalkeepers have been shown to predict the height and direction of the kick more accurately, wait longer to initiate their response, and spend more time fixated on the non-kicking leg (Savelsbergh et al., 2002).

Tactical skills, however, are not limited to sports. Vickers (2007) categorizes locomotion as a tactical skill because "during locomotion the visual field in front changes constantly, and within each visual field there are a number of visual targets and locations that must be attended to in order to navigate safely" (p. 144). Vision serves an important feedforward function in the regulation of locomotion. **Feedforward** control allows information, such as the dimension of an object or details of the terrain, to be sent ahead of the movement to prepare or adjust the movement in advance. For example, when a person is walking up a steep hill, adjustments to stride length, body lean, and arm swing are made in advance to negotiate the terrain and slope of the hill (Kluka, 1999).

Feedforward control is used both to contact and to avoid objects. Lee, Lischman, and Thomson (1982) demonstrated how long jumpers used *tau* to adjust stride length during the long jump approach. In addition to using *tau*, performers used vision to provide predictive information for obstacle negotiation by fixating objects well in advance of reaching them (Hollands, Patla & Vickers, 2002; Patla & Vickers, 1997). Patla and Vickers also found that fixation duration and frequency were a function of object height when the task involved stepping over an obstacle.

### Tips for practitioners

Vision clearly plays an integral role in the performance of skilled movement. Consequently, numerous visual training programs have been created in an effort to improve sports performance. Practitioners should be cautious when examining the claims of such programs. Generalized visual training programs, often referred to as sports vision training and offered by optometrists, lack research support for their effectiveness (Abernethy, 1986; Abernethy & Woods, 2000). Sport-specific perceptual and decision training programs, however, have been shown to be effective in tennis (e.g., Farrow, Chivers, Hardingham & Sasche, 1998; Singer et al., 1994), basketball (e.g., Starkes & Lindley, 1994), baseball (Vickers, Livingston, Umeris & Holden, 1999), and table tennis (e.g., Raab, Masters & Maxwell, 2005).

Central to such programs are the improvement of visual search strategies, pattern recognition, anticipation, and decision-making skills. For example, according to Abernethy and Wollstein (1989), practitioners can improve learners' anticipation in racket sports by providing visual training videos, identifying opponent tendencies, and pointing out information-rich areas, such as the release point of a pitched ball. Magill (1998) also offers several practical tips to help learners develop effective visual search strategies. First, instruction and verbal feedback should direct learners to information-rich areas where critical cues occur. For instance, rather than instructing a hitter to look at how the ball leaves the pitcher's hand, the practitioner should direct the learner's visual attention to the area where the ball is released. Second, practitioners should design appropriate learning experiences that provide extensive practice opportunities in situations that contain common task-relevant cues. For example, providing opportunities to make connections between cues and ultimate event outcomes can facilitate the development of anticipatory skills. Abernethy (1996) further suggests including video training where paused sequences are presented and learners are challenged to anticipate an opponent's action. Finally, the context of learning situations should include a great deal of variability while still requiring learners to search for the same cues on each attempt. This variability will prepare learners to generalize their visual search strategies for performance or game situations. For a comprehensive decision training model, see Vickers (2007).

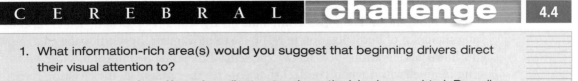

1. What information-rich area(s) would you suggest that beginning drivers direct their visual attention to?

2. Play the game at http://members.iinet.net.au/~pontipak/redsquare.html. Describe the changes in your visual search strategies as a result of this experience.

## PROPRIOCEPTION

**T**he continuous flow of sensory information that is received from receptors located in the muscles, tendons, joints, and inner ear regarding movement and body position is called **proprioception.** Multiple receptors are involved in proprioception. Golgi tendon organs are proprioceptors located at the junction of a tendon with a muscle. When tension is applied to a tendon, Golgi tendon organs relay the corresponding sensory information (intensity of the contraction) to the CNS. One of their functions is to protect tendons and their associated muscles from damage due to excessive tension.

Muscle spindles, another type of proprioceptor, are found between the skeletal muscle fibers in the muscle belly. When a muscle is stretched, the spindle sends a signal to the CNS indicating how much and how fast the muscle's length is changing. Muscle spindles can also cause a reflexive contraction known as a stretch reflex, which contributes to the contractile force that can be generated during a skill. The stretch reflex is created when a muscle is put on stretch just prior to contracting. For example, as in many striking skills, the tennis forehand is preceded by a backswing that stretches the involved muscles and sets up a stretch reflex. Lack of this stretch reflex would change the dynamics of the skill, and practitioners should keep this in mind when designing learning experiences.

Proprioception helps a backpacker make adjustments while walking across a log.

Joint kinesthetic receptors, located in and around synovial joints, respond to pressure, acceleration and deceleration, and excessive strain on a joint. Joint receptors provide feedback about whether movements are too slow, too fast, or in the wrong direction (Kreighbaum & Barthels, 1996).

Finally, the vestibular apparatus is a collective group of receptor organs in the inner ear that respond to changes in posture and balance. The otolithic organs monitor the position of the head, providing sensory information regarding static equilibrium and the maintenance of body position when motionless. They also contribute to dynamic equilibrium, which is the maintenance of body position in response to movement, by monitoring changes in linear acceleration. You have experienced dynamic equilibrium while moving in an elevator, when you feel that you are descending as the elevator starts to ascend. A second aspect of dynamic equilibrium involves angular acceleration of the head, such as when a figure skater does a spin. The cristae in the semicircular ducts of the inner ear are responsible for monitoring changes in the angular acceleration of the head. To better understand proprioception, complete Exploration Activity 4.5.

What would happen if we did not have proprioception? Ian Waterman knows firsthand. When he was 19, a rare virus attacked his nervous system, rendering his proprioception useless. His muscles still worked, but he could no longer sense body position and movement without looking directly at his joints and limbs (Azar, 1998; Cole, 1995). He has had to learn to rely on vision to control his movements, as it has become his only source of feedback. In order to judge the weight of an object he is picking up, for example, Ian has to watch how his hand reacts, instead of receiving feedback from his proprioceptors about the amount of stretch caused in the tendons and muscles as a result of the weight. The faster and higher his hand moves, the lighter the object. This adaptation was demonstrated in a study that required an individual deprived of proprioceptive information to judge different weights (Fleury et al., 1995). When vision was available, the individual could discriminate between weights within 10 g. With the eyes closed, the person's ability to judge the weights was significantly impaired.

**www.**

**Mixed Up in Space**

http://science.nasa.gov/headlines/y2001/ast07aug_1.htm

Similar adaptations are made by astronauts in space. Without gravity, the vestibular system has difficulties sensing which way is up! To learn more, visit the adjoining site.

## exploration   A C T I V I T Y   4.5

## Proprioception

1. To demonstrate the use of proprioception, close your eyes and hold your arms out to the side, forming a T. Now touch your nose with the index finger of your dominant hand. Repeat with your non-dominant hand. Speculate as to why this exercise is sometimes used to test drivers suspected of being intoxicated.

2. Again, close your eyes. Raise your leg so that your thigh is parallel to the floor. Open your eyes and check your leg's position. Repeat the exercise, bringing your arm to a position parallel to the floor. How accurate was your positioning? How did you accomplish this activity in the absence of vision?

To evaluate how visual and proprioceptive information is integrated and modified throughout the learning process, five neurologically normal subjects and one deafferented subject (deprived of proprioception) performed a mirror-tracing task (Lajoie et al., 1992). Subjects were instructed to trace a six-pointed star pattern as fast and accurately as possible while viewing it in a mirror (similar to Exploration Activity 4.1). Normal subjects demonstrated difficulties when drawing oblique lines and changing direction while attempting to trace the star pattern. These difficulties were, however, overcome with practice. These difficulties were not evident in the tracing performance of the deafferented subject, as all trials were consistent in their execution. Because the star is viewed in a mirror, a conflict between visual and proprioceptive information is created for the normal subjects. This conflict does not exist for the deafferented subject. The results of this study demonstrate that there is a tight coupling between visual and proprioceptive feedback in the execution of visuomotor tasks.

## Proprioception and Performance

Combined, proprioceptors function to "make the motor control system more efficient and flexible for the regulation of goal-directed movements" (Park & Toole, 1999; p. 645). Before a movement is initiated, proprioception provides the information about initial body and limb position that serves as the basis for the programming of motor commands. Once initiated, the movement is continuously evaluated for correctness by comparing proprioceptive feedback to the intended goal. If the two do not correspond, an error is detected. At that point, the adjustments needed to correct the movement must be determined, initiated, and accomplished prior to the completion of the response. As we saw with open- and closed-loop systems, the success of this process depends on the time available. If a movement is too rapid, response-produced feedback will be used to make adjustments on the next trial.

As indicated earlier, the intended goal of the movement serves as a frame of reference for error detection, but a learner's level of understanding of that goal depends on her skill level. Because a beginner is still trying to develop an idea of how a movement should be executed, her frame of reference for correct movement has yet to be developed. In contrast, the instant the ball leaves the hand of a skilled free-throw shooter, he can tell whether the shot was a good one by the way it felt at release. To assist beginning learners in developing their frame of reference, practitioners should provide opportunities for learners to experience a variety of positions and movements in a broad assortment of environments (Kreighbaum & Barthels, 1996). In addition, practitioners should focus learners' attention on the feelings associated with a movement. Because we can often see our limbs relative to the environment, we have information regarding movement and body position not only through proprioception but also through visual feedback. Often learners rely too heavily on visual feedback when judging a movement's correctness. Kinesthetic feedback should be stressed for optimal learning.

1. Speculate as to why many practitioners incorporate strategies that focus a learner's attention on the feelings associated with a movement.
2. One such strategy is the use of weighted implements (bats, shots, baseballs). List other devices designed to enhance the feelings associated with movement.

A popular method of teaching a youngster how to swing a bat is to stand next to him or her and manually guide the batter through the movements. This technique, appropriately termed *manual guidance,* is also frequently used in a therapeutic setting. The idea of manual guidance is to move the learner through the desired pattern or range of motion so that he or she can experience the feeling associated with it.

This technique, however, presents an inherent problem. Speculate as to what that problem might be. Try the strategy yourself prior to formulating your response. Based on your response, what conditions might you adhere to when employing this strategy?

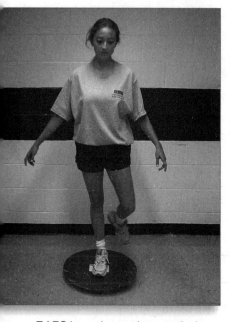

BAPS board exercises assist in reestablishing proprioception.

## Balance and Postural Control

Postural control involves multiple sensory inputs that communicate to the CNS where the body is in space. These information sources include the vestibular apparatus, the somatic senses (touch), and proprioception from the feet and ankles. Vision also provides information regarding vertical orientation, but it is not absolutely necessary—we are capable of maintaining our balance with our eyes closed.

During quiet stance, the maintenance of equilibrium requires postural adjustments that may be either compensatory or anticipatory (Bleuse et al., 2005). Compensatory (feedback) postural adjustments occur after an external perturbation or loss of desirable posture. Anticipatory postural adjustments are activated before a voluntary movement (feedforward control) to counteract a potential loss of stability. For example, a shift in a person's center of gravity will occur when reaching forward from a standing position to lift a weight from a table. Without the activation of anticipatory mechanisms, a loss of stability would occur.

## R E S E A R C H    N O T E S

Taping is often used to counter the proprioceptive deficit that occurs as a result of joint injuries such as ankle sprains. While its use has been shown to be effective in reducing the risk of future sprains, its effects on proprioceptive acuity (ability to sense joint position and movement) remain unclear. To determine whether taping improves proprioceptive acuity, Refshauge and colleagues (2008) examined the movement detection capabilities of 16 participants with recurrent ankle sprains with and without the ankle taped. Participants were seated such that the hip was neutrally rotated and in the middle of the abduction/adduction range and the knee was flexed at approximately 60 degrees. The test foot was placed on a metal footplate with the ankle in the middle of both the plantar flexion/dorsi flexion range and the inversion/eversion range. Movement detection was measured at three velocities (0.1 deg/s, 0.5 deg/s, and 2.5 deg/s) and two directions (inversion and eversion), with the order of testing the taped and untaped conditions randomized. Contrary to the hypothesis, the application of the tape significantly decreased the ability to detect movements of the ankle in the inversion/eversion plane, adding to the conflicting findings regarding taping and proprioceptive acuity. The authors suggest that clinicians continue taping, as studies have found it effective in reducing the reoccurrence of ankle sprains.

## Rehabilitation and Proprioception Training

According to Lepart (2004) and Prentice (2009), the reestablishment of proprioception should be a primary concern for rehabilitation programs. Consequently, athletic trainers commonly include proprioception training in rehabilitation programs following a lower limb musculoskeletal injury. The intent is to regain movement and balance sense that are lost as a result of inactivity or immobilization following an injury or surgery (Leach, 1982; Prentice, 1999). Failure to reestablish proprioception can result in functional instability that may impair performance and predisposes an athlete or patient to recurrent injury (Laskowski, Newcomer-Aney & Smith, 1997). Hence, functional progressions that incorporate balance and proprioception training, such as one-legged standing, double-arm balancing, wobble board exercises, and sport-specific exercises such as cutting and defensive slide drills, are important components of any rehabilitation program designed to return athletes or patients to pre-injury performance levels and prevent the reoccurrence of injury (e.g., Verhagen et al., 2004).

## TRANSMISSION OF INFORMATION: THE SPINAL CORD

**T**he continuous flow of information from the receptors to various levels of the CNS is achieved via the conduction of afferent or sensory nerve impulses. Once the information has been perceived and a decision made as to how to respond, signals are sent by efferent or motor neurons to the muscles to carry out the desired action. An integral component in this process is the spinal cord (see Figure 4.3).

FIGURE **4.3**

Transmission of afferent and efferent information between the body and the brain via the spinal cord.

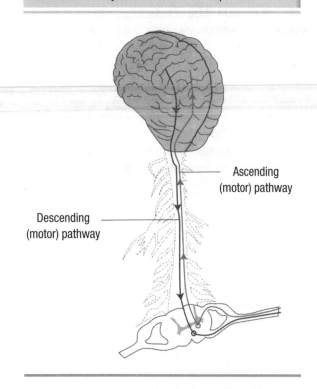

Ascending (motor) pathway

Descending (motor) pathway

The spinal cord performs two major functions. First, it serves as a route for impulse conduction. Sensory impulses travel up the spinal cord to the brain via ascending pathways, while motor impulses travel in the opposite direction along descending pathways. However, not all signals travel to the brain for interpretation. The spinal cord's second function is to integrate some impulses at various levels and to serve as an integrating center for spinal reflexes.

## Sensory and Motor Pathways

Sensory information travels up the spinal cord to the brain via two major routes (ascending pathways) on either side of the cord: the spinothalamic pathway and the posterior or dorsal column pathway. The spinothalamic pathway conducts impulses associated with pain, temperature, crude touch, and deep pressure. Proprioception, discriminative touch, lighter pressure, and vibrations travel to the brain via the dorsal column pathway.

The two descending pathways, which transmit motor impulses to the skeletal muscles that will execute movement, are the pyramidal and extrapyramidal pathways. Nerve impulses leading to the control of skilled voluntary movements travel down the pyramidal pathway. The extrapyramidal pathway conducts nerve impulses that result in more subconscious control of body movements, such as the control of motor activities associated with posture and balance.

## Spinal Reflexes

As noted above, not all impulses travel to the brain for integration. In some cases, the integration of sensory information occurs at the level of the spinal cord. The result is an automatic, involuntary response to stimuli called a **reflex.** Because information is integrated at the spinal cord, reflexes allow the individual to react to a stimulus faster than if conscious thought were involved.

The simplest pathway by which a reflex occurs is known as the **reflex arc.** Its basic components include (1) the receptor; (2) the sensory neuron; (3) the integrating center; (4) the motor neuron, and (5) the effector. When a sensory receptor detects

**common** *myth*

All sensory messages must go to the brain for integration.

a change in the internal or external environment, a sensory neuron is stimulated, and it carries an impulse to the integrating center in the spinal cord (or brain stem). The integrating center then triggers an impulse in a motor neuron, which subsequently stimulates a response in a muscle or gland.

Several types of reflexes exist, which are distinguished by the characteristics of the integrating center.

FIGURE **4.4**

Monosynaptic reflex loop.

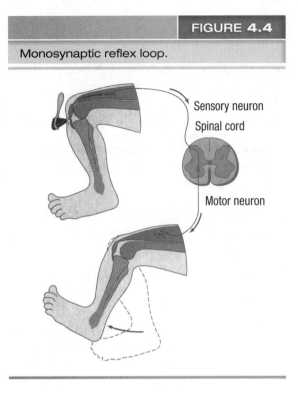

Sensory neuron
Spinal cord
Motor neuron

### Monosynaptic reflex

The simplest reflex involves a single synapse. Hence, a sensory neuron communicates directly with a motor neuron. Because it involves only one synapse, this type of reflex is called a monosynaptic or stretch reflex. The knee-jerk reflex illustrated in Figure 4.4 is one example of a monosynaptic reflex. When an unexpected stretch of the quadriceps occurs, there is a corresponding stretch of the muscle spindles. As we learned earlier, when a muscle spindle is stretched, it sends a signal to the CNS, more specifically the spinal cord, indicating how much and how fast the muscle's length is changing. A single synapse is then made, which prompts an adjustment by increasing the contraction of the quadriceps, resulting in an extension of the leg at the knee. Because only one synapse is involved, the monosynaptic reflex is very fast. Its function in counteracting changes in muscle length, especially those that occur unexpectedly, contributes to our ability to maintain posture and position our limbs. This reflexive action is demonstrated in Exploration Activity 4.8.

### Polysynaptic reflexes

A more common reflex pathway, known as a polysynaptic reflex arc, consists of one or more **interneurons** that lie between a sensory neuron and a motor neuron in a reflex arc (Marieb et al., 2008). Because polysynaptic reflexes involve more than one synapse, they are not as fast as monosynaptic reflexes but still function more quickly than if they required conscious control. The withdrawal reflex, where we pull back from danger, is a polysynaptic reflex. The classic example of the withdrawal reflex is when an individual touches a hot stove. Impulses are generated by heat and pain receptors and sent via sensory neurons to the spinal cord. A synapse occurs there with an interneuron, which in turn synapses with a motor neuron that signals the muscles to withdraw your hand from the hot stove.

# exploration    A C T I V I T Y    4.8

## Knee-Jerk Reflex

### Activity 1

Have a partner sit on a chair and cross his or her legs so that the lower knee fits into the hollow at the back of the upper knee. Now, using the edge of your open hand, firmly tap the soft part just below your partner's kneecap. You may have to try a few times to find the spot that initiates the reflex. Switch places with your partner.

### Activity 2

Repeat the above activity, but this time try to prevent your reflex from occurring. Can you do it?

Another polysynaptic reflex, often associated with the withdrawal reflex, is the crossed extensor reflex. In addition to an interneuron stimulating the motor neuron responsible for the withdrawal signal, a collateral axon conducts an impulse to the opposite side of the spinal cord to a motor neuron that innervates the muscles on that side of the body, causing them to extend. In other words, when the withdrawal reflex occurs in one limb, the crossed extensor reflex may be initiated to cause the opposite limb to extend. The crossed extensor reflex is illustrated in the response to shift one's body weight to prevent a fall. For example, as illustrated in Figure 4.5, if you were walking along the beach and accidentally stepped on a sharp shell, the withdrawal reflex would occur in response to the painful stimuli, while the crossed extensor reflex would cause the opposite leg to extend, creating a weight shift and preventing a fall.

## FIGURE 4.5

Withdrawal and crossed extensor reflex arc.

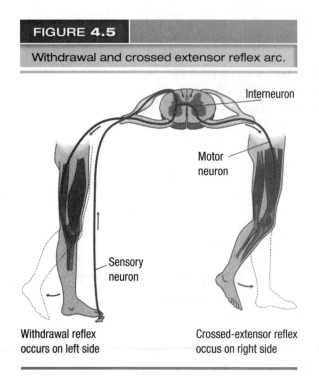

Interneuron

Motor neuron

Sensory neuron

Withdrawal reflex occurs on left side

Crossed-extensor reflex occus on right side

## Damage to the Spinal Cord

Damage to the spinal cord can result in loss of function and/or sensation (feeling). Two factors determine the effects of a spinal cord injury: the type of injury and the level at which the injury occurred.

### Type of injury

Spinal cord injuries may be classified as either complete or incomplete. In a complete injury, function and sensation are lost below the level of the injury on both sides of the body. In an incomplete injury, there is partial damage to the spinal cord, and the effects depend on the area (front, back, side) of the spinal cord affected. Some function and sensation will remain below the level of the injury, and it is possible that the sides of the body will be affected differently. If damage occurs to the ascending pathways, sensations arising from receptors below the level of the injury will be lost. If nerve fibers in the descending tracts are cut, the result will be loss of motor functions.

### Level of injury

The level or location of the injury also determines impairment. In general, the higher up the spinal cord the injury occurs, the greater the extent of disability. An injury to the lower segment of the cord (lumbar and sacral areas), for example, will affect the lower extremities. A cervical (neck) injury, on the other hand, may result in paralysis in both the arms and the legs, as well as loss of many vital involuntary functions, such as breathing.

## THE BRAIN

Composed of about 100 billion neurons, the brain is highly complex in both structure and function. As shown in Figure 4.6, it is divided into four main parts: (1) brain stem, (2) diencephalon, (3) cerebrum, and (4) cerebellum. The brain stem and diencephalon serve many vital functions; their major roles with respect to movement production and control include serving as a reflex center and relaying sensory and motor information between different parts of the brain and between the brain and the spinal cord. The cerebrum and cerebellum, however, contribute more extensively to movement, and they will receive greater attention here.

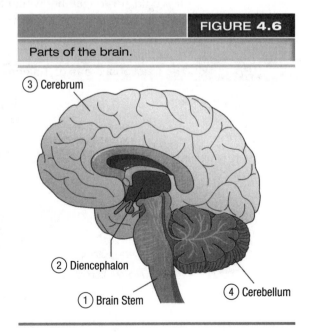

FIGURE 4.6

Parts of the brain.

③ Cerebrum

② Diencephalon

① Brain Stem

④ Cerebellum

## Cerebrum

The cerebrum is the largest portion of the brain. It is divided into left and right cerebral hemispheres, each of which is concerned with the sensory and motor functions of the opposite side of the body. The outermost layer of the cerebrum is the **cerebral cortex.** It is here that we find the centers responsible for higher brain functions.

### Cerebral cortex

The cerebral cortex can be subdivided into three functional areas: (1) sensory areas, (2) motor areas, and (3) association areas. Each of these areas can be further subdivided as depicted in Figure 4.7. This discussion will focus on those areas associated with movement production and control. It should be noted that the areas do not function independently and that a detailed examination is beyond the scope of this text.

**Sensory areas.** The sensory areas interpret information received from the various sensory receptors. The primary somatosensory area receives sensations from cutaneous receptors (touch, pressure, temperature, pain) and proprioceptors in the periphery of the body. In this area, the information is processed and an individual becomes consciously aware of not only the sensation itself, but also the exact location from which the sensation arose. Primary somatosensory area damage from a stroke, for example, will eliminate one's conscious ability to feel and localize touch and pressure on the skin. This in turn will affect grip and object manipulation (Leonard, 1998). In addition, a loss in joint position awareness will result, as the individual will no longer be able to perceive accurate sensory feedback associated with movement. Movements will, therefore, become uncoordinated.

In contrast, the secondary somatosensory area serves to integrate and interpret sensory signals. If damage were to occur in this area of the cerebral cortex, sensory information that would normally be associated with object manipulation would no longer be available. For example, your ability to identify that your hand is feeling a golf ball versus a racquetball would be impaired. In addi-

---

**FIGURE 4.7**    The functional areas of the cerebral cortex.

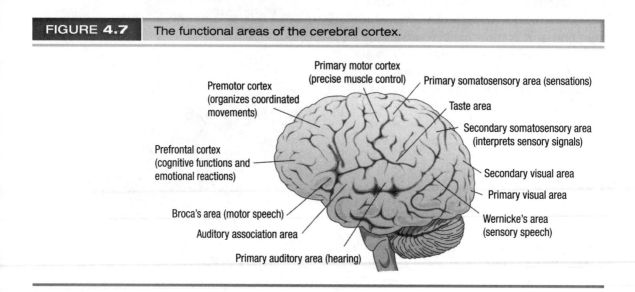

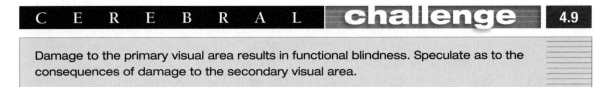

Damage to the primary visual area results in functional blindness. Speculate as to the consequences of damage to the secondary visual area.

tion, because signals to the secondary area are partly processed in the primary somatosensory area before being relayed, impairments similar to those described above for the primary somatosensory area will be manifested.

Given the role of vision in movement, the visual areas deserve attention. The visual areas can also be subdivided into primary and secondary areas. The primary visual area receives visual information regarding the image formed on the retina. Whereas this area detects light and dark spots and determines the orientation of the visual field, it is the function of the secondary visual area to interpret what one is seeing.

**Motor areas.** The function of the motor areas is to coordinate and initiate voluntary movements of skeletal muscles. The primary motor cortex is the region responsible for initiating skilled voluntary movements, including those required for the performance of fine motor skills. Decisions regarding how to initiate those movements are a function of the premotor cortex, which lies just anterior to the primary motor cortex. More specifically, the premotor cortex organizes learned coordinated movements that involve complex sequencing of muscles. For example, if a performer decides to take a step, decisions regarding which muscles to contract, in what order, and to what degree are made in the premotor cortex (Seeley, Stephens & Tate, 1997). Impulses are then sent to the primary motor cortex, which initiates each planned movement.

**Association areas.** The association areas are concerned with the analysis and interpretation of sensory information. For this function, it appears that new sensory inputs are associated with past experiences. The prefrontal cortex's role involves emotional reactions and cognitive functions. Attentiveness, the ability to make accurate judgments, planning for future events, and the motivation to practice depend on prefrontal cortex functioning.

A second area, known as the general interpretive area, plays a primary role in complex thought processing. Situations are interpreted as a result of the integration of sensory information in this region. The interpretation is then sent to the prefrontal cortex, where it is linked with emotion and a decision on how to respond is made.

### Basal ganglia

The basal ganglia are a group of functionally related nuclei that lies deep within the cerebrum. Extensive communication occurs between the basal ganglia and both the cerebral cortex and the brain stem, creating a loop of information flow that is relayed through the thalamus. The basal ganglia is important in the initiation and control of subconscious gross body movements, such as swinging the arms while walking (Tortora, 1997), and plays a key role in regulating the intensity (scaling) of movement parameters. The importance of scaling movement parameters is demonstrated through the functional changes that occur in two different degenerative conditions of the basal ganglia. The first, Parkinson's disease, which is characterized by slow, uncontrollable shaking (tremor) of the limbs and difficulty in initiating voluntary movements, is the result of understimulation of the basal ganglia. Huntington's disease, on the other hand, is the result of an overstimulation of the basal ganglia. An individual with this condition will display uncontrollable jerking movements of the limbs and/or facial muscles.

## Cerebellum

The cerebellum monitors movement by comparing the intended movement that was programmed by the motor areas to what is actually taking place. In other words, it compares the sensory input it receives from proprioceptors and visual receptors to the expected sensory consequences. Consequently, it plays a key role in the detection and correction of errors and works in conjunction with the motor cortex to produce smooth coordinated movements. The cerebellum is also important in the maintenance of posture and balance.

## MEMORY

An exploration of the brain and motor skill acquisition and performance would be incomplete without a discussion about memory. **Memory** is the ability to store and recall information. That information may be a friend's phone number, or it may represent past movement experiences that help with decisions about what motor response to make and how to make it. Several changes have to occur in the CNS in order for an experience to become represented in memory. While portions of the brain, including the association cortex of the frontal, parietal, occipital, and temporal lobes; parts of the limbic system; and the diencephalon, are known to be associated with memory, much about its function remains unknown.

## C E R E B R A L  challenge  4.10

A patient who was not wearing a helmet suffered brain damage as a result of a serious biking accident. The part of the brain affected was the cerebellum. Speculate as to what behaviors this patient would display as a result of trauma to the cerebellum.

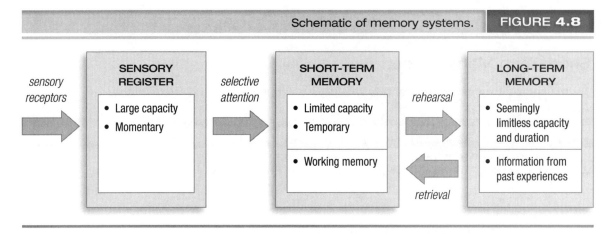

Schematic of memory systems.     FIGURE 4.8

## Composition of Memory

A popular model of memory offered by Atkinson and Shiffrin (1968, 1971) and illustrated in Figure 4.8 proposed that memory is composed of three distinct systems, each of which is defined by its storage and processing characteristics: the sensory register, short-term memory, and long-term memory systems.

### Sensory register

A continuous flow of information is transmitted by the body's sensory receptors and stored momentarily (a few hundred milliseconds) in the sensory register. The information we selectively attend to will be further processed, while that to which we do not attend will be lost.

### Short-term memory (STM)

From the sensory register, the selected information is passed on to the next system, the short-term memory, where we become consciously aware of it. In contrast to the sensory register, the STM has a limited capacity and can hold only seven plus or minus two items or chunks of information at a given time (Miller, 1956). In addition, the information is retained in this temporary storage space for only 20 to 30 seconds unless it is given further attention through processing activities such as repetition, association, or rehearsal. Active processing is also necessary to transfer the information for more permanent storage in long-term memory. Without this transfer, effective learning is not possible. Try Exploration Activity 4.11 to explore the capacity of your own short-term memory.

### Long-term memory (LTM)

Long-term memory is characterized as having a seemingly limitless capacity and duration. LTM consists of three subsystems (Tulving, 1985). The first two, episodic and semantic memory, are concerned with factual information. **Episodic memory**

## exploration    A C T I V I T Y    4.11

### Short-Term Memory Test

Try the short-term memory test at http://faculty.washington.edu/chudler/stm0.html.
Attempt all six trials.

How do your results compare to the limited capacity of seven plus or minus two items? What strategies did you use to remember the letters?

For more memory games and strategies to improve your memory, go to www.exploratorium.edu/memory/dont_forget/index.html.

contains information about personal experiences and events that are associated with a specific time and context. Your high school graduation date is an example of knowledge represented by episodic memory. **Semantic memory,** on the other hand, represents general knowledge that is developed by our experiences but not associated with time. Factual knowledge, such as your school colors, and conceptual knowledge, such as your concept of success, are included in semantic memory. Consequently, episodic and semantic memory store information that we use to decide what to do in a given situation. This information is also termed **declarative knowledge.** The third subsystem, **procedural memory,** retains information regarding how to do something. It is the memory of skills, operations, and actions, or **procedural knowledge,** and is fundamental to our ability to achieve movement goals.

### STM and LTM: Partners in Integration

There is more to memory than simply the storage of information. Short- and long-term memory work together to integrate information about the current situation and past experiences, which, in turn, enables a performer to make, execute, and evaluate strategic and movement decisions. For example, a racquetball player must combine information about the current situation, such as the position of the opponent and her level of fatigue, with information retrieved from LTM about past experiences, such as the opponent's strengths, weaknesses, and probable responses, in order to decide what serve to use. Furthermore, once the serve has been selected, additional information and integration are needed for its execution. These integrative processes take place in STM, which has also been labeled working memory because of its active role in information processing (Baddeley & Hitch, 1974).

### Forgetting

Through practice, learners can transfer increased information into LTM. However, all performers, regardless of skill level, are vulnerable to the phenomenon of forgetting. Two theories have been proposed to explain forgetting. The first, known as the decay theory, suggests that forgetting occurs as a result of the passage of time. A second theory, the interference theory, proposes that forgetting can be attributed to either proactive or retroactive interference. In **proactive interference,** old memories interfere with the retention of newly presented information that is to be remembered. **Retroactive interference** occurs when learning something new interferes with the retention of older memories. Figure 4.9 illustrates these two types of inhibition, using the example of an individual who took surfing lessons over the summer and is now learning how to snowboard. If this person experiences difficulties in remembering a snowboarding movement because of experiences with surfing, then proactive interference is said to occur. On the other hand, if the learner forgets how to perform a surfing movement as a result of interference from newly learned snowboarding skills, this is retroactive interference.

## Tips for Practitioners

Because of limitations in memory capacity, keep instructions, verbal cues, and feedback short and simple. Respect key learning points and provide ample opportunities for physical rehearsal. Since meaningful information is more easily retained, relate the skill being learned to previously learned skills. Use meaningful verbal labels and analogies to strengthen associations. For example, the tibial drop back or sag test is so named because it provides a static view of the amount of posterior translation or sag caused by gravity in a knee with a posterior cruciate ligament tear. Similarly, in tennis, learners are instructed to "shake hands" with the racket rather than provided with a less memorable, detailed explanation to convey the grip. Finally, grouping or "chunking" several movements together into a single unit is an effective method of reducing the amount of information a learner must remember, as demonstrated in Exploration Activity 4.12.

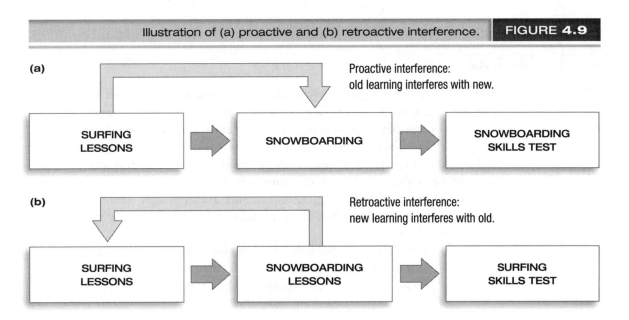

Illustration of (a) proactive and (b) retroactive interference.    **FIGURE 4.9**

# exploration ACTIVITY 4.12

## Chunking

Below is a list of 21 letters. Study the letters for 15 seconds and then close your book. Based on what you remember, write down as many letters as you can.

TRY

CHU

NKI

NGT

HEL

ETT

ERS

How did you do? What strategies did you use to remember the letters?

One strategy that you may have used to recall the letters in this activity is called chunking. If you look at the first three letters, they spell the word *try*. By grouping the letters into a word, you now only have to remember one word instead of three individual letters. Since STM is limited in capacity to seven plus or minus two items, chunking can increase the amount of information that can be remembered. In fact, as you may have realized, the letters spell out the following: TRY CHUNKING THE LETTERS. If you noticed this trick, remembering all 21 letters would have been easy!

# ▶ a look ahead

At this point, the complexity involved in movement production should be apparent. Numerous receptors provide information to various levels of the CNS via afferent pathways for integration. Reflexes are integrated at the spinal cord, while information requiring conscious thought travels up the spinal cord to various locations of the brain, where it is integrated and interpreted. Through the collective efforts of numerous brain structures, including the cerebral cortex and basal ganglia, movements are organized and signals are sent to the effectors to produce the output, which is continuously monitored by the cerebellum.

The focus of Chapters 1 through 4 has been on the behavioral and neurological processes that influence performance. We will now build on this foundational knowledge of how skilled movements are produced and examine the processes involved in their acquisition and refinement. The next chapter begins this discussion by examining the characteristics of learners as they progress from novice to expert.

# ● focus points

After reading this chapter, you should know that . . .

- The nervous system is responsible for the processes that underlie movement preparation, execution, and control.
- Sensory receptors can be classified as exteroceptors, interoceptors, and proprioceptors.
- Vision is the dominant sensory system. Interest in its role in the production of skilled movement has led to the development of a subdiscipline known as sport vision.
- The focal system functions to identify objects primarily located in the central region of the visual field, while the ambient system is responsible for spatial localization and orientation.
- The focal and ambient systems work in conjunction to process visual information during movement.
- Visual search is the manner by which the performer directs his or her attention while trying to locate critical regulatory cues.
- Proprioceptors provide information regarding body position and movement by detecting changes in muscle tension, joint position, and equilibrium through golgi tendon organs, muscle spindles, joint kinesthetic receptors, and the vestibular apparatus.
- Proprioception provides information about initial body and limb position that serves as the basis for the programming of motor commands, evaluates ongoing movements by comparing proprioceptive feedback to the intended goal, and provides response-produced feedback that can be used to make adjustments on the next trial.
- The spinal cord serves as a reflex center and a pathway for the transmission of sensory and motor information.
- The cerebral cortex plays a significant role in movement production and control through three major functional areas (sensory, motor, and association) where interpretive and integrative processes occur.
- The cerebellum plays a key role in error detection and correction and in the maintenance of posture and balance.
- Learning occurs when information is moved from short- to long-term memory.

# ? review questions

1. Which photoreceptor is specialized for vision in dim light? Which one is specialized for visual acuity?

2. Compare and contrast focal and ambient vision. Which one of the two deals with peripheral vision?

3. Define fixation. How can we use fixations to infer visual attention?

4. Describe the different visual requirements for targeting, interceptive, and tactical skills.

5. Compare and contrast golgi tendon organs, muscle spindles, joint kinesthetic receptors, and the vestibular apparatus.

6. What functional problems would be associated with damage to the dorsal column pathways? The extrapyramidal pathway?

7. What are the five components of a reflex arc? Explain why reflexes are faster than voluntary movements.

8. What are the three memory systems? Compare each with respect to capacity and duration.

9. Explain why phone numbers are traditionally seven digits.

10. Why is STM also referred to as working memory?

# REFERENCES

Abernethy, B. (1986). Enhancing sports performance through clinical and experimental optometry. *Clinical and Experimental Optometry, 69,* 189–96.

Abernethy, B. (1991). Visual search strategies and decision-making in sport. *International Journal of Sport Psychology, 22,* 189–210.

Abernethy, B. (1996). Training the visual-perceptual skills of athletes: insights from the study of motor expertise. *The American Journal of Sports Medicine, 24*(6), S-89–S-92.

Abernethy, B. & Wollstein, J. (1989). Improving anticipation in racquet sports. *Sports Coach, 12*(4), 15–18.

Abernethy, B. & Woods, J. (2000). Do generalized visual training programmes for sport really work? An experimental investigation. *Journal of Sports Sciences, 19,* 203–22.

Atkinson, R.C. & Shiffrin, R.M. (1968). Human memory: a proposed system and its control processes. In K.W. Spence and J.T. Spence (Eds.), *The psychology of learning and motivation (vol. 2)* (pp. 89–195). Orlando, FL: Academic Press.

Atkinson, R.C. & Shiffrin, R.M. (1971). The control of short-term memory. *Scientific American, 225,* 82–90.

Azar, B. (1998). Why can't this man feel whether or not he is standing up? *APA Monitor Online, 29*(6).

Baddeley, A.D. & Hitch, G. (1974). Working memory. In G.H. Bower (Ed.), *The psychology of learning and motivation: advances in research and theory (Vol. 8)* (pp. 47–89). New York: Academic Press.

Bahill A.T. & LaRitz, T. (1984). Why can't batters keep their eyes on the ball? *American Scientist, 72,* 249–53.

Bleuse, S., Cassim, F., Blatt, J., Defebvre, L., Derambure, P. & Guieu, J. (2005). Vertical torque allows recording of anticipatory postural adjustments associated with slow, arm-raising movements. *Clinical Biomechanics, 20*(7), 693–99S.

Cole, J. (1995). *Pride and a daily marathon.* Cambridge, MA: MIT Press.

Danion, F., Boyadjian, A. & Marin, L. (2000). Control of locomotion in expert gymnasts in the absence of vision. *Journal of Sports Sciences, 18,* 809–14.

Farrow, D., Chivers, P., Hardingham, C. & Sasche, S. (1998). The effect of video based perceptual training on the tennis return of serve. *International Journal of Sports Psychology, 29,* 231–42.

Fleury, M., Bard, C., Teasdale, N., Paillard, J., Cole, J., Lajoie, Y. & Lamarre, Y. (1995). Weight judgment: the discrimination capacity of a deafferented subject. *Brain, 118,* 1149–1156.

Helsen, W.F. & Pauwels, J.M. (1992). A cognitive approach to visual search in sport. In D. Brogan, A. Gale, and K. Carr (Eds.), *Visual search 2* (pp. 379–88). London: Taylor and Francis.

Hollands, M.A., Patla, A.E. & Vickers, J.N. (2002). Look where you are going! Gaze behavior associated with maintaining and changing direction. *Experimental Brain Research, 143,* 221–30.

Kluka, D.A. (1999). *Motor behavior: from learning to performance.* Englewood, CO: Morton.

Kluka, D.A. & Knudson, D. (1997). The impact of vision training on sport performance. *Journal of Health, Physical Education, Recreation and Dance, 68*(4), 17–24.

Kreighbaum, E. & Barthels, K. (1996). *Biomechanics: a qualitative approach for studying human movement.* San Francisco: Benjamin Cummings.

Lajoie, Y., Paillard, J., Teasdale, N., Bard, C., Fleury, M., Forget, R. & Lamarre, Y. (1992). Mirror drawing in a deafferented patient and normal subjects: visuoproprioceptive conflict. *Neurology, 42*(5): 1104–1106.

Land, M.F. & McLeod, P. (2000). From eye movements to actions: how batsmen hit the ball. *Nature Neuroscience, 3,* 1340–1345.

Laskowski, E.R., Newcomer-Aney, K. & Smith, J. (1997). Refining rehabilitation with proprioception training: expediting return to play. *The Physician and Sportsmedicine, 25*(10), 89–102.

Leach, R.E. (1982). Overall view of rehabilitation of the leg for running. In R.P. Mack (Ed.), *Symposium on the foot and leg in running sports.* St. Louis, MO: Mosby.

Lee, D.N. (1976). A theory of visual control of braking based on information about time to collision. *Perception, 5,* 437–59.

Lee, D.N. (1980). Visuo-motor coordination in space-time. In G.E. Stelmach and J. Requin (Eds.), *Tutorials in motor behavior* (pp. 281–95) Amsterdam: North-Holland Publishing.

Lee, D.N. & Aronson, E. (1974). Visual proprioceptive control of standing in human infants. *Perception and Psychophysics, 15,* 527–32.

Lee, D.N., Lischman, J.R. & Thomson, J.A. (1982). Regulation of gait in long jumping. *Journal of Experimental Psychology: Human Perception and Performance, 8,* 448–59.

Leonard, C.T. (1998). *The neuroscience of human movement.* St. Louis, MO: Mosby-Year Book.

Lepart, S. (2004). Reestablishing neuromuscular control. In W.E. Prentice (Ed.), *Rehabilitation techniques in sports medicine,* 4th ed. (pp. 100–20). Dubuque, IA: WCB/McGraw-Hill.

Magill, R.A. (1998). Knowledge is more than we can talk about: implicit learning in motor skill acquisition. *Research Quarterly for Exercise and Sport, 69*(2), 104–10.

Marieb, E.N., Mallatt, J. & Wilhelm, P.B. (2008). *Human anatomy.* San Francisco: Benjamin Cummings.

Martell, S. & Vickers, J.N. (2004). Gaze characteristics of elite and near-elite ice hockey players. *Human Movement Science, 22,* 689–712.

Mennie, N.N., Hayhoe, M.M., Stupak, N. & Sullivan, B. (2005). Sources of information for catching balls [Abstract]. *Journal of Vision, 5*(8):383.

Miller, G.A. (1956). The magical number seven, plus or minus two: some limits on our capacity for processing information. *Psychological Review, 63,* 81–97.

Milne, C., Buckholz, E. & Cardenas, M. (1995). Relationship of eye dominance and batting performance in baseball players. *International Journal of Sports Vision, 2*(1), 17–21.

Nagano, T., Kato, T. & Fukuda, T. (2004). Visual search strategies of soccer players in one-on-one defensive situations on the field. *Perceptual and Motor Skills, 99,* 968–74.

Panchuk, D. & Vickers, J.N. (2006). Gaze behaviors of goalies under spatial-temporal constraints. *Human Movement Science, 25,* 733–52.

Park, S. & Toole, T. (1999). Functional roles of the proprioceptive system in the control of goal-directed movement. *Perceptual and Motor Skills, 88*(2), 631–47.

Patla, A. & Vickers, J.N. (1997). When and where do we look as we approach and step over an obstacle in the travel path? *NeuroReport, 8*(17), 3661–3665.

Pew, R.W. (1974). Levels of analysis in motor control. *Brain Research, 71,* 393–400.

Prentice, W.E. (1999). Using therapeutic exercise in rehabilitation. In W.E. Prentice (Ed.), *Rehabilitation techniques in sports medicine,* 3rd ed. (pp. 226–43). Boston: WCB/McGraw-Hill.

Prentice, W.E. (2009). *Arnheim's principles of athletic training: a competency based approach.* New York: McGraw-Hill.

Raab, M., Masters, R.S.W. & Maxwell, J.P. (2005). Improving the "how" and "what" decisions of elite table tennis players. *Human Movement Science, 24,* 326–44.

Refshauge, K.M., Raymond, J., Kilbreath, S.L., Pengal, L. & Heijnen, I. (2008). The effect of ankle taping on detection of inversion-eversion movements in participants with recurrent ankle sprain. *The American Journal of Sports Medicine, 0,* 1–5.

Ripoll, H., Bard, C. & Paillard, J. (1986). Stabilization of head and eye movements on target as a factor of successful basketball shooting. *Human Movement Science, 5,* 47–58.

Ripoll, H. & Fleurance, P. (1988). What does keeping one's eye on the ball mean? *Ergonomics, 31*(11), 1647–1654.

Ripoll, H., Fleurance, P. & Cazeneuve, D. (1987). Analysis of the visual strategies involved in the execution of forehand and backhand strokes in table tennis. In J. K. O'Regan and A. Levy-Schoen (Eds.), *Eye movements: from physiology to cognition* (pp. 234–65). Amsterdam: Elsevier Science.

Rodrigues, S.T., Vickers, T.N. & Williams, A.M. (2002). Head, eye and arm coordination in table tennis. *Journal of Sports Sciences, 20,* 187–200.

Savelsbergh, G.J.P., Williams, A.M., van der Kamp, J. & Ward, P. (2002). Visual search, anticipation and expertise in soccer goalkeepers. *Journal of Sports Sciences, 20,* 279–87.

Seeley, R., Stephens, T. & Tate, P. (1997). *Anatomy and physiology,* 3rd ed. St. Louis: Mosby-Year Book.

Shank, M.D. & Haywood, K.M. (1987). Eye movements while viewing a baseball pitch. *Perceptual and Motor Skills, 64,* 1191–1197.

Shea, C.H., Shebilske, W.L. & Worchel, S. (1993). *Motor learning and control.* Englewood Cliffs, NJ: Prentice-Hall.

Singer, R.N., Cauraugh, J.H., Chen, D., Steinberg, G.M., Frehlich, S.G. & Wang, L. (1994). Training mental quickness in beginning/intermediate tennis players. *The Sport Psychologist, 8,* 305–18.

Starkes, J.L., & Lindley, S. (1994). Can we hasten expertise by video simulation? *Quest, 46,* 211–22.

Tortora, G.J. (1997). *Introduction to the human body: the essentials of anatomy and physiology.* Mountain View, CA: Benjamin Cummings.

Tulving, E. (1985). How many memory systems are there? *American Psychologist, 40,* 385–98.

Verhagen, E., van der Beek, A., Twisk, J., Bouter, L., Bahr, R. & van Mechelen, W. (2004). The effect of a proprioceptive balance board training program for the prevention of ankle sprains: a prospective controlled trial. *The American Journal of Sports Medicine, 32,* 1385–1393.

Vickers, J.N. (1992). Gaze control in putting. *Perception, 21,* 117–32.

Vickers, J.N. (1996). Visual control when aiming at a far target. *Journal of Experimental Psychology: Human Perception and Performance, 22,* 342–54.

Vickers, J.N. (2004). The quiet eye: it's the difference between a good putter and a poor one. *Golf Digest, January,* 96–101.

Vickers, J.N. (2007). *Perception, cognition and decision training: the quiet eye in action.* Champaign, IL: Human Kinetics.

Vickers, J.N. & Adolphe, R.A. (1997). Gaze behaviour during a ball tracking and aiming skill. *International Journal of Sports Vision, 4*(1), 18–27.

Vickers, J.N., Livingston, L., Umeris, S. & Holden, D. (1999). Decision training: the effects of complex instruction, variable practice and reduced delayed feedback on the acquisition and transfer of a complex motor skill. *Journal of Sports Sciences, 17,* 357–67.

Williams, A.M. & Davids, K. (1998). Visual search strategy, selective attention, and expertise in soccer. *Research Quarterly for Exercise and Sport, 69*(2), 111–28.

Williams, A.M., Davids, K., Burwitz, L. & Williams, J.G. (1994). Visual search strategies in experienced and inexperienced soccer players. *Research Quarterly for Exercise and Sport, 65*(2), 127–35.

Williams, A.M., Singer, R.A. & Frehlich, S. (2002). Quiet eye duration, expertise and task complexity in a near and far aiming task. *Journal of Motor Behavior, 34,* 197–207.

Witt, J.K. & Proffitt, D.R. (2005). See the ball, hit the ball: apparent ball size is correlated with batting average. *Psychological Science, 16*(12), 937–38.

# Stages of Learning

I n 1927, Babe Ruth hit 60 home runs in a single season. That record would stand for 34 years, until 1961, when the NY Yankees' Roger Maris hit 61. The home run record for a single season was not challenged again until 1998, when the St. Louis Cardinals' Mark McGwire recorded 70 runs, a mark that would be surpassed by Barry Bonds, who hit 73 in 2001.

Who will be the next home run champion? Only time will tell. But for those who pursue this goal, the journey will be a long one. Reaching the high caliber of skill obtained by these great hitters not only requires underlying ability but will take countless hours of hard work and practice—practice that is grounded in the underlying principles discussed thus far that affect skill acquisition and control—practice that is also designed to accommodate the changing needs of the learner as he or she moves through the learning process.

## MODELS OF STAGES OF LEARNING

W hen developing motor skill proficiency, regardless whether it is hitting a baseball or re-learning how to walk after a serious accident, learners progress through stages. Several models, each examining the progression from beginner to expert from a different perspective, have been proposed. These models can assist practitioners in defining the needs of their learners throughout the learning process and, in turn, enable them to select appropriate instructional activities. As you learn about each model, three considerations should be taken into account. First, although the models present each stage as distinct, in reality, transitions between learning stages cannot be clearly delineated, as one stage blends gradually into the next (Christina & Corcos, 1988; Fitts & Posner, 1967). Second, a learner can be in different stages for different skills. A soccer player, for example, might be considered highly skilled in dribbling but only a novice for heading the ball, if the skill is just being introduced. Finally, stages of learning are not dependent on age. Just ask Landon Shuffett, a seventh grader and recognized professional billiards player! You can watch him perform at the adjoining link.

**www.**

**Video story of Landon Shuffett**

www.youtube.com/watch?v=dFl_vsJJG7A

### Fitts and Posner's Three-Stage Model

To facilitate skill acquisition, practitioners must understand what is happening during the learning process from the learners' perspective. A popular model proposed by Fitts and Posner (1967) suggests that learners pass through three distinct stages. These three stages are defined by the behavioral tendencies learners display at various points throughout the learning process, as shown in Figure 5.1.

#### Cognitive stage

The first stage, the **cognitive stage,** is named for its high degree of cognitive activity. During this stage, the learner is first introduced to the new motor skill, and the primary task is to develop an understanding of the movement's requirements. A learner

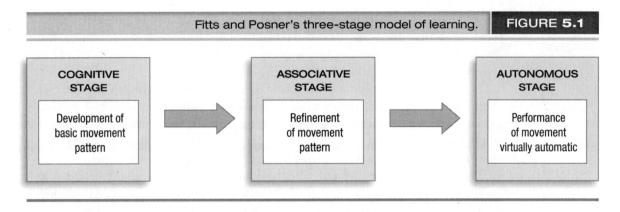

Fitts and Posner's three-stage model of learning. | FIGURE **5.1**

in this stage may have many questions. Think back to your experience with juggling. Questions such as How do I hold onto the balls? How and when do I let go? How high do I throw them? What is the pattern of movement? and countless others likely came to mind. To discover the answers to these questions, learners will often attempt numerous techniques and strategies through a trial-and-error approach. In addition, past movement experiences will be reformulated in an effort to solve the current movement problem. The resulting movements lack synchronization and appear choppy and deliberate. In addition, the attentional demands throughout this process are high and are limited to movement production. Consequently, difficulties will be apparent when learners are required to time their movements in conjunction with an external object or event. Performance at this stage is inconsistent and characterized by numerous errors, which are typically gross in nature.

Through effective verbal instructions and demonstrations, practitioners can facilitate a learner's progression through this stage. These instructions should take into account the fact that learners can more easily reformulate past movement experiences into new patterns if the similarities and differences between them are pointed out. Furthermore, whereas a trained observer may easily recognize the errors being made, the learner lacks the capability to determine the specific cause of an error and, therefore, is unable to determine and make necessary adjustments. Practitioners play a key role not only in the detection and correction of errors but also in the development of the learner's capability to do the same.

### Associative stage

The second stage, the **associative stage,** is characterized by marked performance improvements. Having attempted numerous possible movement strategies, a learner at this stage becomes committed to refining one particular movement pattern. Performance becomes more consistent, with fewer, less gross errors. A setter in the associative stage would, for example, be able to execute a clean pass but not always with the desired accuracy. The ability to time movements with external objects and events also improves as the attentional demands of performing the movement itself decrease, allowing learners to begin attending to other things. This results in a gain in the ability to make adjustments in movement in accordance with various environmental conditions. In this stage, the learner become increasingly capable of not only detecting the cause of errors but also developing appropriate strategies to eliminate them.

Given the changing characteristics of the learner, the practitioner's role at this stage shifts from one of predominantly providing instruction to that of designing constructive practice experiences. For open skills, those experiences should aid the development of visual search strategies as learners become increasingly able to direct their attention toward aspects of the performance environment. Finally, the provision of effective feedback continues to play an important role throughout this stage, not only to guide skill refinement but to further develop learners' error detection and correction capabilities by teaching them to relate response-produced feedback to the resulting performance outcome.

### Autonomous stage

Transition to the final stage in Fitts and Posner's model, the **autonomous stage,** requires countless hours of practice. In fact, this final stage is one that not all learners will reach. In the autonomous stage, performance reaches the highest level of proficiency and has become automated. Learners' attention during this stage is reallocated to strategic decision-making. In addition, the learner can perform multiple tasks simultaneously. Finally, learners in this stage are consistent and confident, make few errors, and can generally detect and correct those errors that do occur.

One might falsely assume that when a learner has reached this stage, the role of the practitioner is minimal at best. It is important to remember that while skill proficiency has reached the highest levels, there remains room for improvement. Practice design and error detection and correction remain responsibilities of the practitioner. Performance improvements are difficult to obtain at this level, and advances occur so gradually that learners can become discouraged and lose the motivation necessary to strive to obtain them, so the practitioner must serve in the capacity of motivator to assist learners in reaching their potential. Use Exploration Activity 5.2 to apply Fitts and Posner's stages to real-world performers.

## C E R E B R A L  challenge  5.1

Create a chart with column headings as shown below. Choose a skill or task and generate a list of practical tips practitioners could follow based on Fitts and Posner's description of the behavioral characteristics of the learner for their three-stage model.

Skill/Task:

| COGNITIVE | ASSOCIATIVE | AUTONOMOUS |
|-----------|-------------|------------|
|           |             |            |

## exploration  A C T I V I T Y  5.2

### Stage of Learning Analysis

*Task 1*

Observe and compare the forearm pass performance for each individual at the following web links:

>    www.youtube.com/watch?v=pkfDDtZMR_Q&feature=related
>    www.youtube.com/watch?v=IFwltz8xAgE

Based on your observations, determine which stage of learning each performer is in, using Fitts and Posner's model, and list the specific behavioral characteristics that led you to your decision.

*Task 2*

Observe a youth sport competition or practice in a skill of your choice. Choose five individuals to watch closely. Based on your observations, determine which stage of learning each performer is in, using Fitts and Posner's model, and list the specific behavioral characteristics that led you to your decision.

## Gentile's Two-Stage Model

Rather than simply describing the characteristics of the learner in each phase of the learning process, Gentile (1972, 1987) approached the identification of learning stages from the learners' perspective. More specifically, Gentile's model, illustrated in Figure 5.2, emphasizes the goal of the learner and the influence of task and environmental characteristics on that goal.

### *"Getting the idea of the movement" stage*

The first stage of learning in Gentile's model is termed **"getting the idea of the movement."** According to Gentile, the goal of the learner introduced to a new motor skill is to develop an understanding of the movement requirements that are necessary to meet the demands imposed by the characteristics of the task and the environment in which the task is to be performed and to organize a corresponding movement. Paramount to the learner's success in achieving this goal is the ability to discriminate between regulatory conditions and nonregulatory conditions. As you will recall from Chapter 1, regulatory conditions are environmental conditions that specify the movement characteristics necessary to perform the task. In contrast, nonregulatory conditions are those factors that are not inherently related to producing the appropriate motor response. To produce a movement pattern that meets the demands imposed by task and environmental conditions, the learner must be able to selectively attend to relevant information while ignoring irrelevant information.

| FIGURE 5.2 | Gentile's two-stage model of learning. |

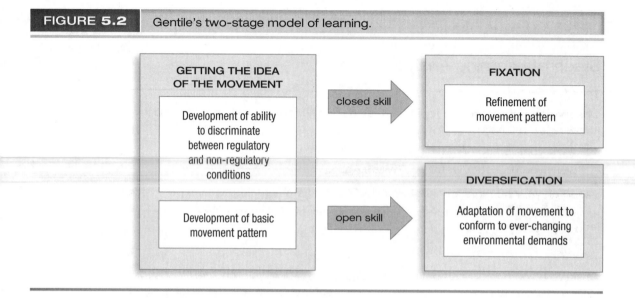

Instruction and practice during the initial stage of learning should facilitate learners' development of a basic movement pattern. To accomplish this, the practitioner must clearly communicate to the learner the goal of the task, through verbal instructions and demonstrations. In addition, the practitioner must point out those features of the environment that are regulatory and nonregulatory and direct learners' attention and visual search toward those stimuli that are relevant.

### Fixation/diversification stage

Once a general idea of the requisite movement pattern is acquired, the learner advances to the second and final stage, **fixation/diversification**. During this stage, the learner's goal is one of refinement. The nature of that refinement is a function of the predictability of the environment in which the skill is to be performed. Consequently, the learner's objective will be different for closed versus open skills. Closed skills, such as taping an ankle, performing a balance beam routine, or playing a musical instrument, are performed in a fixed, stable environment. Successful performance of such skills requires that the learner be able to replicate the movement pattern consistently and accurately (fixation). Open skills, on the other hand, are performed in an unpredictable, ever-changing environment. Accordingly, the performer must be able to adapt his or her responses continually to conform to these ever-changing demands (diversification). With open skills, the learner's objective is to diversify the movement pattern. An individual confined to a wheelchair, for example, must be able to change directions, traverse various surfaces and inclinations, and negotiate obstacles. Similarly, a hockey player must be able to shoot the puck from countless angles, distances, and positions, as well as negotiate around the movements of teammates and defenders.

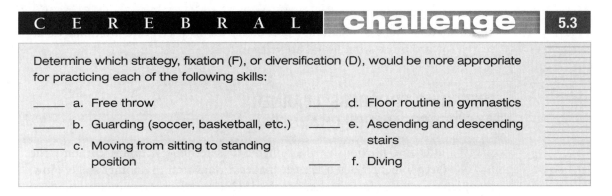

C E R E B R A L **challenge** 5.3

Determine which strategy, fixation (F), or diversification (D), would be more appropriate for practicing each of the following skills:

_____ a. Free throw

_____ b. Guarding (soccer, basketball, etc.)

_____ c. Moving from sitting to standing position

_____ d. Floor routine in gymnastics

_____ e. Ascending and descending stairs

_____ f. Diving

Once the learner has reached the fixation/diversification stage, the instructional strategies employed will depend on whether the skill is open or closed. For a closed skill, such as the free throw, where the regulatory conditions remain fixed during each successive performance attempt, practice should reflect these fixed conditions (basket is same height, shot taken from behind free throw line, etc.), while also subjecting the learner to the variety of nonregulatory cues that would normally occur (performer's level of fatigue, crowd noise, importance of the shot). If the regulatory conditions change across trials, as is the case in golf, learners should practice under the various regulatory conditions that may occur in the criterion condition (e.g., putts from various locations and distances on the green, including different slopes). This is also true of practice for open skills. Because learners performing open skills must be able to respond proficiently under ever-changing and often unpredictable environmental conditions, variations in regulatory conditions that simulate possible criterion conditions should be systematically introduced in practice. This approach not only assists the learner to acquire a larger repertoire of movement possibilities but also aids in the development of vital decision-making skills. Because decision-making depends on the learner's ability to detect regulatory cues and ignore nonregulatory stimuli,

C E R E B R A L **challenge** 5.4

Create a chart with column heads as shown below. Choose a skill or task and generate a list of practical tips practitioners could follow based on Gentile's two-stage model of learning.

Skill/Task: _____

| GETTING THE IDEA OF THE MOVEMENT | FIXATION | DIVERSIFICATION |
|---|---|---|
|  |  |  |

practitioners should continue to highlight those features of the environment that are regulatory and nonregulatory and direct the learner's attention and visual search toward those stimuli that are relevant.

## INFERRING PROGRESS: LEARNER AND PERFORMANCE CHANGES

As indicated previously, it is difficult to determine with any certainty the exact moment when a learner makes a transition to another stage. How, then, can we tell that learning has occurred? One of the most common methods of assessing an individual's progress is to note changes in observable motor behavior over time. The following section discusses a number of performance indicators that have been identified through the study of novice versus expert performers and can provide clues for the practitioner as to the progress of the learner.

### Movement Pattern

It would not be difficult to distinguish between the swing of a professional baseball player and that of a novice. While both may be able to achieve the goal of the task, hitting the ball, the movement pattern that they produce to do so will be quite different. As the novice hitter's skill level improves, however, these differences will diminish.

#### Increase in coordination and control

A learner's progression in skill acquisition characteristically results in several changes related to movement production, and perhaps the most notable changes are in coordination and control. As we learned in Chapter 3, the organization of a movement pattern that will effectively achieve the goal of the task requires that the learner coordinate and control numerous independent elements or degrees of freedom. In the early stages of skill acquisition, the learner attempts to accomplish this by freezing or fixing the possible movements of a joint so that the limb(s) will function as a single unit or segment. In other words, novices will reduce the available degrees of freedom to a more manageable quantity in order to accomplish the goal of the task. This strategy, termed **freezing the degrees of freedom** (Bernstein, 1967; Whiting, 1984) results in stiff, rigid, inefficiently timed movements. As learners progress in skill development, those degrees of freedom once constrained will be gradually released and collectively reorganized into a new movement pattern that is smoother, faster, and more closely resembling the correct movement.

Consider the swing pattern produced by a novice racquetball player compared to that of a highly skilled player. The novice will attempt to control the swing by restricting the movement that occurs at each joint. Consequently, the

FIGURE 5.3

Kinematic illustration of (a) freezing and (b) freeing the degrees of freedom for the arm and racket during a racquetball kill shot.

**(a)** Freezing     **(b)** Freeing

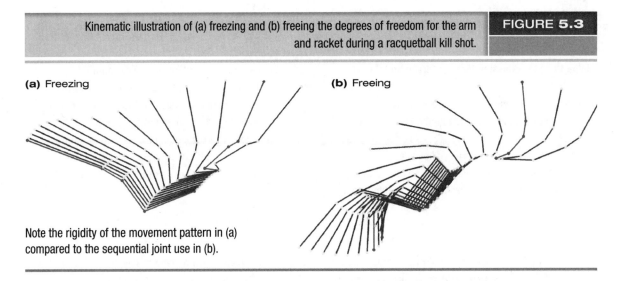

Note the rigidity of the movement pattern in (a) compared to the sequential joint use in (b).

novice will initially use a straight-arm swing, where the racquet is simply treated as a rigid extension of the arm. Furthermore, it is likely that the lower body will remain inactive. The pattern of coordination exhibited by a highly skilled player, depicted in Figure 5.3(b), incorporates multiple and sequential joint action (both upper and lower body), and, because of its biomechanical efficiency, the movement is significantly faster. Support for this resulting increase in velocity, as well as the notion of freezing and then gradually releasing or unfreezing the available degrees of freedom, has been found in studies investigating the acquisition of the forehand shot in racquetball (Southard & Higgins, 1987), kicking (Anderson & Sidaway, 1994), and learning a slalom skill on an indoor ski apparatus (Vereijken, van Emmerik, Whiting & Newell, 1992).

Recently, however, the notion of moving from freezing to freeing degrees of freedom during skill acquisition has come into question, and it has been suggested that the emergence of a particular pattern of coordination depends on the task (Newell, Broderick, Deutsch & Slifkin, 2003). In fact, studies have reported novices demonstrating larger ranges of motion initially and a freezing of the degrees of freedom as a result of practice. One example is a case study by Hodges, Hayes, Horn, and Williams (2005) where coordination changes were examined for a ball kicking task. Specifically, the task required a scoop-like movement over a low barrier to a target. With practice, range of motion (ROM) of the knee and ankle joints decreased, whereas an increased ROM was found at the hip. Similar findings were reported by Chow, Davids, Button, and Koh (2007), who investigated movement patterns that emerged as a function of the interaction between task constraints and stage of learning for a kicking task. For a soccer chip shot, they reported a movement pattern that involved greater ROM at the distal joints with less joint involvement at the proximal segments for skilled and intermediate players, versus the larger ranges of mo-

Using the soccer in-step kick, Anderson and Sidaway (1994) examined changes in coordination as a result of practice. Six novices, who were enrolled in a beginning soccer class, were given an initial demonstration of the skill. They then performed 15 to 20 shots for each of 20 practice sessions. Performance was videotaped before and after the practice period, and hip and knee peak angular velocities, timing variables, and joint range of motion were analyzed, along with maximum linear velocity of the foot (using motion analysis software). Results of the kinematic analysis revealed a change in the fundamental pattern of coordination for the skill as a result of practice. A corresponding increase in the maximum resultant linear velocity of the foot was also found, indicating the adoption of a more effective movement pattern.

tion of the kicking leg demonstrated by novices. The authors suggested that "it is possible that skilled and intermediate players are better able to optimize the intersegmental dynamics about the hip and knee to allow a functional movement to emerge" (p. 477). In other words, the optimal movement solution for the imposed task constraints, which was not discovered until later stages in learning, required greater ROM at one joint and less ROM at another.

Additional research is necessary to explore the interaction of task constraints and skill level for variations in coordination. Regardless, practitioners must be highly proficient not only in their knowledge of skill-specific performance indicators but also in skill analysis.

### More fluid muscle activity

Accompanying the reorganization of the system to produce a new pattern of coordination is a change in muscular activity. As the learner becomes more proficient, the number of muscles activated to produce a movement will be reduced to only those fundamental for correct performance. In addition, the timing and sequence with which the muscles are activated will be altered. Skilled movement is the result of cooperative actions of muscle groups (Hall, 2006). Early in the learning process, however, the cycle of muscle activation is mistimed. This has been found to be the case in sport skills (e.g., Jaegars et al., 1989; Lay, Sparrow, Hughes & O'Dwyer, 2002), rapid finger and arm movement tasks (e.g., Carson & Riek, 2001; Gabriel & Boucher, 1998; Schneider, Zernicke, Schmidt & Hart, 1989), and aiming tasks (e.g., Shemmell et al., 2005). With practice, correct activation patterns are achieved and movements become more fluid.

A professional cyclist uses only the essential muscles needed to create a skilled, fluid movement that appears effortless.

## More efficient energy expenditure

Unlike experts, whose movements appear effortless, beginners are mechanically inefficient. This can be readily seen with beginning swimmers who are learning to flutter kick. Because of poor mechanics, many beginners will initially lack forward progress, and some will even move backward in the water! Puzzled by their lack of movement across the pool, they will quite often kick harder, but to no avail. Fatigue will eventually set in, and the learner will have to rest before attempting the skill again.

Understandably, beginning swimmers will expend a great deal of energy (and frustration) through their efforts. We know, however, that with practice comes improved coordination, the use of only those muscles necessary, and increased accuracy of muscle activation. You can observe this firsthand by visiting a local pool and answering the questions in Exploration Activity 5.5. Through practice, movements become more efficient, and the amount of energy needed to perform them will be reduced. Eventually, this decreased energy expenditure will enable a once-frustrated swimmer to travel greater distances with less frequent rest periods.

## Increased consistency

Another means of assessing a learner's progress is through changes in performance consistency. Recall from Chapter 1 that learning is defined as a relatively permanent change in a person's capability to execute a motor skill, as a result of practice or experience. Indicative of a relatively permanent change is increased consistency (Yang & Scholz, 2005). It should be noted, however, that although a learner may be able to reproduce an action consistently, this does not necessarily mean that the skill is being performed correctly. Practitioners should consider several performance variables prior to making a judgment about learning.

## exploration ACTIVITY 5.5

### Observation: Expert versus Novice Swimmers

Visit a local swimming pool.

a. Watch a beginning swimmer performing freestyle for several minutes. Describe his or her technique. List the muscles that are involved in accomplishing this technique. Now watch an individual who is more proficient at the freestyle stroke. Describe his or her technique. Again, note the muscles involved in the performance.

b. What physical differences did you observe between the two learners' execution of the freestyle stroke?

Traditionally, increased movement consistency has been considered an indicator of skill development. Recently, however, it has been suggested that variability in the movement patterns of advanced performers may be an essential element that provides flexibility in adapting to perturbations (disturbances in motion). To examine this notion, Wilson, Simpson, van Emmerik, and Hamill (2008) examined the influence of skill on the coordination variability of the lower extremity in expert triple jumpers. They hypothesized that coordination variability would increase as skilled performance increased.

Five expert triple jumpers (personal best jumps = 70% of the current world record) performed 10 jumps. Three-dimensional kinematic data and ground reaction forces were recorded for the hop-step transition phase of the jump. De-scriptive data revealed that the participants who were least and most skilled displayed the highest coordination variability, whereas individuals of intermediate skill produced the most consistent movement coordination patterns. More specifically, higher variability was found for the swing leg of the least skilled participants, while the most skilled athletes displayed higher variability in the stance leg. Given the stance leg's role in impact and transitional actions, the authors speculate that it is likely to experience greater perturbations than the swing leg and that increased variability enables highly skilled athletes to cope with movement disruptions imposed by environmental or task constraints. Due to a number of limitations, including a small sample size, additional studies are necessary to explore this phenomenon further.

While increased consistency can be a sign of learning, practitioners can also look at the onset of *inconsistent* performance for clues about skill acquisition. As suggested above, a learner may develop a consistent movement pattern that is fundamentally flawed. Unless the movement is corrected, future progress will be impeded. To change a fundamentally flawed movement, the learner must learn new invariant characteristics, which means learning a new motor program. In the terms of the dynamic systems theory, the learner must move from one state of stability to a new state of stability (a phase shift). This transition, regardless of how we describe it, will first be characterized by increased inconsistency as the learner tries to abandon the old movement for the new coordination pattern. Eventually, with practice, the learner will begin to produce the new movement, and with continued practice, the movement will become consistent.

## Attention

Changes in both the amount of conscious attention focused on movement execution and the allocation of visual attention also accompany skill development. These changes lead to quicker and more accurate movement preparation and a corresponding reduction in response times.

### Attention to skill execution

Initially, learners concentrate on how to perform each technical component of a skill. Their undivided attention is focused solely on the skill's execution. As

Having just introduced a beginning soccer class to dribbling, the teacher designs a drill where the learners pair up and one dribbles to the other end of the field while avoiding the other person, who tries to take away the ball. Will this be an effective drill? Justify your answer.

their skill proficiency develops, the need to attend consciously to each aspect of the movement decreases, and eventually (after a great amount of practice) performance becomes virtually automatic. Conscious thought is no longer required to perform the movement. Throughout this transition, overt performance shifts, and an initial hesitancy with a robotic appearance becomes a smooth, free-flowing, and apparently effortless performance.

Once a learner reaches the point where the skill can be performed with little or no conscious control, two consequences emerge. First, the learner can now reallocate attentional resources to other factors of performance. For example, in the volleyball spike, rather than concentrating on the technique that will successfully result in ball contact, the learner can focus on game strategy, such as where to place the ball in the opponent's court. The learner becomes better able to focus on and evaluate the environmental context and, hence, able to respond more quickly and appropriately to performance conditions.

Now observe what happens in Exploration Activity 5.7. From this activity, you can see a second consequence of automaticity: once it is achieved, conscious control of the movement may actually be detrimental to performance. When a performer consciously focuses on the specifics of a well-learned skill that is normally performed automatically, the information needed to coordinate the muscle pattern is slowed (Byers, 2000). The resulting performance becomes hesitant and

**exploration** A C T I V I T Y 5.7

## Automatic Behaviors

Each able-bodied person has a walking pace that is natural for him or her. If able, determine your natural pace by walking down a hallway several times.

*Questions*

1. Describe what happened when you tried to determine your natural walking pace.
2. When a practitioner asks a patient to walk naturally across the clinic in order to evaluate his or her gait, would you expect to see similar results? Give suggestions to help ensure an accurate assessment.

## R E S E A R C H   N O T E S

To explore differences in attentional mechanisms as a function of skill level, Beilock, Carr, McMahon, and Starkes (2002) examined the dribbling performance of novice and experienced soccer players through a slalom course under a dual-task condition and a skill-focused condition. The dual-task condition involved dribbling through the course while concurrently monitoring a list of words and repeating the target word out loud each time it was heard. In the skill-focused condition, participants were prompted to focus on a specific component of the dribbling task. Participants performed the task under both conditions with both their dominant and non-dominant foot. As expected, for dominant-foot dribbling, novices were distracted during the dual-task condition and performed at a lower level than they did in the skill-focused condition, which was designed to draw their attention to the performance of the movement. The opposite pattern of results was found for the experienced players, whose performance declined when they focused on skill execution.

choppy. Adopting a "non-awareness" strategy, where the performer simply "lets the movement happen," is recommended.

When undergoing gait analysis, patients may become conscious of their movements and change their natural walking pattern.

### Allocation of visual attention

As we saw in Chapter 4, differences exist between experts and novices with respect to where their visual attention is allocated. Recall the study by Shank and Haywood (1987) showing that expert hitters not only direct their visual attention toward information-rich areas but also are able to ignore non-regulatory cues. Beginners, on the other hand, pay attention to too many things and have difficulty discriminating between environmental cues that are relevant and those that are irrelevant to performance. A superior visual attention allocation strategy, combined with extensive knowledge of the sport, enables highly skilled performers to recognize, predict, and respond to performance situations more accurately and rapidly than their less skilled counterparts (Abernethy, 1997).

## Knowledge and Memory

It stands to reason that changes in a learner's knowledge base regarding the activity would accompany performance changes. Quite simply, accomplished performers know more about the skill than do their less proficient counterparts. They have higher levels of both declarative knowledge (e.g., rules) and procedural knowledge (e.g., what to do in a given situation), giving them a larger knowledge base from which to draw (Thomas and Thomas, 1994).

C E R E B R A L **challenge** 5.8

List examples of declarative and procedural knowledge for a skill of your choice.

Skill: _____

Declarative: _____

_____

_____

Procedural: _____

_____

_____

The structure of that knowledge base (specific to the activity) has been found to be more complex in skilled performers and organized in a manner that facilitates pattern recognition and recall. This was demonstrated by Allard, Graham, and Paarsalu (1980), who found expert basketball players to be superior to novices in a recall study. Participants were shown two sets of slides that depicted basketball game situations. The difference between the two was that one set displayed structured situations and the other unstructured situations. At the end of a four-second viewing period, participants were asked to recreate the slide using magnets representing players on a magnet board that simulated half of a basketball court. The results found the experts to be superior to the novices at recalling the structured situations only. Since the experts' superiority only was evident in the game condition, it appears that experts are able to build a better representation of the problem because of their ability to organize or chunk information into meaningful units (Allard, 1982). This ability, along with a larger knowledge base, enables them to access information more efficiently, focus on higher-level concepts, make more connections between concepts, and, therefore, solve problems more quickly and with fewer errors (McPherson & Thomas, 1989; Thomas, French & Humphries, 1986). Similar results have been found in chess (Chase & Simon, 1973), snooker (Abernethy, Neal & Koning, 1994), and dance (Smyth & Pendleton, 1994).

## Error Detection and Correction

Another indicator of skill development is the increased ability of the learner to detect and correct performance errors. With practice, learners develop the capability to monitor and interpret the exteroceptive and proprioceptive feedback provided by the various sensory receptors. This information can be used either to make corrections during a movement (time permitting) or to direct future attempts.

As their error detection and correction capabilities improve, learners will become less dependent on practitioners. Questions such as "What did I do that time?" will decrease, and the questions will become more specific. Learners will also display behaviors indicating that they know they have made an error. For example, when performing the tennis serve, if the ball toss is off, less skilled learners will likely attempt to hit it anyway, jeopardizing the outcome, but more proficient learners will be able to recognize a bad ball toss and will let the ball drop so that they may re-toss it.

### Self-Confidence

As learners become more skilled, their confidence in their ability to perform the skill will increase. With increased confidence comes increased motivation to improve further. Consequently, when designing learning experiences, practitioners should ensure that each learner experiences some degree of success during each practice period.

## MEASURING PROGRESS

In addition to evaluating an individual's progress subjectively by observing variations in performance over time, a number of objective assessment measures may be used to evaluate the effectiveness of training or instructional strategies. These techniques allow the practitioner to document changes in proficiency by quantifying learning based on skilled performance indicators such as time, distance, and frequency.

### Performance Curves

A performance curve is obtained by systematically plotting the results from repeated measurements of a specific performance variable across time. The resulting graph offers the practitioner two pieces of information. First, the general direction of the curve is indicative of improvement. Second, by examining successive trials, the practitioner can make inferences about consistency.

To construct a performance curve, first select a performance variable to evaluate that is an appropriate indicator of skill. For example, the Functional Reach Test (Duncan, Weiner, Chandler & Studenski, 1990) may be used to evaluate the impact of a rehabilitation program designed to assist a patient in regaining postural control. To perform the test, the patient stands with feet shoulder width apart and one shoulder flexed to 90 degrees, so that the arm is parallel to the floor. The patient then reaches as far forward as possible while maintaining balance. The distance reached is measured and recorded. In Figure 5.4, the patient was tested once a week for a period of 12 weeks. On the graph, the distance reached is plotted on the y-axis and the number of weeks on the x-axis.

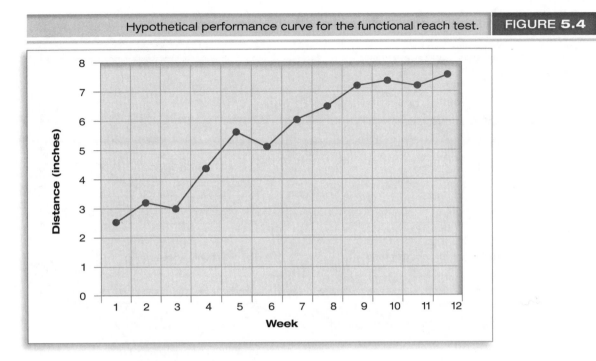

Hypothetical performance curve for the functional reach test.   **FIGURE 5.4**

## Types of performance curves

Performance curves generally follow one of four patterns (see Figure 5.5):

1. *A negatively accelerating curve*, reflects the **power law of practice:** when learning a new skill, there tends to be a large initial improvement in performance, which slows later in practice (Newell & Rosenbloom, 1981). This is the most common performance curve.

2. *A positively accelerating curve* is characterized by little initial improvement with larger gains occurring later.

3. *A linear curve* reflects a direct relationship between performance and time.

4. *An S-shaped curve* is a combination of the negative and positively accelerating curves.

When reading performance curves, keep in mind that the nature of the curve depends on what is being measured. For example, if the performance variable being measured is time and a decrease in the time required to execute the skill indicates improved performance, then the curve will be reversed.

## Limitations of performance curves

Although a popular method of documenting progress, performance curves do possess several limitations. To understand the first limitation, we must review the

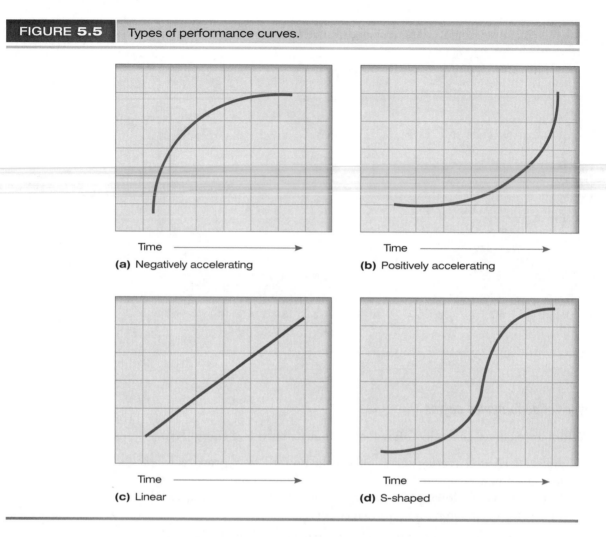

**FIGURE 5.5**    Types of performance curves.

**(a)** Negatively accelerating    Time

**(b)** Positively accelerating    Time

**(c)** Linear    Time

**(d)** S-shaped    Time

characteristics that distinguish between performance and learning. Recall that learning results in a relatively permanent change in a person's capability to execute a motor skill, whereas performance is simply the act of executing a skill. Because the measures for performance curves are taken during the practicing of a skill, they represent temporary effects and, therefore, cannot establish relative permanence. It is for this reason they are labeled performance curves rather than learning curves.

A second limitation is that the measurements used to construct the curve are often obtained by calculating the mean of several trials in a particular session. Two learners may have the same mean number of catches, but their performances for each trial could be very different. Examine the data of two learners' juggling performance in Table 5.1, for example. Each learner performed 10 trials in one session, and their resulting means are equal. However, learner A's performance is relatively consistent across trials, whereas learner B displays a much broader

## C E R E B R A L   **challenge**   5.9

Three learners were asked to practice juggling 10 minutes per day for 10 consecutive days. The mean number of catches per day was calculated by dividing the total number of catches by the number of trials. The mean number of catches per day for each learner is graphed below.

1. Categorize each participant's performance curve based on the four patterns depicted in Figure 5.5.
2. What conclusions can you make based on the data presented?

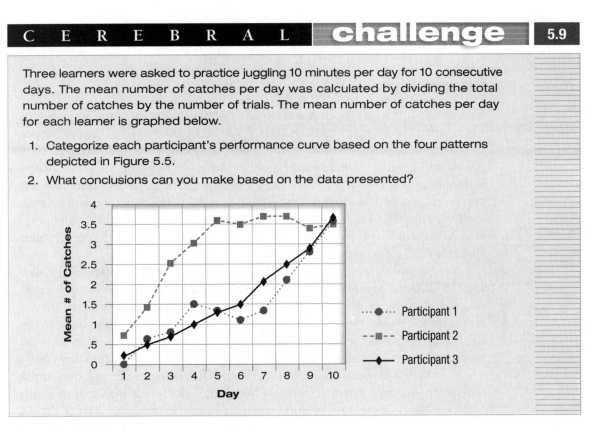

| TRIAL | LEARNER A | LEARNER B |
| :---: | :---: | :---: |
| | Individual juggling data (number of catches per trial in a 10-trial session) for two different learners. | TABLE **5.1** |
| 1 | 5 | 1 |
| 2 | 5 | 6 |
| 3 | 4 | 0 |
| 4 | 4 | 11 |
| 5 | 5 | 3 |
| 6 | 4 | 6 |
| 7 | 5 | 2 |
| 8 | 5 | 2 |
| 9 | 4 | 14 |
| 10 | 4 | 0 |
| MEAN | 4.5 | 4.5 |

range of scores. If we look only at the mean, valuable information regarding the learning process may be lost.

## Retention Tests

One method of inferring that a relatively permanent change in a performance has occurred is through a retention test. A **retention test** measures the persistence of improved skill performance. Unlike a **post-test,** which is administered directly following a practice period (which could be one session or multiple sessions) and is used to find out what a learner can do after practicing a skill, a retention test is given after a period of no practice (see Figure 5.6). The resulting performance level is compared to the initial performance level of that same skill (before practice). If the comparison indicates a high degree of improvement, you can infer that learning has occurred.

For example, at the beginning of a handball unit, The Tyson 30-Second Volley test (1970) could be administered to establish a baseline of the learner's skill proficiency prior to the practice period. To perform this particular skills test, the learner stands behind the short line of the court. When the signal is given, the student tosses the handball against the front wall and volleys it as many times as possible in 30 seconds. For a volley to be counted, it has to be made from behind the short line.

A common practice is to retest the learner following the completion of the unit, or to give a post-test. A post-test however, is not a true indicator of learning, as it does not measure performance persistency. Instead, the learner should be given a retention test, that is, retested following a period of no practice, such as one week after the completion of the handball unit.

## Transfer Tests

A second type of assessment that may be used to distinguish between temporary and permanent performance changes is a transfer test. A **transfer test** measures the degree to which a learner can adapt the practiced skill to a different performance situation. Variations in the skill itself or the environment in which it is performed can serve to test adaptability and permit the practitioner to infer learning. For example, a transfer test for a patient learning to execute a sit-to-stand

**FIGURE 5.6**    Retention test timeline.

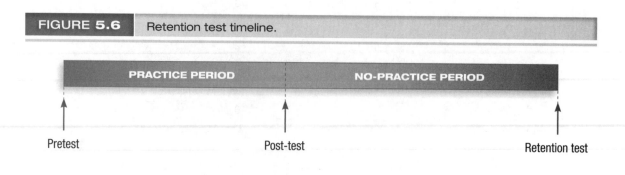

movement might involve a novel chair height or surface (e.g., firm versus padded). A transfer test for handball volleying might require the learner to strike the ball after it bounces off the back wall instead of the front wall. A useful resource for designing transfer tests is Gentile's (2000) taxonomy, discussed in Chapter 1.

## PERFORMANCE PLATEAUS

**P**ractitioners must be careful not to assume that learning has ceased when performance improvement subsides. It may be that the learner is experiencing a **performance plateau**—a period of time during the learning process in which no overt changes in performance occur. Again, it is important that practitioners be able to distinguish between temporary changes in performance and relatively permanent changes, which are indicative of learning.

**common** *myth*

Unless a learner displays some overt changes in performance, he or she is no longer learning.

Remember that learning is not directly observable. We cannot see what someone perceives, we cannot see what someone is thinking, and we cannot see changes in underlying behavioral and neurological processes. Thomas and Thomas (1994) remind us that "knowing when and how is not synonymous with the execution of the activity" (p. 296). Plateaus often represent transitional periods in the learning process where the integration of task components (and perhaps strategy) is being resolved. Consequently, performance plateaus do not necessarily indicate that the learner has stopped learning but are instead a normal part of the learning process. A second reason for the occurrence of performance plateaus is that performance may temporarily be affected by variables such as fatigue, anxiety, or lack of motivation. Finally, a plateau may be the result of limitations in the performance measurement used. Ceiling and floor effects occur when there is a maximum or minimum achievable score on a task. For example, if a learner's average number of successful free throws out of 10 were plotted on a performance curve, as he or she approached the ceiling (10), the performance curve would begin to plateau.

## ▶ a look ahead

Learners progress through distinct stages of learning as they acquire skill. Each stage is characterized by both behavioral changes and alterations in the goal of the learner. In addition, a number of learner and performance indicators have been identified to assist practitioners' inference of skill development. Understanding the characteristics of each learning stage, in addition to being able to assess a learner's proficiency level, can assist a practitioner's decision-making with respect to the delivery of instructions, the design of practice and experiences, and the provision of feedback. The next chapter begins our discussion of how to design appropriate learning environments by examining pre-instructional considerations that influence communication.

# ● focus points

After reading this chapter, you should know that . . .

- According to Fitts and Posner, learners pass through three distinct stages:
  1. Cognitive stage: development of basic movement pattern
  2. Associative stage: refinement of movement pattern
  3. Autonomous stage: performance of movement becomes virtually automatic
- Gentile's two-stage model emphasizes the goal of the learner and the influence of task and environmental characteristics on that goal.

   Stage 1: getting the idea of the movement

   Stage 2: fixation (closed skills)/diversification (open skills)
- To infer learning, the practitioner can assess numerous performance changes, including changes in coordination and control, muscle activity, energy expenditure, consistency, attentional focus, knowledge and memory, error detection and correction, and self-confidence.
- Progress can also be assessed through performance curves, retention tests, and transfer tests.
- Retention tests measure the persistence of improved skill performance.
- Transfer tests measure the degree to which the learner can adapt the practiced skill to a different performance situation.
- A performance plateau is a period of time during the learning process in which no overt changes in performance occur. Plateaus often represent transitional periods in the learning process where the integration of task components (and perhaps strategy) is being resolved; they are not necessarily indicative of a cessation in the learning process.

# ? review questions

1. Explain how the role of the instructor shifts as a learner progresses through Fitts and Posner's three stages of learning.
2. How does Gentile's model differ from that of Fitts and Posner?
3. Define fixation and diversification, and explain their relationship to closed and open skills.
4. List five performance characteristics that can help you infer learning has occurred.
5. What does "freezing the degrees of freedom" mean?
6. What are the two consequences of automaticity?

7. Explain how expert performers are able to build a better representation of the movement problem.

8. What can you look for to determine whether a learner's error detection and correction capabilities have improved? Do you have any suggestions beyond those listed in the chapter?

9. Why might it be a false assumption that someone is no longer learning if the person does not display any performance improvements?

10. Compare and contrast retention tests and transfer tests.

## REFERENCES

Abernethy, B. (1997). Motor control adaptations to training. In B. Abernethy, V. Kippers, L.T. Mackinnon, R.J. Neal and S. Hanrahan (Eds.), *The biophysical foundations of human movement* (pp. 334–53). Champaign, IL: Human Kinetics.

Abernethy, B., Neal, R.J. & Koning, P. (1994). Visual-perceptual and cognitive differences between expert, intermediate and novice snooker players. *Applied Cognitive Psychology, 8,* 185–211.

Allard, F. (1982). Cognition, expert performance and sport. In J.H. Salmela, J.T. Partington and T. Orlick (Eds.), *New paths of sport learning and excellence* (pp. 22–27). Ottawa: Sport in Perspectives.

Allard, F., Graham, S. & Paarsalu, M.F. (1980). Perception in sport: basketball. *Journal of Sport Psychology, 2,* 14–21.

Anderson, D.I. & Sidaway, B. (1994). Coordination changes associated with practice of a soccer kick. *Research Quarterly for Exercise and Sport, 65*(2), 93–99.

Beilock, S.L., Carr, T.H., McMahon, C. & Starkes, J.L. (2002). When paying attention becomes counterproductive: impact of divided versus skill focused attention on novice and experienced performance of sensorimotor skills. *Journal of Experimental Psychology, 8,* 6–16.

Bernstein, N. (1967). *The coordination and regulation of movements.* Oxford, England: Pergamon Press.

Byers, B.B. (2000). "Just do it": commercial slogan or movement principle? *Journal of Physical Education, Recreation and Dance, 71*(9), 16–19.

Carson, R.G. & Riek, S. (2001). Changes in muscle recruitment patterns during skill acquisition. *Experimental Brain Research, 138*(1), 71–87.

Chase, W.G. & Simon, H.A. (1973). Perception in chess. *Cognitive Psychology, 4,* 55–81.

Chow, J.Y., Davids, K., Button, C. & Koh, M. (2007). Variation in coordination of a discrete multiarticular action as a function of skill level. *Journal of Motor Behavior, 30,* 463–79.

Christina, R.W. & Corcos, D.M. (1988). *Coaches guide to teaching sport skills.* Champaign, IL: Human Kinetics.

Duncan, P.W., Weiner, D.K., Chandler, J. & Studenski, S. (1990). Functional reach: a new clinical measure of balance. *Journal of Gerontology: Medical Sciences, 45*(6), M192–M197.

Fitts, P.M. & Posner, M.I. (1967). *Human performance.* Belmont, CA: Brooks/Cole.

Gabriel, D.A. & Boucher, J.P. (1998). Practice effects on the timing and magnitude of agonist activity during ballistic elbow flexion to a target. *Research Quarterly for Exercise and Sport, 69,* 30–37.

Gentile, A.M. (1972). A working model of skill acquisition with application to teaching. *Quest, Monograph, 17:*3–23.

Gentile, A.M. (1987). Skill acquisition: action, movement, and the neuromotor processes. In J.H. Carr, R.B. Shepard, J. Gordon, A.M. Gentile and J.M. Hind (Eds.), *Movement science: foundations for physical therapy in rehabilitation* (pp. 93–154). Rockville, MD: Aspen.

Gentile, A.M. (2000). Skill acquisition: action, movement, and the neuromotor processes. In J.H. Carr and R.B. Shepard (Eds.), *Movement science: foundations for physical therapy in rehabilitation* (pp. 111–80). Rockville, MD: Aspen.

Hall, S.J. (2006). *Basic biomechanics*. New York: McGraw-Hill.

Hodges, N.J., Hayes, S.J., Horn, R.R. & Williams, A.M. (2005). Changes in coordination, control and outcome as a result of extended practice with the non-dominant foot on a soccer skill. *Ergonomics, 48*, 1672–1685.

Jaegars, S.M.H.J., Peterson, R.F., Dantuma, R., Hillen, B., Geuze, R. & Schellekens, J. (1989). Kinesiologic aspects of motor learning in dart throwing. *Journal of Human Movement Studies, 16*, 161–71.

Lay, B.A., Sparrow, W.A., Hughes, K.M. & O'Dwyer, N.J. (2002). Practice effects on coordination and control, metabolic energy expenditure, and muscle activation. *Human Movement Science, 21*, 807–30.

McPherson, S.L. & Thomas, J.R. (1989). Relation of knowledge and performance in boys' tennis: age and expertise. *Journal of Experimental Child Psychology, 48*, 190–211.

Newell, K.M., Broderick, M.P., Deutsch, M. & Slifkin, A.B. (2003). Task goals and change in dynamical degrees of freedom with motor learning. *Journal of Experimental Psychology: Human Perception and Performance, 29*, 379–87.

Newell, A., & Rosenbloom, P.S. (1981). Mechanisms of skill acquisition and the law of practice. In J.R. Anderson (Ed.), *Cognitive skills and their acquisition* (pp. 1–51). Hillsdale, NJ: Lawrence Erlbaum.

Schneider, K., Zernicke, R.F., Schmidt, R.A. & Hart, T.J. (1989). Changes in limb dynamics during the practice of rapid arm movement. *Journal of Biomechanics, 22*, 805–17.

Shank, M.D. & Haywood, K.M. (1987). Eye movements while viewing a baseball pitch. *Perceptual and Motor Skills, 64*, 1191–1197.

Shemmell, J., Tresilian, J.R., Riek, S., Barry, B.K. & Carson, R.G. (2005). Neuromuscular adaptation during skill acquisition on a two-degree-of-freedom target-acquisition task: dynamic movement. *Journal of Neurophysiology, 94*, 3058–3068.

Smyth, M.M. & Pendleton, L.R. (1994). Memory for movement in professional ballet dancers. *International Journal of Sport Psychology, 25*, 282–94.

Southard, D. & Higgins, T. (1987). Changing movement patterns: effects of demonstrations and practice. *Research Quarterly for Exercise and Sport, 58*, 77–80.

Thomas, J.R., French, K.E. & Humphries, C.A. (1986). Knowledge development and sport performance: directions for motor behavior research. *Journal of Sport Psychology, 8*, 259–72.

Thomas, K.T. & Thomas, J.R. (1994). Developing expertise in sport: the relation of knowledge and performance. *International Journal of Sport Psychology, 25*, 295–311.

Tyson, K.W. (1970). A handball skills test for college men. Unpublished Master's Thesis, University of Florida, Gainesville, FL.

Vereijken, B., van Emmerik, R.E.A., Whiting, H.T.A. & Newell, K.M. (1992). Free(z)ing degrees of freedom in skill acquisition. *Journal of Motor Behavior, 24*(1), 133–42.

Whiting, H.T.A. (1984). *Human motor actions: Bernstein reassessed*. Amsterdam: North-Holland.

Wilson, C., Simpson, S.E., van Emmerik, R.E.A. & Hamill, J. (2008). Coordination variability and skill development in expert triple jumpers. *Sports Biomechanics, 7*(1), 2–9.

Yang, J.F. & Scholz, J.P. (2005). Learning a throwing task is associated with differential changes in the use of motor abundance. *Experimental Brain Research, 163*, 137–58.

CHAPTER

**6**

The Learner: Pre-instruction
Considerations

135

A t a college track meet, Coach Hernandez was talking with Jackson, a pole vaulter, after he performed a warm-up vault. The coach was giving Jackson verbal instructions to assist in correcting a technical flaw. When Coach Hernandez finished his explanation, he asked Jackson if he understood what he had said. Jackson replied that he did and returned to the end of the runway. When he got there, he turned to one of his teammates and said, "Can you show me what Coach was saying?" Once the technique was demonstrated, he understood perfectly.

Perhaps the single greatest factor that influences a learner's ability to understand new concepts and achieve movement proficiency is communication. Practitioners communicate both verbally and non-verbally through instructions, demonstrations, and feedback. Effective communication occurs when messages are clear, concise, and match the level of the receiver. However, learners are different in how they receive new information and attempt to make sense of it. Recognizing the influence of individual differences such as learning style, past experiences, and level of motivation on how learners receive information enables the teacher, coach, or therapist to provide instruction and design experiences that are meaningful for each learner.

## LEARNING STYLES

A ll learners have unique preferences for receiving and processing new information. These preferences constitute the person's individual **learning style**. Research has shown that when instructional style and learning style match, learners are able to process information more effectively and, as a result, achieve greater learning (Bruner & Hill, 1992; Cano, Garton & Raven, 1992; Dunn, Beaudry & Klavis, 1989; Dunn & Dunn, 1975; Lovelace, 2005; Murray, 1979; Onwuegbuzie & Daley, 1998; Price, Dunn & Sanders, 1981; Ross, Drysdale & Schulz, 1999). Since no two individuals possess identical learning styles, it is important to incorporate instructional strategies that accommodate each learner when designing the learning environment. The athlete in the scenario described above, for example, better understood the movement when shown a demonstration rather than given verbal instructions. Had Jackson's coach known of and accommodated his preference for visual information, he would not have needed to turn to another source.

Among the many theories and models regarding individual learning styles—including Gardner's Multiple Intelligences (2006), Kolb's Learning Styles Inventory

**C E R E B R A L  challenge**  **6.1**

Discuss the importance of effective communication for teachers, coaches, and therapists. In your discussion, specify those with whom you will have to communicate and when you will use communication throughout the learning process.

(2005), and Gregorc's Mind Styles Model (2006)—the Learning Styles Inventory of Dunn, Dunn, and Price (2000) has often found informal use in a motor skill acquisition setting. Dunn and Dunn (1992, 1993, 1975) contend that an individual's learning style is an integrative collection of multiple levels and may be determined through the assessment of five areas:

1. *Instructional environment preferences* for sound, light, temperature, and class design
2. *Emotionality preferences,* including motivation, persistence, responsibility, and structure
3. *Sociological preferences* for individual, pair, peer, team, adult, or varied relations
4. *Physiological preferences* regarding perception, intake (e.g., chewing gum), time, and mobility
5. *Psychological preferences* based on analytic mode (movement from details to big picture or vice versa), hemisphericity (associated with right or left brain dominance), and action

Some of the elements of Dunn and Dunn's model, such as intake, are not directly related to a skill acquisition setting, but others can easily be accommodated. Bruner and Hill (1992) altered their coaching strategies and redesigned the varsity high school wrestling room layout represented in Figure 6.1 to accommodate

Wrestling room layout accommodating sociological and perceptual preferences. **FIGURE 6.1**

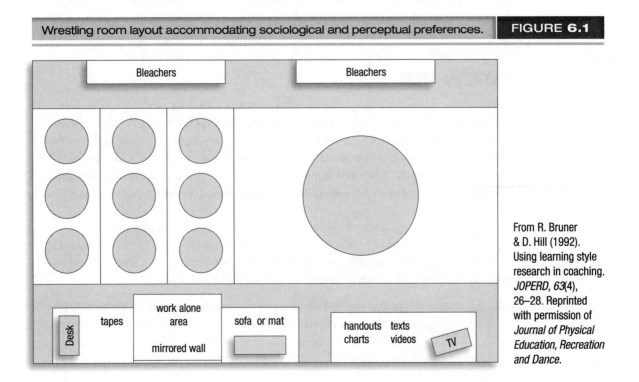

From R. Bruner & D. Hill (1992). Using learning style research in coaching. *JOPERD, 63*(4), 26–28. Reprinted with permission of *Journal of Physical Education, Recreation and Dance.*

individual preferences for two of the elements of Dunn and Dunn's model, perceptual mode and sociological inclination. According to learners' perceptual preference, Bruner and Hill provided opportunities to attempt new skills, videotapes, handouts, charts, and verbal presentations. They redesigned the wrestling room to accommodate sociological preferences by providing distinct areas where wrestlers could work alone, in pairs, or in groups. Although their program was not examined through a formal research study, Bruner and Hill reported positive changes in wrestlers' athletic skill, academic achievement, and self-esteem as a result of matching instructional style with individual learning styles.

Not only are the individual elements of Dunn and Dunn's model important considerations in designing the learning environment, but many have been found to correlate with two learning profiles that are based on processing preferences—that is, whether an individual is considered a global learner, an analytic learner, or a combination of the two (Dunn et al., 1990; Dunn, Cavanaugh, Eberle & Zenhausern, 1982). **Global learners** learn more easily when they are first presented with the big picture and then asked to concentrate on details. Humor, anecdotes, and graphics are helpful for introducing global learners to new information. **Analytical learners,** on the other hand, prefer to have new information presented in a step-by-step, sequential manner that builds toward the main concept. Rules, guidelines, and procedures are helpful for analytical learners. Interestingly, individuals who work in science-based professions, such as medical personnel, tend to fall within the analytical profile, while most patients do not (Samelson, 1997). Complete Exploration Activity 6.2 and the activities presented at the adjoining website to gain a better understanding of your own learning preferences.

**www.**

**Abiator's Online Learning Styles Inventory**

www.berghuis.co.nz/abiator/lsi/lsiframe.html

## Perceptual Mode

Although a person's learning style consists of many variables, perhaps the easiest to accommodate for motor skill learning is preferred perceptual mode. Perceptual mode is the way information is received and processed. Learners preferentially take in and process information in different ways. The preferred mode is referred to as the individual's **modal strength.** When giving instructions and designing practice environments, practitioners should consider four types of learner, based on their modal strength:

1. *Visual learners* understand new concepts better when explanations include visual cue words such as "watch," "see," and "look." Demonstrations, videotapes, pictures, models, and the use of mirrors are all effective methods for accommodating learners whose modal strength is visual.

2. *Kinesthetic learners* strive to understand what the desired movement feels like. Once they achieve this understanding, they use it as a frame of reference with which to compare future attempts. Instructional strategies such as simulations, guidance, repeated practice, and incorporating cue words such as

# exploration A C T I V I T Y 6.2

## Exploring Your Learning Preferences

Several elements from Dunn and Dunn's learning style model are presented below. For each element, circle the description that better suits your preference when learning new information.

| ELEMENT | OPTION A | OPTION B |
|---------|----------|----------|
| Sound | Work best in silence | Work best when there is background noise or music |
| Lighting | Prefer room to be well-illuminated | Prefer soft lighting |
| Design | Prefer to work at a desk, table, or other "work-like" setting | Prefer to work in an easy chair, on bed, in another comfortable setting |
| Persistence | Need to finish a task once started | Need frequent breaks; prefer to work on several tasks simultaneously |
| Structure | Prefer guidelines, specifications, procedures, and rules | Prefer less structure that allows for creativity |
| Social | Prefer to learn alone or with a practitioner | Prefer to learn with peers |
| Intake | Rarely eat, drink, smoke, or have other distracters while learning | Prefer to eat, drink, smoke, or have other distracters while learning |

Analytical learners will tend to select responses under Option A, while global learners are more inclined to choose responses provided under Option B. Remember that all learners are different, and some individuals may have a combined profile.

"feel," "move," and "experience" all assist the kinesthetic learner to develop a sense of what the correct movement feels like.

3. *Analytical learners* approach the desired movement in a problem-solving fashion. Scientific concepts and principles and cue words such as "analyze," "investigate," and "why" assist the analytical learner in solving the movement problem.

4. *Auditory learners* prefer sounds and rhythms. Cue words such as "hear," "pace," and "tempo" will assist auditory learners in learning the movement pattern. Auditory learners also benefit from verbal descriptions such as the one given by the coach in the story that opened this chapter.

Table 6.1 offers cue words and teaching strategies for each type of learner. Some learners, however, do not have a particular modal strength but instead have multiple modal preferences. To accommodate these learners, combine strategies to target each of the preferred modes.

| | VISUAL | KINESTHETIC | ANALYTICAL | AUDITORY |
|---|---|---|---|---|
| **TABLE 6.1** | Examples of cue words and strategies to target each perceptual mode. | | | |
| Sample Cue Words | see | feel | analyze | hear |
| | look | touch | think | listen |
| | watch | sense | examine | detect |
| | observe | move | compare | tempo |
| Sample Teaching Strategies | demonstrations | simulations | principles | clapping |
| | pictures | guidance | testing | music |
| | video | trial and error | investigating | sound |

## CEREBRAL challenge 6.3

Go back to the story at the beginning of the chapter about the pole vaulter. What was the athlete's preferred perceptual mode? Suggest alternative strategies that the coach could have used to better accommodate the athlete's learning style.

## Accommodating Your Learners

How do you find out each individual's learning style? Formal testing instruments are available, such as Kolb's Learning Style Inventory (2005) and Dunn, Dunn, and Price's Learning Style Inventory (2000). Exercise caution when using such instruments, however, as they were designed for traditional classroom settings, and it has been found that learning styles shift depending on whether the task is predominantly a cognitive or motor one (Coker, 1995, 2000). If formal testing instruments are used, respondents must be instructed to answer the questions as they apply to a motor setting.

Informal assessment is also possible, and it can be a powerful and reliable technique. For informal assessment, pay attention to the clues that learners provide about their learning preference. Listen to the descriptive words they use to assess their performance and the questions they ask. Do the words consistently fall into one of the four perceptual mode categories? Do the learners ask for clarification through a different mode? The athlete in the opening story was a visual learner. When the coach verbally explained Jackson's mistakes (auditory mode) and how to fix them, the athlete did not completely understand. As a result, he sought out an alternative way to get the information through his modal strength, vision. His teammate's demonstration gave him all he needed to understand what the coach had been trying to explain to him.

| Example of eclectic approach for the basketball set shot. | TABLE **6.2** |
| --- | --- |

| PREPARATION | ACTION |
| --- | --- |
| Toes and shoulders face the basket (visual) | Knees bend slightly with tension felt in quads (kinesthetic) |
| Eyes focus on the front of the rim (visual) | Smooth sequential rhythm begins from knees and ends at fingers (auditory) |
| Feel weight distributed evenly over both feet (kinesthetic) | Force for shot comes from legs [discuss why generating force with legs is more efficient] (analytical) |
| Position ball between shoulders and eye level (kinesthetic) | See arm extend through the ball (visual) |

When you utilize only one presentation style, you deny learners comparable opportunities to understand the information presented. Instead, rearrange the learning environment as suggested by Dunn and Dunn (1993, 1992). Get to know your instructional tendencies and make an effort to expand your repertoire to incorporate strategies for all learning styles. Research suggests that an individual's learning style preference influences that person's teaching style. As a result, practitioners will tend to focus almost exclusively on their preferred style when giving instructions, and these natural instructional tendencies may not match the needs of learners (Heikkinen, Pettigrew & Zakrajsek, 1985; MacNeil, 1980; McDaniel, 1986). Practitioners must make a conscious effort to employ alternate strategies that are compatible with learners' preferences. When working one-on-one with an individual, the practitioner should provide instruction and feedback through the learner's preferred perceptual mode so as to capitalize on the learner's strengths (return to Table 6.1 for ideas). With large groups of learners, providing instruction and feedback through each individual's preferred mode is not feasible. In this situation, the practitioner should instead use an eclectic approach as shown in Table 6.2, constantly varying the mode through which information is presented so that all modes are used. Recognizing and accommodating learning styles will result in more meaningful communication and translate to enhanced learning.

## exploration A C T I V I T Y  6.4

### Self-Analysis

Record yourself teaching a 10-minute lesson on a skill of your choice. Review your video and, using the box on the following page, tabulate the number of cue words and strategies that you use in each of the four perceptual mode categories: visual,

*(continued)*

kinesthetic, auditory, and analytical (see Table 6.1). Do you tend to teach the way you prefer to learn, as research suggests? Do you incorporate all four modes of presentation, or do you tend to use only one mode? Suggest areas on the video where you could have used a different mode. Give a specific example of an alternative cue word or strategy for each of these areas.

| VISUAL | KINESTHETIC | ANALYTICAL | AUDITORY |
|--------|-------------|------------|----------|
|        |             |            |          |
|        |             |            |          |
|        |             |            |          |
|        |             |            |          |

Opportunities for using a different mode: _____

_____

_____

Alternative cue word or strategy: _____

_____

_____

## C E R E B R A L  challenge  6.5

Below are examples of strategies for accommodating specific modal strengths in physical education offered by Reed, Banks, and Carlisle (2004). Determine which modal preference (visual, kinesthetic, analytical, auditory) would best be accommodated by each suggestion.

_____ a. Demonstrate five patterns of jumping.

_____ b. Create a fitness plan for you and your family to follow over summer vacation.

_____ c. Create a series of diagrams that explain a strategy or tactic used in a game.

_____ d. Design a flow chart that explains _____.

_____ e. Create a dance that expresses the way you value physical education.

_____ f. Create a poster of the four most important things a good dribbler does.

# TRANSFER OF LEARNING

**A**nother individual difference that the practitioner should consider to enhance communication and design optimal learning experiences is the learner's past experience. Throughout a person's lifespan, experience with movement accumulates. The sum of past experiences influences the individual's ability to learn new skills in both positive and negative ways. The phenomenon in which the learning of a new skill or performance of a skill under novel conditions can be influenced by past experience with another skill or skills is known as **transfer.**

## Types of Transfer

Three types of transfer exist: positive, negative, and zero. **Positive transfer** occurs when a learner's past experience with one skill facilitates the learning of a new skill or the use of a skill in a different context. The zone defenses used in football and basketball, for example, share many commonalities. In this instance, a learner's past experience with a zone defense in football will likely accelerate the rate at which he or she learns the zone defense in basketball. **Negative transfer** occurs when a learner's past experience with one skill hinders or obstructs the learning of a new skill or the performance of a skill under novel conditions. Despite the fact that swinging a bat in softball and in baseball shares similar movement characteristics, the task of tracking the oncoming pitch differs significantly in the two sports. In baseball, the pitcher uses an overarm throwing motion, causing the ball's trajectory to move from high to low. In softball, the pitcher uses an underhand throwing motion, and the ball rises as it approaches the plate. Previous experience in baseball could, therefore, temporarily interfere with hitting performance in softball. Finally, when two skills are completely unrelated, such as swimming the butterfly stroke and goaltending in waterpolo, **zero transfer** occurs, because experience with the first skill has no influence on the second.

Positive transfer is helpful, and practitioners should capitalize on it. Negative transfer often results from having to learn a new response to a well-learned stimulus. A classic example of negative transfer occurs when a skilled badminton player decides to learn tennis. In badminton, the forehand drive requires a wrist snap. This is not the case in tennis, where the wrist contribution is minimal. Initially, the badminton player may attempt to incorporate a wrist snap in the tennis forehand. Fortunately, most negative transfer effects are temporary and can be overcome with practice.

## Theories of Transfer

Understanding the theoretical underpinnings of transfer will assist the teacher, coach, or therapist in designing learning experiences that foster positive transfer. This understanding will also help the practitioner account for difficulties that individuals display during initial attempts as a result of negative transfer.

### Identical elements theory

The identical elements theory originally hypothesized that transfer was based on the number of common elements shared by two skills (Thorndike, 1914). It was thought that the more identical elements shared by two skills, the greater the positive transfer from one skill to the other. Accordingly, we would expect positive transfer to occur between the skills of picking up buttons and picking up coins, whereas the amount of transfer between putting and an instep kick in soccer would be negligible.

The identical elements theory was amended by Osgoode (1949), who specified that, rather than identical elements, it was the similarities between the stimulus and response conditions of the two tasks that were fundamental. Consequently, we would expect a high degree of positive transfer when the stimulus and response conditions for the previously acquired task were the same as for the task being learned.

Learning difficulties arise when two skills have opposite stimulus–response requirements. For example, we would predict negative transfer when the skill being introduced has an identical stimulus to a previously learned skill but requires a different response. An individual who purchases a new mountain bike, for example, will experience some temporary frustration if the gear-shifting mechanism is different from the previously owned bike.

Skill progressions assume that experience with simplified versions, such as diving from the side of a pool, will positively transfer to more advanced skill performance, such as diving from a board.

### Transfer appropriate processing theory

The identical elements theory does not account for all possible transfer conditions. Strategic and conceptual aspects of games or tasks can also transfer. As a result, the **transfer appropriate processing theory** was proposed to account for cognitive processing similarities that occur between practice conditions and the performance criterion (Bransford, Franks, Morris & Stein, 1979; Lee, 1988; Morris, Bransford & Franks, 1977). According to the transfer appropriate processing theory, we would expect positive transfer when practice conditions require learners to engage in problem-solving processes similar to those that the criterion task requires.

In volleyball, when a spike is hit around a block, the defensive player may use one of the four main defensive skills: the forearm pass, the roll, the dive, or the sprawl. The technique that the defensive player chooses depends on a number of factors that have to be assessed instantaneously. To facilitate the player's ability not only to choose the appropriate skill but also to execute it correctly, proponents of transfer appropriate processing would recommend practicing each defensive skill during the same practice period, but in a random order, rather

Chen, Kang, and colleagues (2007) investigated the training effects of a virtual reality intervention on the reaching behaviors of children with spastic cerebral palsy (CP). Wearing a sensor glove, four children practiced three activities (butterfly, peg-board, and pick-and-place blocks) in a three-dimensional virtual environment. They received virtual reality interventions for two hours per week over the course of a month. All three activities were designed to train the reaching and grasping of stationary or moving objects in different directions, and the children were encouraged to reach as quickly as possible toward the virtual object that appeared. Both auditory (banging sound as hand hit virtual object) and visual feedback (e.g., change in color of object as it came within grasping range) was provided. The results indicated that three of the four children demonstrated some improvement in reaching behavior (kinematics) during the intervention. Those practice effects were partially maintained in a four-week follow-up test. The researchers concluded that participation in the virtual reality training program appeared to

improve the quality of reaching in children with CP.

Information about other virtual reality applications can be found at the links below.

Basic information about virtual reality:

www.pri.univie.ac.at/workgroups/csport/index.php?m=D&t=main&c=show&CEWebS_what=Virtual~32~Reality

Designing sport training simulators:

www.asme.org/NewsPublicPolicy/Newsletters/MechanicalAdvantage/Lab_Subject_Sports.cfm

Exploring virtual reality applications across numerous fields:

www.scienceclarified.com/scitech/Virtual-Reality/The-Virtual-Classroom-Virtual-Reality-in-Training-and-Education.html

Video of Toyota Driving Simulator:

www.youtube.com/watch?v=zkwskWtA2jE

than practicing each skill independently (to make use of a phenomenon known as contextual interference). Furthermore, continuously changing the direction, speed, position, and trajectory of the oncoming ball would help assure maximum positive transfer. This practice strategy, known as variable practice, forces the learner to engage in realistic cognitive processing, since the learner will never be in exactly the same situation twice. Both contextual interference and variable practice will be discussed in more detail in Chapter 9.

## Transfer and Instructional Design

Many instructional decisions regarding presentation sequence and the use of instructional aids are based on the principles of transfer. For example, simplified versions of skills, drills, and games serve as precursors to more complex forms that will be introduced in the future. Skill progressions, such as that of diving into a swimming pool, where learners are first taught to dive from a kneeling position and then advance to a crouched position, a stride position, and finally a standing position, are based on the assumption that experience with simplified versions will positively transfer to the actual movement, facilitating its acquisition. Similarly, lead-up games, such as T-ball, sideline soccer, five hundred in softball or baseball, keep away in basketball, and three-hit volleyball, have been adopted to assist the leaner.

A Resusci Anne mannequin allows the learner to simulate CPR.

Other modifications may be made when the skill involves a potential risk of injury or is expensive, when practice facilities are lacking, or when practice in a real-life setting is not possible. Gymnasts first learn complex and potentially dangerous skills with some type of instructional aid, such as a harness, to minimize the risk of injury. Bicycles are equipped with training wheels. Fighter pilots train on flight simulators that allow countless practice trials with minimal risk and expense. Astronauts train underwater, as it simulates the weightless environment that they will experience in space. In the clinical environment, the BTE Work Simulation device allows patients to simulate activities such as driving, turning a key, pulling a knob, and applying brakes, and the Resusci Anne mannequin (Laerdal Medical) aids in learning rescue breathing and CPR. All of these modifications attempt to capitalize on positive transfer.

Until recently, much of the support for designing instructional methodology that capitalizes on the notion of positive transfer was anecdotal. Recently, however, a study examined transfer of learning in a practical physical education setting. O'Keeffe, Harrison, and Smyth (2007) demonstrated that participants improved in the practiced skill, the overarm throw, and also showed significant learning effects for the badminton overhead clear and the javelin throw, supporting the idea of positive transfer between fundamental motor skills and sport-specific skills.

### Fostering positive transfer

The following guidelines, based on the theories of transfer, provide a starting point for practitioners to create learning experiences that will foster positive transfer.

**Analyze the skill.** Given that transfer is based on similarity between skills, the ability to analyze skills effectively is indispensable for designing instructional strategies that will facilitate learning. We can examine four subcomponents of skills to determine their degree of similarity and assess the potential for positive transfer.

1. *The fundamental movement pattern.* The last three steps of the lay-up, for example, are comparable to those of the high jump. A learner who is proficient at the lay-up will have an advantage in learning the high jump if the practitioner were to associate the two during instruction.

2. *The strategic and conceptual aspects of the game or task.* For example, the "give and go" strategy is used in a variety of sports. If a learner has performed a "give and go" in one sport, pointing out the similarities to a "give and go" in a different sport should facilitate learning. Similar examples include the use of a pelvic tilt in numerous therapeutic and fitness activities, and the influence of head position on balance.

3. *Perceptual elements.* Whitewater kayaking and whitewater rafting may lack similarities with respect to physical skills, but both activities require the person to know how to read the water to choose the best route. The regulatory cues, as well as the visual search strategies used for their detection, would be quite similar in both skills.

4. *Temporal and spatial elements.* Many skills require the performer to ensure that an implement meets an object at both the ideal time and location, including the racket sports of squash, tennis, and racquetball.

Prior to providing instruction, then, practitioners should become familiar with their learners' past experience with various motor skills. Those skills should be analyzed to determine if similarities exist in fundamental movement pattern, strategic and/or conceptual aspects, perceptual elements, and temporal and spatial elements between the skill being taught and those with which the learner is familiar. Comparisons, like the one in Figure 6.2, may then be made throughout the instructional process to facilitate understanding. Observe examples of positive transfer by visiting your school's athletic training room or a rehabilitation or physical therapy clinic and answering the questions in Exploration Activity 6.6.

## exploration A C T I V I T Y 6.6

### Observation: Transfer

For this activity, arrange to observe at your school's athletic training room or a local rehabilitation or physical therapy clinic.

1. How many examples of equipment, instructions, exercises, and so on can you find that are designed to elicit positive transfer? List them.

2. For each example on your list, determine which component(s) of the skill will transfer (fundamental movement pattern, strategic and conceptual aspects, perceptual elements, or temporal and spatial elements).

| EXAMPLE | FUNDAMENTAL MOVEMENT PATTERN | STRATEGIC AND CONCEPTUAL ASPECTS | PERCEPTUAL ELEMENTS | TEMPORAL AND SPATIAL ELEMENTS |
|---|---|---|---|---|
| Training Staircase | X | X | | X |
| | | | | |
| | | | | |
| | | | | |

**FIGURE 6.2**

There is a high degree of similarity between the hand position for (a) catching a football above the waist and (b) setting a volleyball.

(a)  (b)

**Determine the cost–benefit tradeoff.** Lead-up games, simulators, and skill analysis should be evaluated for cost effectiveness prior to their use. Unless there is a high degree of similarity between the designed experience and the criterion, implementation of some preliminary activities and drills may not be warranted. For example, the volleyball drill that requires teammates to form a circle and bump the ball to the next person in a clockwise direction will transfer poorly to a game situation and may in fact teach players the bad habit of swinging their arms to the side rather than facing their target.

Note that even when a high degree of similarity exists, transfer is generally found to be relatively small. Accordingly, efforts to design instructional methodology that capitalizes on positive transfer are not always worthwhile, such as when the time spent learning a lead-up game (cost) exceeds the positive transfer benefit.

**Get to know the learner.** All learners have many past experiences that may influence their ability to acquire new skills. Get to know your learners. Find out what types of experiences they have had that you might use as a comparison with a skill you are introducing. In rehabilitation, for example, patients will see greater success if clinical practice conditions closely match the real-world functional activities in which they will engage (Stevans & Hall, 1998). Determining the real-world demands imposed on each patient is prerequisite to designing an effective rehab program.

**Point out similarities and differences.** Once you have determined the similarities and differences between the skills already learned and the skill about to be learned, point them out to the learner. Learners are not always able to

C E R E B R A L **challenge** 6.7

Analyze the following pairs of skills to determine their similarities and differences. Be sure to compare the fundamental movement pattern, strategic and conceptual aspects, perceptual elements, and temporal and spatial elements. Based on your analysis, assess the potential for transfer, either positive or negative, for each pairing. Justify your answer.

a. Cane walking and using a walker
b. Downhill skiing and waterskiing
c. Kickball and baseball
d. Mountain biking and whitewater kayaking

Coldwells and Hare (1994) conducted an experiment to determine if short tennis skills positively transferred to lawn tennis. Short tennis is a modified version of tennis designed for children. The rackets are smaller and made of plastic, making them lighter and easier to swing. The ball, made of foam, bounces lower and slower. The court is smaller with a lower net, and the rules are simplified.

Sixteen subjects were divided into two groups. The experimental group received 10 hours of short tennis instruction and 10 hours of lawn tennis instruction. The control group received 20 hours of lawn tennis instruction only. A pre- and post-test using the Dyer Backboard test was administered and videotaped. Three experienced coaches then analyzed the videotape, judging each subject's backswing, follow-through, ball placement, and positioning (position of the player relative to the bounce of the ball). Results revealed that the experimental group improved more than the control group on the Dyer Backboard test ($p < .05$). In addition, the video analysis indicated that the experimental group performed significantly better on the backswing and the follow-through, while the control group was significantly better at positioning and ball placement. A second study, limited to eight hours of total instruction and focusing only on ground strokes, revealed no significant differences between groups for the test but found the experimental group to be significantly better on the backswing, follow-through, and placement and the control group better at positioning. The authors concluded that because the experimental group was superior in the backswing and follow-through in both experiments, positive transfer of those actions occurred. They further concluded that the positioning superiority of the control group was probably due to greater experience with the bounce of a tennis ball. Consequently, negative transfer for reading ball bounce likely resulted between the foam ball used in short tennis and the tennis ball.

**QUESTION:**

How could this study be redesigned to test the authors' hypothesis regarding the control group's superiority with positioning?

make connections between skills on their own. Stating that inline skating and ice skating are similar is insufficient—you must point out specifically which aspects of the two skills are similar and which are dissimilar. For example, the push-off to start in inline skating and ice skating is comparable, but stopping is very different. With inline skates, the "brake" is located at the back of the boot, and it must be forced in front of the participant to engage. In ice skating, stopping may be performed several ways, depending on the learner's experience. An individual who learned how to skate in hockey skates will probably stop by turning to the side with the feet parallel. A person who learned how to skate using figure skates, however, may simply dig the pick into the ice and drag it. Consequently, blanket statements are misleading and may impede initial performance rather than facilitate it.

**Make sure that the skills you refer to have been well learned.** Anytime you attempt to capitalize on the use of transfer, it is important to be sure that the skill or concept you refer to has been well learned. Shoveling snow and scooping up a ball in lacrosse share a similar movement pattern, but a person who lives in the Southwest will have limited experience with shoveling snow. Another example is comparing the overhead throwing motion to the volleyball serve. If the individual has an immature throwing pattern to begin with, this strategy may backfire. Unless the skills you refer to are well learned, the example will not be meaningful, and the idea you are trying to convey will not be communicated effectively.

**Use analogies.** Another technique to elicit positive transfer is the use of analogies. Learners create a mental image of how a skill is to be executed based on the practitioner's explanation. The practitioner can simplify new concepts by relating the new information to a familiar model. For example, to teach the correct grip in tennis, instructors often ask students to "shake hands" with the racquet. This analogy relates the grip to something familiar, a handshake, enhancing the learner's mental picture of the task.

Liao and Masters (2001) suggest that the benefit of using analogies is that the essential rules of the new skill do not need to be explicated. In their study, participants were to hit a table tennis ball to a target area with topspin using a forehand stroke. To teach topspin, the researchers used an analogy to a right-angled triangle, and participants were told to "strike the ball while bringing the bat up the hypotenuse of the triangle" (p. 310). Other participants were given a set of 12 basic techniques for generating topspin. The findings suggest that analogy learning was implicit in nature and was an effective strategy for learning the topspin forehand stroke in table tennis.

**Maximize similarities between practice and performance.** When teaching for positive transfer, provide practice opportunities that have a high degree of similarity to the actual performance context. For example, the movement required to step up stairs is one that is used in a variety of situations. A patient learning this motion will use it not only to climb stairs of differing heights but also to step over curbs, step into the bathtub, and step onto an escalator. Similarly, a second baseman needs to be able to throw accurately to first, second, third, and home from a variety of fielding positions. Providing opportunities to use newly learned skills in a variety of situations and designing drills that simulate actual performance will foster maximum positive transfer.

**Consider the skill level of the learner.** Transfer is more beneficial for a beginning learner than for one who has intermediate or advanced levels of skill. Comparing aspects of an overhand volleyball serve to a tennis serve can assist a beginner to create a mental image in order to generate initial attempts. Once the learner has demonstrated an idea of the desired movement, however, he or she must focus on skill-specific cues to improve.

C  E  R  E  B  R  A  L    challenge    6.8

On a separate sheet, for a sport or activity of your choice, list 10 analogies that you could use to assist a learner in creating a mental picture of a corresponding skill.

Think back to the last time you had to learn something that you weren't interested in. Why were you not motivated to learn? How much effort did you put into learning? What other consequences to the learning process resulted from your lack of motivation?

## MOTIVATION TO LEARN

**M**otivation is an internal condition that incites and directs action or behavior. Motivation influences learners' receptivity to instruction. Learners who are motivated will explore, practice, think, and attempt to master the task. Practitioners should recognize that although some individuals are excited to learn, others may be apprehensive, have misconceptions about the skill being introduced, or simply not see the importance of learning it. Regardless of the reason, lack of motivation hinders learning.

**common** *myth*

All learners are motivated to learn the skills presented to them.

The introduction of a new skill should captivate learners' interest. Simply explaining the objective of the skill is not always enough to do this. Learners must be given a reason why it is important to learn that particular skill. The reason may be to develop a good foundation on which to build future skills, to gain an edge in competition, or to regain the use of a limb that has been injured. Learners' interest in the skill may also be increased through exposure to elite role models and performances on videotape or in live demonstrations. Finally, creating a learning environment that is positive, supportive, and challenging but also realistic and that provides opportunities for success can reduce apprehensions and increase motivation. Other ideas for increasing motivation are presented in Table 6.3.

| Suggestions for increasing motivation (Blankenship, 2008). | TABLE 6.3 |
| --- | --- |

- Give learners choices.
- Provide opportunities for learners to initiate activities and be self-directed.
- Allow freedom of expression and flexibility in criteria for success.
- Establish clear expectations and consequences (positive and negative).
- Give positive feedback for good performances and corrective feedback for less successful performances.
- Offer opportunities to demonstrate competence as well as to become successful.
- Use cooperative activities and stress cooperation.

From *The Psychology of Teaching Physical Education,* Bonnie T. Blankenship. Holcomb Hathaway, 2008. Used with permission.

# C E R E B R A L challenge 6.10

1. How might you motivate an injured athlete to learn and complete a rehabilitation program? How would your suggestions differ for physical education students who perceive volleyball to be boring?

2. Generate a more extensive list of reasons students, athletes, or patients may not be motivated to learn, then develop specific strategies that could stimulate their interest.

## ▶ a look ahead

The learning process is highly dependent on quality practitioner–learner interactions. Recognizing the influence of individual differences—such as learning style, past experiences, and level of motivation—on how learners receive information enables the teacher, coach, or therapist to provide instruction and design experiences that are meaningful for each learner. We will continue to apply these concepts as we explore methods for presenting novel skills in the next chapter.

## ● focus points

After reading this chapter, you should know that . . .

- All learners have unique preferences for receiving and processing new information, which define their learning style.

- Greater learning gains have been shown when the instructional style is matched to the learner's learning style.

- Four perceptual modes should be considered when giving instructions and designing practice environments: visual, kinesthetic, analytical, and auditory.

- When the learning of a new skill or its performance under novel conditions is influenced by the individual's past experience with another skill or skills, transfer is said to occur.

- While practitioners should capitalize on positive transfer, negative transfer is often the result of having to learn a new response to a well-learned stimulus.

- To determine the similarity between two skills and assess the potential for positive transfer, four factors should be compared: fundamental movement pattern, strategic and conceptual aspects of the game or task, perceptual elements, and temporal and spatial elements.

- Considerations for fostering positive transfer include:
  - determining the cost–benefit tradeoff of its implementation

- understanding the past experiences of learners
- determining and highlighting the similarities and differences between skills already learned and those being learned
- ensuring that the skills being used for transfer have been well learned
- using analogies
- maximizing similarities between practice and performance
- adjusting instruction to the skill level of the learner.

■ Motivation is an internal condition that incites and directs action or behavior.

■ In order to learn, an individual must be motivated to do so.

## ? review questions

1. What are the characteristics of effective communication?
2. Define learning style.
3. What is the significance of matching presentation style and learning style?
4. Two major theories have been proposed to account for transfer. Compare and contrast them.
5. What four subcomponents of a skill would you assess to determine the similarities and differences between two skills?
6. Explain why it is important to point out to learners both the similarities and differences when comparing two skills for the purpose of transfer.
7. What is motivation, and why is it a pre-instruction consideration?

## REFERENCES

Blankenship, B.T. (2008). *The psychology of teaching physical education*. Scottsdale, AZ: Holcomb Hathaway.

Bransford, J.D., Franks, J.J., Morris, C.D. & Stein, B.S. (1979). Some general constraints on learning and memory research. In L.S. Cermak and F.I.M. Craik (Eds.), *Levels of processing in human memory* (pp. 331–54). Hillsdale, NJ: Erlbaum.

Bruner, R. & Hill, D. (1992). Using learning styles research in coaching. *Journal of Physical Education, Recreation and Dance, 63*(4), 26–28.

Cano, J., Garton, B.L. & Raven, M.R. (1992). The relationship between learning and teaching styles and student performance in a methods of teaching agriculture course. *Journal of Agricultural Education, 33*(3), 16–22.

Chen, Y.P., Kang, L.J., Chuang, T.Y., Doong, J.L., Lee, S.J., Tsai, M.W., Jeng, S.F. & Sung, W.H. (2007). Use of virtual reality to improve upper-extremity control in children with cerebral palsy: a single subject design. *Physical Therapy, 87*, 1441–1457.

Coker, C.A. (1995). Learning style consistency across cognitive and motor settings. *Perceptual and Motor Skills, 81*, 1023–1026.

Coker, C.A. (2000). Consistency of learning styles of undergraduate athletic training students across the traditional classroom vs. the clinical setting. *Journal of Athletic Training, 35*(4), 441–44.

Coldwells, A. & Hare, M.E. (1994). The transfer of skill from short tennis to lawn tennis. *Ergonomics, 37*(1), 17–21.

DeCecco, J.P. (1968). *The psychology of learning and instruction.* Englewood Cliffs, NJ: Prentice-Hall.

Dunn, R., Beaudry, J.S. & Klavis, A. (1989). Survey of research on learning styles. *Educational Leadership, 46*(6), 50–58.

Dunn, R., Bruno, J., Sklar, R., Aenhausern, R. & Beaudry, J. (1990). Effects of matching and mismatching minority developmental college students hemispheric preferences on mathematics scores. *Journal of Educational Research, 83*(5), 283–88.

Dunn, R., Cavanaugh, D., Eberle, B. & Zenhausern, R. (1982). Hemispheric preference: the newest element of learning style. *The American Biology Teacher, 44*(5), 291–94.

Dunn, R. & Dunn, K. (1975). *Educator's self-teaching guide to individualizing instructional programs.* Nyack, NY: Parker.

Dunn, R. & Dunn, K. (1992). *Teaching elementary students through their individual learning styles.* Boston: Allyn and Bacon.

Dunn, R. & Dunn, K. (1993). *Teaching secondary students through their individual learning styles.* Boston: Allyn and Bacon.

Dunn, R., Dunn, K. & Price, G. (2000). *Learning styles inventory: grades 5–12.* Lawrence, KS: Price Systems.

Gardner, H. (2006). *Multiple intelligences: new horizons.* New York: Basic Books.

Gregorc, A.F. (2006). *The mind styles model: theory, principles, and applications.* Columbia, CT: Gregorc.

Heikkinen, M., Pettigrew, F. & Zakrajsek, P. (1985). Learning styles vs. teaching styles: studying the relationship. *NASSP Bulletin, 69*(478), 80–85.

Kolb, D. (2005). *Learning styles inventory: version 3.1.* Boston: HayGroup.

Lee, T.D. (1988). Transfer appropriate processing: a framework for conceptualizing practice effects in motor learning. In O.G. Meijer and K. Roth (Eds.), *Complex motor behavior: the motor action controversy* (pp. 201–15). Amsterdam: Elsevier Science.

Liao, M. & Masters, R.S.W. (2001). Analogy learning: a means to implicit motor learning. *Journal of Sports Sciences, 19,* 307–27.

Lovelace, M.K. (2005). Meta-analysis of experimental research based on the Dunn and Dunn model. *Journal of Educational Research, 98,* 176–83.

MacNeil, R.D. (1980). The relationship of cognitive style and instructional style to the learning performance of undergraduate students. *Journal of Educational Research, 22,* 354–59.

McDaniel, T.R. (1986). A primer on classroom discipline: principles old and new. *Phi Delta Kappan, 66*(1), 63–67.

Morris, C.D., Bransford, J.D. & Franks, J.J (1977). Levels of processing versus transfer appropriate processing. *Journal of Verbal Learning and Verbal Behavior, 16,* 519–33.

Murray, M. (1979). Matched preferred cognitive mode with teaching methodology in learning a novel motor skill. *Research Quarterly, 50,* 80–87.

O'Keeffe, S.L., Harrison, A.J. & Smyth, P.J. (2007). Transfer or specificity? An applied investigation into the relationship between fundamental overarm throwing and related sport skills. *Physical Education and Sport Pedagogy, 12*(2), 89–102.

Onwuegbuzie, A.J. & Daley, C. (1998). Similarity of learning styles of students and a teacher in achievement in a research methods course. *Psychological Reports, 82,* 163–68.

Osgoode, C.E. (1949). The similarity paradox in human learning: a resolution. *Psychological Review, 56,* 132–43.

Price, G., Dunn, R. & Sanders, W. (1981). Reading achievement and learning style characteristics. *The Clearing House, 54,* 223–26.

Reed, J.A., Banks, A.L. & Carlisle, C.S. (2004). Knowing me, knowing who? Getting to know your students' preferred learning style. *Teaching Elementary Physical Education, 15*(4), 25–27.

Ross, J.L., Drysdale, M.T.B. & Schulz, R.A. (1999). Learning style in the classroom: towards quality instruction in kinesiology. *Avante, 5*(3), 31–42.

Samelson, T.C. (1997). Getting information across to patients. *Medical Economics, 74*(3), 105–08.

Stevans, J. & Hall, K.G. (1998). Motor skills acquisition strategies for rehabilitation of low back pain. *Journal of Orthopedic Sports Physical Therapy, 28* (3), 165-167.

Thorndike, E.L. (1914). *Educational psychology.* New York: Columbia University.

# Skill Presentation

A 34-year-old patient is referred for physical therapy after surgery to repair a torn anterior cruciate ligament (ACL). A component of the rehabilitation program prescribed for this patient is core stability training using a therapeutic ball. Since the patient is unfamiliar with therapeutic ball exercises, the therapist will have to introduce them. How is that best accomplished? Should the therapist use verbal instructions to introduce the exercises? Should he demonstrate them? What must he consider in order to ensure the skills are presented most effectively?

When introduced to a new skill or task, the learner uses the information provided in instructions and demonstrations to develop an idea of the movement's requirements. This idea helps the learner formulate a movement plan that serves as a guide during initial attempts of the skill or task. The development of an accurate movement plan depends on the instructor's ability to analyze a skill, determine the information that is important to convey, organize that information, and communicate it effectively (Rink, 2005). Facilitating the learner's understanding of a newly introduced skill is the focus of this chapter.

## LEARNER PREPARATION

Regardless of the method to be used to present a skill, before instruction begins the practitioner must consider two factors that will directly influence learning. First, it is critical to capture learners' undivided attention before introducing the skill. The practitioner can accomplish this by arranging the learners in a location that is free of background distractions. The formation should allow all to see and hear the instructor clearly, and if instruction takes place outdoors, the learners should be positioned with their backs to the sun. Finally, the instructor should direct learners to place equipment such as balls, hand weights, surgical tubing, and rackets away from the gathering area to eliminate any temptation to play with them. Lack of attention, even for a brief moment, will result in the learner missing important information needed for successful skill development (Abernethy, 1993).

C E R E B R A L  **challenge**  7.1

For a motor skill that you teach or will teach in your professional field, list variables that might compete for your learners' attention while you are giving instructions. Then, develop suggestions that you could implement to reduce these attention problems. For example:

- Patient's cell phone is vibrating.
- Student is pestering a peer.

The second factor to consider is the introduction of the skill. Once the learners are settled, the instructor should introduce the skill in a manner that stimulates interest. As discussed in Chapter 6, motivated learners are more receptive to instruction. Enthusiasm is contagious! The practitioner should present the skill dynamically and emphasize its importance.

## VERBAL INSTRUCTIONS

**H**ave you ever tried to teach a child how to tie his or her shoelaces? You probably wouldn't think it would be that difficult. You have been tying your own shoelaces for years. In fact, you could probably be considered an expert at tying shoelaces. But the ability to provide effective instructions requires more than a thorough understanding of the skill. You have to be able to convey that knowledge to the learner. Suddenly, a seemingly simple skill like tying your shoelaces becomes incredibly complex when you try to describe it! Test your verbal instruction effectiveness by performing the tasks in Exploration Activity 7.2.

## exploration ACTIVITY 7.2

### Verbal Instructions

**Part A. Tying Shoelaces**

Find a partner whose shoes have shoelaces and who is willing to forget temporarily how to tie them. Using verbal descriptions alone, provide instructions for your partner to assist him or her in tying the shoelaces.

**Part B. Replicating a Drawing**

For this activity you will need a partner, a piece of paper, and a pencil. Your partner should sit facing away from you with the paper and pencil. Your task is to describe the following diagram so that your partner can replicate it. Throughout the exercise, you should not look at your partner's attempt, and your partner should not look at the diagram. Your partner may ask you questions but may not use gestures. Once you have completed your description and your partner has finished his or her interpretation of what you described, compare diagrams.

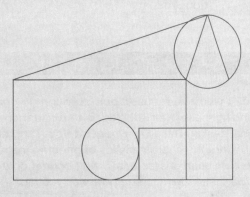

*(continued)*

Perform the exercise again, using the following diagram and switching roles. This time, the "drawer" is not permitted to ask any questions. Compare diagrams when you are finished.

**QUESTIONS:**

1. How accurate was your partner's reproduction of the diagram you described? Do the differences give you any hints about how you communicate?

2. What type of clarification questions did your partner ask? Do these questions give you any hints about how you communicate?

3. How did you feel during the second part, when questions were not permitted? Can you generalize any of that information to other learning situations?

4. What changes, if any, could you make to improve your communication effectiveness in the future?

Familiarity with the skill being taught is an obvious asset. A thorough understanding of the skill enables the practitioner to determine what information is important to convey to the learner. That same skill familiarity, however, can negatively influence how the instructor conveys that information. The practitioner may unknowingly provide excessive descriptions, use confusing technical terminology, or leave out important details. The result is a frustrated learner who ultimately loses interest. Effective instructions send clear messages to the learner. This can be accomplished only if individual differences are considered in instructional design.

**common** *myth*

Experts are always the most effective instructors.

**C E R E B R A L   challenge**   **7.3**

To this point we have focused our attention on characteristics of the learner. Understanding the learner enables us to make more effective decisions regarding instructional design. Based on your understanding of the learner to this point, what do you think are the characteristics of effective instructions? Support your ideas by explaining how each characteristic will accommodate the learner. Continue reading about verbal instructions to see how well you did.

Example:   *Characteristic:* Instructions should be brief.

   *Rationale:* Limited capacity of short-term memory.

## Role of Task Instructions

Task instructions serve two distinct roles. First, they introduce a learner to a new skill. In this capacity, instructions must communicate a general idea of the goal of the skill or task and make learners aware of major technical features or critical elements (Siedentop & Tannehill, 2001). Once this general idea of the movement has been conveyed, the focus of instructions shifts, and skill refinement becomes the goal. Instructions in this capacity serve to develop the learners' skill level so that they can perform the skill under criterion conditions.

## Introducing the Skill

As indicated in the previous section, initial instructions should focus learners' attention on the critical elements of the new motor skill (Rink, 2005; Siedentop & Tannehill, 2001). Beginners often have difficulty discriminating between relevant and irrelevant stimuli. For example, the juggling activity presented in Chapter 1 provided little direction on how to juggle. If you had not tried juggling before, you probably had an enormous number of questions about how to perform the task, including "How high do I throw the balls?" "When do I let go?" and "What type of rhythm should I use?" Because the key elements of the juggling task were not pointed out to you, you probably discovered later, through trial and error, that many of the elements you chose to attend to really had no bearing on learning the task. By drawing the learner's attention to the critical elements of the skill, the instructor does not leave the learner guessing what to focus on, as was the case when you were juggling.

## Amount of Information

Keep explanations short and simple. Long, detailed instructions challenge learners' attentional capacity and short-term memory, which, as discussed in Chapter 4, has a limited capacity. After capturing learners' interest with your introduction, take advantage of it! Learners will be eager to try the skill themselves. Supply only the key elements of the skill. An explanation about how to grip the bat is appropriate for a first batting lesson, but specific techniques to produce an optimal hip turn for the generation of maximum force are not. Those specifics should be addressed later, when the learner is striving to refine the movement pattern.

C E R E B R A L   **challenge**   7.4

Reflect on your juggling experience in Exploration Activity 1.1. What variables did you choose to attend to but later abandon because you discovered they were irrelevant to the task? What variables did you discover were relevant to successful performance? How might your juggling experience have been different had you had an effective instructor?

## Precise Language

When giving instructions, be sure to provide learners with enough information to relay the concept while using developmentally appropriate terminology. The phrase "choke up on the bat" may be familiar to some learners, but to a beginner with limited sporting experience, it may make little sense. Telling an individual who is learning how to do empty can exercises for rotator cuff rehabilitation to "raise your arm" will elicit a different response from telling her to "raise your arm to the point where your upper arm is parallel with the floor."

Lack of specificity can lead to misunderstandings. In one instance, a coach instructed a middle school quarterback to "throw faster" after noticing that the player was short arming his throws, resulting in poor ball speed. Unfortunately, this resulted in the player's using an even greater short arming technique, as the athlete's interpretation of the instructions was to release the ball sooner, rather than to use a full range of motion to develop additional velocity. Choose your words carefully. By using specific, developmentally appropriate terminology that matches the skill level of the learner, you can significantly increase the likelihood that the instructions will be clearly understood.

## Internal versus External Focus

Where should learners be instructed to focus their attention when practicing a movement? The common practice of instructing learners to focus their conscious attention on their own body movements has been questioned. Wulf and Weigelt (1997) demonstrated that instructions prompting learners to adopt an **internal focus** of attention, by directing them to concentrate on a specific body movement while learning a slalom-type movement on a ski simulator, degraded performance compared to when no instructions were given at all. These results suggest that, in addition to degrading the execution of automated skills, allocating conscious attention to one's own body movements may also have a negative impact on the acquisition and refinement of new skills.

Given the negative impact on learning found when learners adopt an internal focus, Wulf, Hofl, and Prinz (1998) studied the effectiveness of using an external focus. In their experiment, using a ski simulator task, instructions that directed learners' attention to the effects of their actions on the environment (**external focus**) were compared to those that prompted an internal focus. The results indicated that instructions that focused the learners' attention on the force they exerted on the simulator's platform wheels (external focus) were more effective than those where the learners' focus of attention was directed to the feet that were exerting the force (internal focus). Advantages of adopting an external focus of attention have also been demonstrated for the learning and performance of pitch shots in golf (Wulf, Lauterbach & Toole, 1999; Wulf & Su, 2007), basketball free throws (Zachry, Wulf, Mercer & Bezodis, 2005), tennis stroke (Wulf et al., 2000), volleyball serves and soccer passes (Wulf, McConnel, Gärtner &

To study how instructions influence motor skill learning, Wulf, McNevin, and colleagues (2000) compared the relative effectiveness of two effect-related (external) attentional focus conditions. Two groups of 13 subjects hit golf balls with a 9-iron to a target. The "club" group was instructed to focus on the movement of the club, while the "target" group was instructed to direct their attention to the ball's trajectory and the target. More specifically, the club group was asked to concentrate on allowing the club to perform a pendulum motion, and the target group was asked to anticipate the arc of the ball and its outcome relative to the target. Although both groups became more accurate during the 80-shot practice phase, the club group significantly outperformed the target group. This superior performance was also seen in the retention test. The authors concluded that instructions that focus the learner's attention on technique-related effects were more effective for both learning and performance than attentional focus instructions that were related to the outcome of the action.

Schwarz, 2002), and a number of balance tasks (e.g., Landers, Wulf, Wallmann & Guadagnoli, 2005; Totsika & Wulf, 2003; Wulf & McNevin, 2003).

Given these findings, it appears that instructions directing learners how to focus their attention can affect motor skill acquisition and performance (see Wulf 2007a and b for a comprehensive review). Although additional research is necessary to understand fully which contexts would most benefit from the adoption of an external focus, a viable instructional strategy may be to have, for example, a patient who is re-learning how to walk imagine kicking a ball during the terminal swing phase of the gait cycle rather than focusing attention on heel strike (McNevin, Wulf & Carlson, 2000). Other examples include instructing a percussionist to focus on the movement of the drumsticks rather than those of the wrist, focusing on the target in horseshoes instead of the arm movement, and focusing a patient's attention on the position of an object to be moved rather than on the hand and finger movements used to move the object (Wulf, 2007a).

## Awareness of Regulatory Conditions

In open skills, early detection of task-relevant information can reduce response delays and enhance performance. As a result, instructions are commonly given that direct the learner's attention toward such information in an attempt to facilitate learning. For example, a person learning to bat may be instructed to look for certain hand positions when a pitcher releases the ball in order to identify or predict the oncoming pitch. Preliminary research indicates, however, that this strategy may not only be unnecessary but may in fact hinder learning (Hodges & Franks, 2002; Masters & Maxwell, 2004).

Using a computer-simulated catching task, Green and Flowers (1991) found that participants were able to determine the predictive relationship of ball flight without being made aware of it through explicit verbal instructions. Moreover, this **implicit learning** group showed greater performance improvement than those in the **explicit learning** group, who were instructed about the underlying rules of the relationship. The authors attributed the poorer performance of the group that received instructions to an overload of the available attentional resources as a result of trying to remember the rule and its application along with meeting the demands of performing the movement itself.

Additional support for the notion that conscious awareness might not be necessary for acquisition of knowledge about the environmental regulatory features of a motor skill has been provided by Magill (1998). In a tracking study, participants once again were able to exploit an embedded relationship without being made aware of it through verbal instructions. Magill suggests that instructors direct learners' attention at information-rich areas, such as the area where the ball is released, rather than instructing learners to look for specific cues, such as how the ball leaves the pitcher's hand. In addition, learners should be exposed to a variety of performance situations that contain the critical environmental regulatory cues to facilitate their acquisition.

## Learning Styles

Recall that all learners are unique in how they prefer to receive new information, and instructions are more meaningful if delivered through the learner's preferred mode. "See your fingers point to the floor after you release the ball" and "Feel the tension in your wrist after you release the ball" both provide a frame of reference for what the learner should experience if the follow-through in the free throw is performed correctly. The first statement appeals to a visual learner, while the second is more meaningful to a kinesthetic learner. Explanations that accommodate learning preferences enable learners to process information more effectively and achieve greater learning gains (e.g., Ross, Drysdale & Schulz, 1999).

## Previously Learned Skills

According to the principles of transfer, when a skill is introduced, the learner will derive greater meaning from the explanation if it is related to some previous experience. For example, for an individual with extensive volleyball experience, understanding the arm position at contact for a tennis serve will be easier if the instructor makes a comparison to that of the volleyball serve. Such a connection simplifies the new concept for the learner and accelerates the development of an accurate movement plan.

## Verbal Cues

A **verbal cue** is a word or concise phrase that focuses the learner's attention or prompts a movement or movement sequence (Masser, 1993). For example, "Feet shoulder-width apart," focuses the learner's attention on a key element of the skill, and "Free ball," used in volleyball, prepares the defense, indicating that the ball will be passed over the net because an attack was not possible. The cue "Step" prompts a movement, and the cue "Right, right, left, together" prompts a movement sequence, the series of foot contacts that occur in the triple jump.

Practitioners frequently use verbal cues to facilitate learning. Learners also develop and use cues to guide themselves through an action or a movement sequence. This technique is referred to as **self-talk** or verbal rehearsal, because the learners essentially talk to themselves while performing a task. Saying "right, right, left, together" to cue the steps in the triple jump is a good example. Planned instructional self-talk has been shown to enhance skill acquisition (e.g., Hatzigeorgiadis, Theodorakis & Zourbanos, 2004; Landin & Hebert, 1999; Perkos, Theodorakis & Chroni, 2002).

The following four guidelines can help you develop effective practitioner and self-directed cues:

1. *Cues must be concise.* Self-talk cues are most effective if they contain only one or two words (Ziegler, 1987). For practitioner-directed cues, phrases should ideally be no longer than four words (Masser, 1993).

2. *Cues must be accurate.* Unless cues clearly represent skill components, they will be ineffective. To develop critical cues that accurately represent key movement components, you need to be familiar with the skill.

3. *The number of cues should be limited.* Too many cues will not only increase the chances of forgetting but could also interfere with the natural rhythm of the skill. Remember that cues are used to focus the learner's attention. Breaking a skill down into too many components in an effort to simplify it for the learner may negatively affect the overall timing of the skill. Learning to drive a car with a manual transmission is a good example. If the cues "Push in the clutch," "Shift," "Let out the clutch," and "Step on the accelerator" are attended to as separate steps, the learner may be surprised when the car stalls or leaps forward!

4. *The same cues should be used repeatedly.* Repetition assists the learner in developing a strong association between the cue and the task. This association will, in turn, have a positive effect on retention.

## Check for Understanding

Instructions can elicit the desired response only if they are understood. Rather than waiting to assess learners' understanding of instructions until they attempt to carry them out, provide an opportunity for learners to ask questions after the skill presentation. Asking learners to restate the key elements of the skill can help you further assess their comprehension of the instructions. With a quick check for understanding, you will avoid having to reassemble the learners to repeat or clarify instructions.

## CEREBRAL challenge 7.5

Performing a task analysis (see Chapter 1) will assist the practitioner in developing verbal cues. First, break the skill into its phases. Second, determine the key elements of each phase. Finally, develop verbal cues based on the key elements. For example, putting can be broken down into the grip, set-up, and stroke. Below are examples of key elements of the stroke and examples of corresponding cues:

| KEY ELEMENT | VERBAL CUE |
|---|---|
| Shoulders, elbows, hands, and putter swing back and forth as a unit | Pendulum swing<br>No wrist break |
| Putter accelerates in the front swing | Swing through the ball |
| Back swing and front swing should move through the same distance | Maintain swing ratio |

**www.**

**PE Central Activity Cues**

www.pecentral.org/lessonideas/
cues/cuesmenu.asp

Choose a motor skill with which you are very familiar and perform this process. How would you perform this process for a skill you are not familiar with? For a resource to assist you in determining activity cues, visit the adjoining website. Find and list three additional resources that you could refer to in the future.

## CEREBRAL challenge 7.6

1. List behaviors or mannerisms that suggest that the learner may not have understood the instructions given.
2. Speculate as to whether asking learners if they have any questions or asking the learners to restate the key elements of a skill may be more effective when checking for understanding. Give reasons for your response.

## DEMONSTRATIONS

Let's revisit the experience of teaching an individual how to tie his or her shoelaces. It probably didn't take too long before you realized that verbally describing the subtleties of shoelace tying in a meaningful way would not only require a great amount of detail but would involve a rather lengthy explanation, neither of which would facilitate learning. In fact, your first instinct when presented with this challenge most likely involved *showing* the learner how to do it. Certainly, because a demonstration will quickly provide the learner with a meaningful visual picture of the skill, it is a preferred instructional method.

# Theories of Observational Learning

Demonstrations, also referred to as modeling or observational learning, rely on the ability of the learner to acquire information through observation of another individual, or model, performing the movement. Currently, two theories offer explanations of how a demonstration facilitates skill acquisition.

## Social cognitive theory of observational learning

The social cognitive theory of observational learning (Bandura, 1986) suggests that when a learner observes another individual performing a movement, the learner processes the information conveyed by the model and transforms it into a cognitive memory representation of the activity. This cognitive representation, formed by symbolic coding and cognitive rehearsal, not only serves to guide the learner's subsequent movement attempts but also provides a frame of reference for error detection and correction.

## Dynamic interpretation of modeling

The dynamic interpretation of modeling (Scully & Newell, 1985) presents an alternative perspective on how observational learning facilitates skill acquisition. In this perspective, the key information that the learner acquires from a demonstration is the relative features of the movement pattern or, in other words, the pattern of coordination of the limbs relative to one another. This information is directly perceived and enables the learner to coordinate body movements to reproduce the observed relative motion. Further, the coordinated motion is scaled according to individual specifications. Consequently, the need to create a cognitive representation of the skill, as suggested by Bandura, is disputed.

Although the dynamic theory offers an intriguing alternative perspective, the social cognitive theory is currently widely accepted and has been the theory of focus in the literature. Further research is needed to determine whether either perspective or a combination of the two most accurately explains how demonstrations facilitate learning.

# Designing Effective Demonstrations

If a demonstration is to be effective in conveying information that will assist the learner with subsequent movement attempts, the practitioner must make five decisions regarding its design:

1. What should be demonstrated?
2. Who should demonstrate?
3. How should the demonstration be organized?
4. When should the demonstration occur?
5. How often should the demonstration occur?

## Content: What should be demonstrated?

It is obvious that the demonstration should focus on the skill to be taught, but several additional considerations are important. The specific content of the demonstration is, therefore, the first decision facing the practitioner.

**Coordination versus control.** Although demonstrations are one of the most popular techniques for presenting skills, learners seem to benefit most from those that focus on a new pattern of coordination, such as the technique used to cradle a lacrosse ball or to crutch walk (Magill & Schoenfelder-Zohdi, 1996). Studies show that learners who have observed a model demonstrate a movement pattern or form characteristics similar to the model's relative motion or coordination (Al-Abood, Davids & Bennett, 2001; Horn, Williams & Scott, 2002; Horn, Williams, Scott & Hodges, 2005; Schoenfelder-Zhodi, 1992). On the other hand, when demonstrations emphasize variables that control well-learned patterns of movement, such as speed and force, observational learning is no more effective than other forms of instruction (Magill, 1998; Williams & Hodges, 2005).

**Entire versus partial.** Since the purpose of the initial demonstration is to provide the learner with a general idea of the movement's requirements, the skill should be performed in its entirety, as it would occur in a competitive or criterion situation. Seeing the whole skill not only gives the learner an idea of the movement and its intended outcome but also shows the interrelationships among its component parts (Hodges & Franks, 2004). The content of subsequent demonstrations depends on the skill's complexity and the ease with which it can be broken down into components. After a demonstration of the breaststroke, for example, a swimming instructor may want to focus learners' attention on how to execute the whip kick and perform a demonstration isolating the kick.

**Real time versus slow motion.** Instructors often use slow motion to direct the learner's attention to a particular aspect of a skill. However, its use should be limited, because viewing the skill in real time is important for the development of a frame of reference for the skill (Williams, 1986), and it allows the learner to appreciate the natural timing of the movement. Hence, the initial demonstration of the skill should occur in real time, and once the learner comprehends a concept being emphasized with slow motion, the demonstration should be shown again at the original speed.

## Characteristics of the model: Who should demonstrate?

The second decision the practitioner must make for a demonstration is who should perform it, because the characteristics of the model will affect the demonstration's effectiveness.

**Expert versus learning model.** Learners create a cognitive representation, or "perceptual blueprint" (Lee, Swinnen & Serrien, 1994), of a skill based on

McCullagh and Meyer (1997) examined the efficacy of using a learning model for demonstration of the free weight squat. Forty female participants were assigned to one of four learning conditions: (1) physical practice plus feedback, (2) learning model with model feedback, (3) correct model with model feedback, or (4) learning model without model feedback. Each participant performed five 30-second acquisition trials. Prior to their first trial and during the two-minute inter-trial rest period, participants viewed a videotape model and were given feedback statements that corresponded to their assigned experimental condition. Results indicated that viewing a correct model and viewing a learning model with model feedback were equally effective for learning correct squat technique.

their observation of a demonstration. Since this representation serves to guide the learners' subsequent movement attempts and error detection and correction, it stands to reason that the model should perform the skill correctly. The more a learner sees the skill performed correctly, the stronger the blueprint. The stronger the blueprint, the greater the ability to replicate the skill. However, increasing evidence challenges the exclusive use of an expert model. An equally if not more effective strategy is the use of a learning model—an unskilled model who is learning the skill. The key to this technique is that the learners not only view another learner practicing the skill but also benefit from listening to the instructor's feedback and watching the individual attempt to correct the errors that were identified (Hebert & Landin, 1994). Support for this strategy has been found for simple timing tasks (McCullagh & Caird, 1990), complex video games (Pollock & Lee, 1992), bimanual coordination patterns (Hirose, Tsutsui, Okuda & Imanaka, 2004), and sport skills such as tennis (Hebert & Landin, 1994) and weightlifting (McCullagh & Meyer, 1997).

**common** *myth*

For an observer to learn a movement, the demonstration must be performed correctly.

Comparisons of demonstrations by experts versus learning models suggest a significant difference in the degree to which learners are actively engaged in the learning process. The use of an expert model may encourage learners to imitate movements rather than explore movement. On the other hand, after observation of a learning model, learners must generate personal movement solutions. This not only encourages self-discovery through the exploration of a variety of possible task solutions but also increases learners' cognitive effort. Furthermore, learners may better identify with a learning model. Expert and learning models are compared in Table 7.1.

**Model-observer similarity.** What influence do variables such as the model's status, age, gender, and similarity to observers have on how well a movement pattern or skill is ultimately learned? In several studies, when participants viewed models whom they perceived as similar to themselves, they performed better than when they viewed models they perceived as dissimilar (Gould & Weiss, 1981;

| TABLE 7.1 | Characteristics of expert model versus learning model (Darden, 1997). | |
|---|---|---|
| | **EXPERT MODEL** | **LEARNING MODEL** |
| Model Characteristics | ■ High skill proficiency<br>■ High status | ■ Level of skill proficiency slightly above that of observer<br>■ Similar status to observer |
| Content of Demonstration | ■ Skill is performed correctly<br>■ Verbal cues accompany demonstration<br>■ Learner's attention is directed to correctness of performance | ■ Performance may include both correct and incorrect aspects<br>■ Verbal cues plus instructor feedback accompany demonstration<br>■ Learner's attention is directed to both correct and incorrect aspects of performance |
| Outcome | ■ Passive engagement of observer<br>■ Encourages movement imitation | ■ Active engagement of observer<br>■ Encourages movement exploration |

McCullagh, 1987). Moreover, when participants view an unfamiliar model, the skill level rather than the status of the model may be more significant to the observer's perception of similarity (Lirgg & Feltz, 1991).

These results may be attributed to increased self-efficacy beliefs (Gould & Weiss, 1981; McAuley, 1985; Schunk & Hanson, 1985). Essentially, when observers view a similar model successfully performing the skill, their perception that they, too, will be able to reproduce the skill successfully increases. Consequently, improvements in performance may be the result of increases in observer attention or motivation. Care must be taken when interpreting these results. Note that the increases found were in performance. To date, little direct evidence exists to support the influence of model characteristics on learning.

**Alternative mediums.** Live models are not the only kind of model available for demonstrating concepts and movements. With advances in technology, video demonstrations have become popular. They not only free up the instructor but also permit learners to view the movement and specific aspects of it repeatedly, from numerous angles (some of which may be difficult to see during a live demonstration), and at various speeds. Disadvantages of using video demonstrations are that for large groups, not everyone may be able to hear and see well, and that commercial videos may not show all of the pertinent elements and angles.

Another effective way to demonstrate concepts and movements is to supplement a live or video model with drawings or still photos. Still pictures, such as those in Figure 7.1, allow the instructor to show relationships between performers and implements or opponents, isolate key positions, and highlight hard-to-see aspects of the skill or formation.

**Still pictures that represent specific aspects of a movement.**    FIGURE **7.1**

**(a)** Freestyle technique.

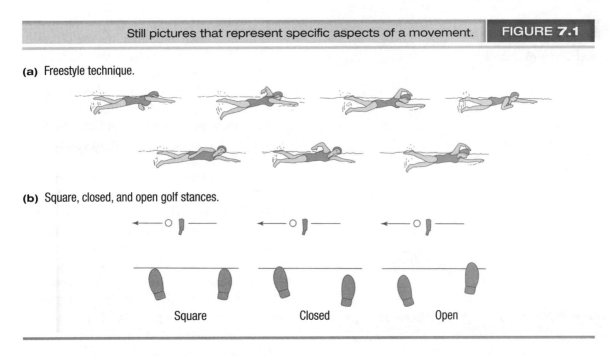

**(b)** Square, closed, and open golf stances.

Square          Closed          Open

Finally, Shea, Wulf, Park, and Gaunt (2001) demonstrated that auditory modeling enhanced learning of the relative-timing features of a task. In other words, highlighting the internal rhythm or tempo of a skill through sound can facilitate skill acquisition. The last five steps in the javelin run-up, for instance, generally have the rhythm: medium, medium, long, short, short. A live model could reproduce the step pattern for the observer, but clapping the pattern to isolate the rhythm may better increase understanding, especially for auditory learners. The use of a metronome in dance is another example. Furthermore, many sport skills have consequent sounds. For example, a different sound results when a softball is caught in the pocket than when it is caught in the palm of a glove. A demonstration of consequent sounds can provide learners with a frame of reference for the correctness of their movements.

## Mechanics of effective demonstrations: How should the demonstration be organized?

Determining how the demonstration will be organized is the third decision the practitioner must make. The instructor must ensure that all learners have a good viewing angle and that they focus on the key elements of the demonstration. The following guidelines will help you organize effective demonstrations.

**Use an appropriate formation.** All learners must be able to see and hear the demonstration clearly. Some formations lend themselves quite well to this objective, while others are problematic. An example of a problematic forma-

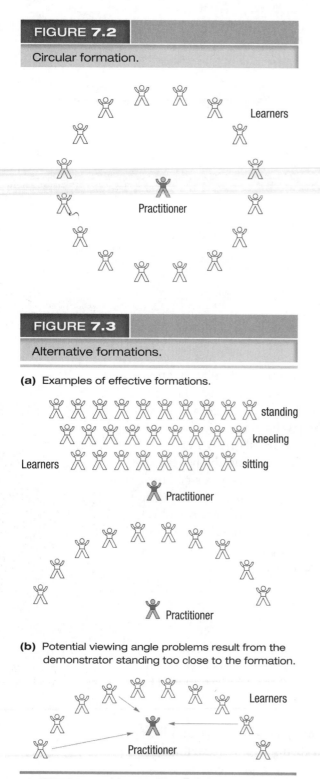

**FIGURE 7.2**

Circular formation.

**FIGURE 7.3**

Alternative formations.

**(a)** Examples of effective formations.

**(b)** Potential viewing angle problems result from the demonstrator standing too close to the formation.

tion is a circle with the model in the center, as in Figure 7.2. Obviously, it will be more difficult for a learner who is positioned to the left of a right-handed model to attend to the key elements of the skill. Likewise, a learner who is positioned behind the model will not be able to hear cues and instructions well. Another problem with a circle is that all learners cannot view the demonstration from the same perspective. Some learners will see it from the front, others from the rear, and others from the side. Alternative formations designed to resolve these concerns are illustrated in Figure 7.3a. The demonstrator must not be positioned too close to the learners, or the learners at the ends of the formation will have a different viewing angle from those in the center, as illustrated in Figure 7.3b.

Demonstrating a skill from a number of different viewpoints will enhance learners' understanding of the movement requirements. Different viewpoints highlight different aspects of the skill. For example, a patient who is learning the use of a walker can see the overall movement pattern from the front, while a side view will provide information about the placement of the walker in relation to the body prior to stepping. Similarly, a side view of the gliding action in the shot put enables learners to focus on the movement of the legs, while a rear view highlights the position of the shoulders. Seeing the demonstration from multiple viewing angles presents a more complete picture of the skill.

Sometimes viewing a skill from the front is problematic. The grapevine in an aerobics class is a good example. If a model demonstrates this skill while facing the group, the learners must reverse what they observed in order to perform the steps using the same limbs, which can be quite confusing. In this situation, viewing the model from behind will aid the learners in imitating the movement.

Alternatively, the instructor could present a mirror image by facing the group but performing the skill in the same direction that the group is moving.

**Explain how the demonstration will proceed and what to watch for.** It has been stressed throughout this chapter that the learners' attention must be directed to the relevant features of the movement, or instructions are likely to be worthless. To this end, avoid using the phrases "like this" and "like that" in conjunction with the demonstration. These phrases are not specific enough to direct the learners' attention. Instead, tell the learners how the demonstration will proceed and what, specifically, to watch for. For example, the initial demonstration of a new skill should encompass the whole skill, as it would be performed in competitive or criterion situations. Since the intent here is to give the learner a general idea of the movement's requirements, appropriate instructions would be simply to watch the skill in its entirety. In subsequent demonstrations of either the whole skill or part of the skill, learners should be precued to direct their attention to specific aspects of the movement, such as watching how the toes are pointed during the flutter kick (Janelle, Champenoy, Coombes & Mousseau, 2003; McCullagh, Steihl & Weiss, 1990; Weiss & Klint, 1987; Zetou, Tzetzis, Vernadakis & Kioumourtzoglou, 2002).

**Avoid product options.** Although the initial demonstration of a new skill should encompass the whole skill, as it would be performed in competitive or criterion situations, subsequent presentations should be designed to avoid product options. In other words, design the demonstration so that the outcome is eliminated. As humans, we are very curious creatures. We want to know if the ball went in, how far the javelin flew, and whether or not the catch was made. Unfortunately, this curiosity often distracts our focus from the key aspects of the movement that produced the outcome (the process). Removing the outcome—throwing a modified javelin into a net, for example—makes learners less likely to track the implement and more likely to focus on the key elements of the movement.

**Demonstrate for both right and left limb dominance.** If you are demonstrating to a group, be aware of the composition of that group with respect to limb dominance. If all

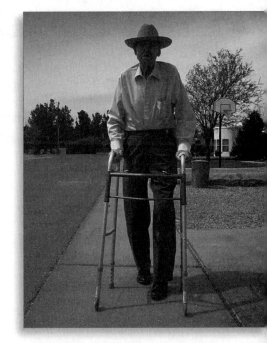

A front view provides information about the timing of the movement.

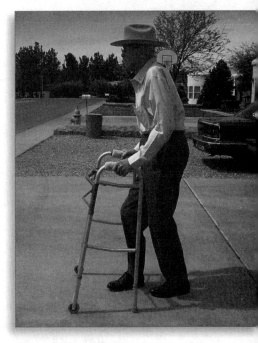

The side view offers a more specific demonstration of the placement of the walker.

Janelle, Champenoy, Coombes and Mousseau (2003) examined the effectiveness of different cueing conditions during observational learning on the outcome and form of the inside-of-the-foot soccer pass toward a target. Sixty participants were randomly assigned to one of six groups: discovery learning, verbal instruction, video model with visual cues, video model with verbal cues, video model with visual and verbal cues, and video model only. Each participant performed eight blocks of 10 trials. Blocks 1 and 2 constituted the practice phase, where no manipulation was provided. Blocks 3 through 6 were considered the acquisition phase, as all groups received their corresponding instructional modality (manipulation administered). Finally, 24 hours following the acquisition phase, participants completed blocks 7 and 8, the retention phase, where no manipulation was given. Results indicated that participants who were exposed to video modeling with visual and verbal cueing performed with less error and a more refined movement pattern compared with those who used alternative modeling modalities or learning strategies. These results lend additional support to the notion that the provision of cues during observational learning facilitates skill acquisition.

learners are right-handed, demonstrating the tennis serve with the left hand may not be necessary. However, if both limb preferences are represented in the group, demonstrate the skill both ways. Telling left-handed learners simply to switch everything you said to the other side increases the complexity of the task.

### Distribution and frequency: When and how often should demonstrations occur?

The use of a demonstration to complement initial instructions when introducing a new skill seems intuitive. But practitioners must also decide whether to intersperse additional demonstrations throughout the practice session, and if so, how often? Research exploring this question suggests that, for learning movement form, a schedule that combines viewing a demonstration several times before practicing with inter-practice observations early in the learning process (demonstrations interspersed throughout the practice period) is superior to either pre-practice viewing only or an interspersed-only schedule (Weeks & Anderson, 2000).

To determine the frequency of demonstrations, consider the skill level of the learner and complexity of the task. In general, more experienced learners need fewer demonstrations than inexperienced learners (Wrisberg, 2007). Additional demonstrations will likely be necessary as skills become more complex. To individualize instruction, consider giving learners the opportunity to control their viewing frequency. Research indicates that learners who were able to self-select their model viewing frequency (i.e., see a demonstration when they chose) acquired movement form equally well to those who viewed a model before each practice attempt (Wrisberg & Pein, 2002; Wulf, Raupach & Pfeiffer, 2005). When learners were given the opportunity to control their model viewing frequency, they primarily elected to view the model during the early stages

| | | Demonstration considerations. | | TABLE **7.2** |
|---|---|---|---|---|
| **WHAT** | **WHO** | **HOW** | **WHEN** | **HOW OFTEN** |
| New pattern of coordination | Expert model vs. learning model | Formation and viewing angle | Introduction of skill | Imposed vs. self-regulated schedule |
| Whole vs. part | Observer–model similarity | Limb preference | Interspersed throughout practice | |
| Real time vs. slow motion | Video, still pictures, audio | Direction of movement | | |
| | | Avoidance of product options | | |

of learning, suggesting that demonstrations serve to provide the learner with a "general idea of the movement pattern or perhaps to adjust their movements following an inaccurate performance" (Wrisberg & Pein, 2002; p. 794). Refer to Table 7.2 for a summary list of demonstration considerations, and complete Exploration Activity 7.7 to assess skill presentation effectiveness.

## exploration  A C T I V I T Y  7.7

### Evaluating skill presentation effectiveness

*Part A*

Using the information presented in this chapter, design an evaluation checklist for determining skill presentation effectiveness.

Examples:

1. Did the practitioner use a clear signal to call the learners together?
2. Did the practitioner demonstrate the skill for both right and left limb dominant learners?

*Part B*

Observe a teacher, coach, or therapist presenting a new skill. Using the checklist you designed in Part A, evaluate the effectiveness of the skill presentation.

*Part C*

Now record yourself presenting a new skill. Review the video, using the checklist from Part A to evaluate your performance. How might you improve your demonstration effectiveness?

## DISCOVERY LEARNING

**A** n effective alternative to the "show and tell" approach to presenting skills is **discovery learning** (Araújo et al., 2004; Mosston, & Ashworth, 1994; van Emmerik, den Brinker, Vereijken & Whiting, 1989; Vereijken, Whiting & Beek, 1992; Wulf & Weigelt, 1997). As you may recall from Chapter 3, discovery learning is advocated under the constraints-led approach. In discovery learning, the practitioner creates a learning environment where the learner attempts to solve the movement problem by exploring a variety of possible task solutions. The practitioner's role is to facilitate this process by manipulating the individual, environmental, and task constraints to shape learners' skill development (Williams & Hodges, 2005).

Learning to ice skate in a forward direction without losing one's balance is a good example of a task that could benefit from discovery learning. Rather than providing specific instructions on how to skate, the practitioner simply introduces the movement problem and goal. The learner is encouraged to discover the ideal solution to the movement problem through trial and error. In this example, once a basic solution has been discovered, the practitioner can then use instructions, demonstrations, and other strategies for skill refinement. Visit the adjoining website for other examples and videos of discovery learning.

**WWW.**

**The PE Central Challenge**

www.pecentral.org/pecchallenge/
challenges/challengelist.html

### Guided Discovery

In some cases, discovery learning can be too general, allowing the learner too many options, and the result may be a coordination mode that might initially work but may inhibit progress beyond a certain point. In these instances, a variation of discovery learning known as **guided discovery** may be more effective. In guided discovery, the practitioner asks a sequence of questions, each of which elicits a single correct response discovered by the learner (Mosston & Ashworth, 1994). This step-by-step process leads to the eventual discovery of the intended concept or principle. The adjoining websites offer examples of and more information on guided discovery.

**WWW.**

**Examples of guided discovery**

http://82.195.132.34/uploadedfiles/PSC/
PEGExemplar_1.pdf

www.educ.uvic.ca/faculty/thopper/
Unitplan452/default.html

**More information on guided discovery**

www.powerade.co.nz/default,592,a_
new_coaching_approach.sm

To implement this technique, the practitioner must design a series of questions or clues regarding the new movement or concept. The first question is delivered, the learner is given the opportunity to answer, and the practitioner either reinforces the response or redirects the learner. Once the correct answer has been discovered, the practitioner asks the next question in the sequence. For example, while introducing the skill of dribbling a soccer ball, the learner might be asked, "What is the goal of the defenders?" Once the learner identifies the goal of the defender as stealing the ball, subsequent questions lead to the learner's discovery of kicking the ball softly and with the side of the foot as opposed to the toe. Gradually, the learner will not only learn the technique but also develop an understanding of why that technique is used.

## MANUAL GUIDANCE

In manual guidance, another strategy often used in physical education, sport, and rehabilitation settings, a practitioner or device correctly moves the learner through the goal movement (Sidaway et al., 2008). Examples of manual guidance include a therapist moving a patient's limb through the desired range of motion; the use of a safety belt for diving, gymnastics, and acrobatic stunts; the golf swing ring; and training wheels on a bicycle. The use of manual guidance techniques is based on the assumption that they provide the learner with a clearer understanding of the goal movement, help reduce errors, and allow potentially dangerous movements to be practiced in a safe manner (Wulf, Shea & Whitacre, 1998).

Activities such as ice skating could benefit from discovery learning.

However, leading a learner passively through a movement presents several potential problems (Wrisberg, 2007). First, one of the premises behind manual guidance is that learners will experience what the correct movement feels like, but assisted movements produce different response-produced feedback (feeling) than unassisted ones. Second, learners are likely to be less attentive when they are passively led through a movement. Third, manual guidance eliminates learners' opportunity to detect and correct their own movements.

Given these concerns, practitioners should use this strategy sparingly. In fact, research indicates that while a high frequency of manual guidance facilitates practice performance, it has a detrimental effect on retention (Sidaway et al., 2008; Winstein, Pohl & Lewthwaite, 1994; Wulf et al., 1998). In other words, marked performance improvements will likely be seen in practice or

C E R E B R A L **challenge** | 7.8

If you were the therapist in the story that opened this chapter, what technique(s) would you use to teach the patient therapeutic ball exercises? Explain your answer.

during treatment, but long-term maintenance of those effects is unlikely (Sidaway et al., 2008). Consequently, although occasions exist where manual guidance may initially be helpful (e.g., injury prevention, developing a basic understanding of a skill), unassisted practice should be introduced as soon as possible.

## ▶ a look ahead

When presenting a new skill, the instructor's initial goal is to convey to learners the information they need in order to develop a basic understanding of the movement's requirements and formulate an initial movement plan. Once this is accomplished, the focus shifts to one of skill refinement. Five techniques—instructions, demonstrations, discovery learning, guided discovery, and manual guidance—facilitate both initial skill understanding and skill refinement. However, motor skill acquisition also requires that learners be provided with ample opportunities to practice new skills. Issues related to designing optimal practice opportunities are the focus of the next chapter.

## ● focus points

After reading this chapter, you should know that . . .

- When giving instructions:
  - Keep explanations short and simple
  - Use developmentally appropriate terminology
  - Direct learners' attention to critical elements of the skill during initial instructions
  - Provide learners with a frame of reference for correctness
  - Consider learners' learning styles and previous experiences
- Instructions focusing learners' conscious attention on specific body movements have been shown to influence learning negatively.
- Verbal cues are used to focus learners' attention or prompt a movement or movement sequence and should be concise, accurate, limited in number, and used repeatedly throughout the learning process.
- When planning a demonstration, the practitioner should consider its content, the characteristics of the model, how the demonstration will be organized, and its distribution and frequency.
- When providing an initial demonstration, the practitioner or model should perform the whole skill in real time to give learners an idea of the movement.

- Learners benefit from demonstrations that focus on a new pattern of coordination.

- The use of a learning model encourages movement exploration and active involvement in the learning process.

- For an effective demonstration, all learners should have a good viewing angle and should be focused on the key elements being demonstrated.

- The complexity of the skill and the extent to which the learner understands the information will dictate when and how often a demonstration should be provided.

- In discovery learning, the practitioner acts as a facilitator and the learner is given the opportunity to explore a variety of possible solutions to a given movement problem.

- Guided discovery gives learners the opportunity to explore possible movement solutions but is more structured than discovery learning, in that the practitioner asks a sequence of questions, each of which elicits a single correct response to be discovered by the learner.

- Manual guidance may be used to convey skill requirements and for safety purposes but should be withdrawn as soon as possible.

## ? review questions

1. Why is it critical to capture learners' attention before skill instruction begins?
2. Explain why practitioners who are highly familiar with their subject matter are not always the most effective instructors.
3. What is the function of a verbal cue?
4. Compare and contrast instructor-directed verbal cues and self-talk.
5. What guidelines should the practitioner follow to optimize the use of cues?
6. Compare and contrast the social cognitive theory of observational learning and the dynamic interpretation of modeling.
7. Which of the four subprocesses in Bandura's observational learning theory might be influenced by model characteristics? Justify your answer.
8. What is a learning model? What are some advantages of using a learning model?
9. For a motor skill of your choice, explain what decisions you would make regarding the mechanics of its demonstration. Justify your answers.
10. Compare and contrast demonstrations and discovery learning.
11. List the potential problems associated with using a high frequency of manual guidance.

# REFERENCES

Abernethy, B. (1993). Attention. In R.N. Singer, M. Murphy and L.K. Tennent (Eds.), *Handbook of Research on Sport Psychology* (pp. 127–70). New York: MacMillan.

Al-Abood, S.A., Davids, K. & Bennett, S.J. (2001). Specificity of task constraints and effects of visual demonstrations and verbal instructions in directing learners' search during skill acquisition. *Journal of Motor Behavior, 33,* 295–305.

Araújo, D., Davids, K., Bennett, S.J., Button, C. & Chapman, G. (2004). Emergence of sport skills under constraints. In A.M. Williams and N.J. Hodges (Eds.), *Skill acquisition in sport: research, theory and practice* (pp. 409–33). London: Routledge, Taylor and Francis.

Bandura, A. (1986). *Social foundations of thought and action: a social cognitive theory.* Englewood Cliffs, NJ: Prentice Hall.

Darden, G.F. (1997). Demonstrating motor skills: rethinking that expert demonstration. *Journal of Physical Education, Recreation and Dance, 68*(6), 31–35.

Green, T.D. & Flowers, J.H. (1991). Implicit vs. explicit learning processes in a probabilistic, continuous fine motor catching task. *Journal of Motor Behavior, 23,* 239–300.

Gould, D. & Weiss, M. R. (1981). The effects of model similarity and model talk on self-efficacy and muscular endurance. *Journal of Sport Psychology,* 17-29.

Hatzigeorgiadis, A., Theodorakis, Y. & Zourbanos, N. (2004). Self-talk in the swimming pool: the effects of ST on thought content and performance on water-polo tasks. *Journal of Applied Sport Psychology, 16,* 138–50.

Hebert, E.P. & Landin, D. (1994). Effects of a learning model and augmented feedback on tennis skill acquisition. *Research Quarterly for Exercise and Sport, 65*(3), 250–57.

Hirose, T., Tsutsui, S., Okuda, S. & Imanaka, K. (2004). Effectiveness of the use of a learning model and concentrated schedule in observational learning of a new bimanual coordination pattern. *International Journal of Sport and Health Science, 2,* 97–104.

Hodges, N. & Franks, I.M. (2002). Modelling coaching practice: the role of instruction and demonstration. *Journal of Sports Sciences, 20,* 793–811.

Hodges, N. & Franks, I.M. (2004). Instructions and demonstrations: creating and constraining movement options. In A.M. Williams and N.J. Hodges (Eds.), *Skill acquisition in sport: research, theory and practice* (pp. 145–74). London: Routledge.

Horn, R.R., Williams, A.M. & Scott, M.A. (2002). Learning from demonstrations: the role of visual search from video and point-light displays. *Journal of Sports Sciences, 20,* 253–69.

Horn, R.R., Williams, A.M., Scott, M.A. & Hodges, N.J. (2005). Visual search and coordination changes in response to video and point-light demonstrations without KR. *Journal of Motor Behavior, 37,* 265–74.

Janelle, C.M., Champenoy, J.D., Coombes, S.A. & Mousseau, M.B. (2003). Mechanisms of attentional cueing during observational learning to facilitate motor skill acquisition. *Journal of Sports Sciences, 21,* 825–38.

Landers, M., Wulf, G., Wallmann, H. & Guadagnoli, M.A. (2005). An external focus of attention attenuates balance impairment in Parkinson's disease. *Physiotherapy, 91,* 152–85.

Landin, D. & Hebert, E.P. (1999). The influence of self-talk on the performance of skilled female tennis players. *Journal of Applied Sport Psychology, 11,* 263–82.

Lee, T.D., Swinnen, S.P. & Serrien, D.J. (1994). Cognitive effort in learning. *Quest, 46*(32), 328–44.

Lirgg, C.D. & Feltz, D.L. (1991). Teacher vs. peer models revisited: effects on motor performance and self-efficacy. *Research Quarterly for Exercise and Sport, 62*(2), 217–24.

Magill, R.A. (1998). Knowledge is more than we can talk about: implicit learning in motor skill acquisition. *Research Quarterly for Exercise and Sport, 69*(2), 104–10.

Magill, R.A. & Schoenfelder-Zohdi, B. (1996). A visual model and knowledge of performance as sources of information for learning a rhythmic gymnastics skill. *International Journal of Sport Psychology, 27,* 7–22.

Masser, L.S. (1993). Critical cues help first grade students' achievement in handstands and forward rolls. *Journal of Teaching Physical Education, 11,* 301–12.

Masters, R.S.W. & Maxwell, J.P. (2004). Implicit motor learning, reinvestment and movement disruption: what you don't know won't hurt you? In A.M. Williams and N.J. Hodges (Eds.), *Skill acquisition in sport: research, theory and practice* (pp. 207–28). London: Rutledge.

McAuley, E. (1985). Modeling and self-efficacy: a test of Banduras model. *Journal of Sport Psychology, 6,* 283–95.

McCullagh, P. (1987). Model similarity effects on motor performance. *Journal of Sport Psychology, 9,* 249–60.

McCullagh, P. & Caird, J.K. (1990). Correct and learning models and the use of model knowledge of results in the acquisition and retention of a motor skill. *Journal of Human Movement Studies, 18,* 107–16.

McCullagh, P. & Meyer, K.N. (1997). Learning versus correct models: influence of model type on the learning of a free-weight squat lift. *Research Quarterly for Exercise and Sport, 68,* 56–61.

McCullagh, P., Steihl, J. & Weiss, M.R. (1990). Developmental modeling effects on the quantitative and qualitative aspects of motor performance acquisition. *Research Quarterly for Exercise and Sport, 61,* 344–50.

McNevin, N.H., Wulf, G. & Carlson, C. (2000). Effects of attentional focus, self-control and dyad training on motor learning: implications for physical rehabilitation. *Physical Therapy, 80*(4), 373–85.

Mosston, M. & Ashworth, S. (1994). *Teaching physical education* (4th Ed.). New York: MacMillan.

Perkos, S., Theodorakis, Y. & Chroni, S. (2002). Enhancing performance and skill acquisition in novice basketball players with instructional self-talk. *The Sport Psychologist, 16,* 368–83.

Pollock, B.J. & Lee, T.D. (1992). Effects of the model's skill level on observational motor learning. *Research Quarterly for Exercise and Sport, 63,* 25–29.

Rink, J.E. (2005). *Teaching physical education for learning.* New York: McGraw-Hill.

Ross, J.L., Drysdale, M.T.B. & Schulz, R.A. (1999). Learning style in the classroom: towards quality instruction in kinesiology. *Avante, 5*(3), 31–42.

Schoenfelder-Zhodi, B. (1992). Investigating the informational nature of a modeled visual demonstration. Unpublished doctoral dissertation, Louisiana State University, Baton Rouge, La.

Schunk, D.H. & Hanson, A.R. (1985). Peer models: influence on children's self-efficacy and achievement. *Journal of Educational Psychology, 77,* 313–22.

Scully, D.M. & Newell, K.M. (1985). Observational learning and the acquisition of motor skills: towards a visual perception perspective. *Journal of Human Movement Studies, 11,* 169–86.

Shea, C.H., Wulf, G., Park, J. & Gaunt, B. (2001). Effects of an auditory model on the learning of relative and absolute timing. *Journal of Motor Behavior, 33,* 127–38.

Sidaway, B., Ahn, S., Boldeau, P., Griffin, S., Noyes, B. & Pelletier, K. (2008). A comparison of manual guidance and knowledge of results in the learning of a weight-bearing skill. *Journal of Neurologic Physical Therapy, 32,* 32–38.

Siedentop, D. & Tannehill, D. (2001). *Developing teaching skills in physical education.* New York: McGraw-Hill.

Totsika, V. & Wulf, G. (2003). The influence of external and internal foci of attention on transfer to novel situations and skills. *Research Quarterly for Exercise and Sport, 74,* 220–25.

van Emmerik, R.E.A., den Brinker, B.P.L.M., Vereijken, B. & Whiting, H.T.A. (1989). Preferred tempo in the learning of a gross cyclical action. *The Quarterly Journal of Experimental Psychology, 41,* 251–62.

Vereijken, B., Whiting, H.T.A. & Beek, W.J. (1992). A dynamical systems approach to skill acquisition. *The Quarterly Journal of Experimental Psychology, 45A*(2), 323–44.

Weeks, D.L. & Anderson, L.P. (2000). The interaction of observational learning with overt practice: effects on motor skill learning. *Acta Psychologica 104,* 259–71.

Weiss, M.R. & Klint, K.A. (1987). "Show and tell" in the gymnasium: an investigation of developmental differences in modeling and verbal rehearsal of motor skills. *Research Quarterly for Exercise and Sport, 58,* 234–41.

Williams, A.M. & Hodges, N.J. (2005). Practice, instruction and skill acquisition in soccer: challenging tradition. *Journal of Sport Sciences, 23*(6), 637–50.

Williams, J.G. (1986). Perceiving human movement: review of research with implications for the use of demonstrations during motor learning. *Physical Education Review, 9*(1), 53–58.

Winstein C., Pohl P. & Lewthwaite R. (1994). Effects of physical guidance and knowledge of results on motor learning: support for the guidance hypothesis. *Research Quarterly for Exercise and Sport, 65,* 316–23.

Wrisberg, C.A. (2007). *Sport skill instruction for coaches.* Champaign, IL: Human Kinetics.

Wrisberg, C.A. and Pein, R.L. (2002). Note on learners' control of the frequency of model presentation during skill acquisition. *Perceptual and Motor Skills, 94,* 792-794.

Wulf, G. (2007a). *Attention and skill learning.* Champaign, IL: Human Kinetics.

Wulf, G. (2007b). Attentional focus and motor learning: a review of 10 years of research. *E-Journal Bewegung und Training,* 1–11.

Wulf, G., Hofl, M. & Prinz, W. (1998). Instructions for motor learning: differential effects of internal vs. external focus of attention. *Journal of Motor Behavior, 30,* 169–79.

Wulf, G., Lauterbach, B. & Toole, T. (1999). The learning advantages of an external focus of attention in golf. *Research Quarterly for Exercise and Sport, 70*(2), 120–26.

Wulf, G., McConnel, N., Gärtner, M. & Schwarz, A. (2002). Feedback and attentional focus: enhancing the learning of sport skills through external-focus feedback. *Journal of Motor Behavior, 34,* 171–82.

Wulf, G. & McNevin, N. (2003). Simply distracting learners is not enough: more evidence for the learning benefits of an external focus of attention. *European Journal of Sport Science, 3*(5), 1–13.

Wulf, G., McNevin, N., Fuchs, T., Ritter, F. & Toole, T. (2000). Attentional focus on complex skill learning. *Research Quarterly for Exercise and Sport, 71*(3), 229–39.

Wulf, G., Raupach, M. & Pfeiffer, F. (2005). Self-controlled observational practice enhances learning. *Research Quarterly for Exercise and Sport, 76,* 107–11.

Wulf, G., Shea, C. & Whitacre, C. (1998). Physical-guidance benefits in learning a complex motor skill. *Journal of Motor Behavior, 30,* 367–80.

Wulf, G. & Su, J. (2007). An external focus of attention enhances golf shot accuracy in beginners and experts. *Research Quarterly for Exercise and Sport, 78,* 384–89.

Wulf, G. & Weigelt, C. (1997). Instructions about physical principles in learning a complex motor skill: to tell or not to tell. *Research Quarterly for Exercise and Sport, 68*(4), 363–67.

Zachry, T., Wulf, G., Mercer, J. & Bezodis, N. (2005). Increased movement accuracy and reduced EMG activity as a result of adopting an external focus of attention. *Brain Research Bulletin, 67,* 304–09.

Zetou, E., Tzetzis, G., Vernadakis, N. & Kioumourtzoglou, E. (2002). Modeling in learning two volleyball skills. *Perceptual and Motor Skills, 94,* 1131–1142.

Ziegler, S.G. (1987). Effects of stimulus cueing on the acquisition of groundstrokes by beginning tennis players. *Journal of Applied Behavioral Analysis, 20,* 405–11.

# Principles of Practice Design

A lthough it will be two more hours before the sun appears over the horizon, the alarm clock is going off. It is the dead of winter, and Anna has 30 minutes before she has to be on the deck of the pool warming up for morning practice. When Anna was 7, she watched the diving competitions during the 2000 Australian Summer Olympics. Ever since, she has dreamed of being an Olympic diver—but this morning, that dream is a distant one. She hasn't been diving well recently, and she doesn't feel like practicing. She hits the snooze button and falls back asleep. Five minutes later, her father pokes his head in and says encouragingly, "Come on, Anna, practice makes perfect!"

Several misconceptions regarding skill acquisition and control have been mentioned in this text, but perhaps the most widespread is the old adage, "Practice makes perfect." In reality, practice does not guarantee that a learner will become more proficient. Only practice designed according to the ways the learner, the task, and the environment influence the learning process leads to optimal gains in skill proficiency. This chapter will focus on several contributors to effective practice design, including skill progressions, sequencing, and psychological strategies.

## BREAKING DOWN SKILLS: PROGRESSIONS AND SEQUENCING

W hen designing effective practices and rehabilitative experiences, practitioners face several decisions regarding the breakdown of skills. When should a skill be broken down into parts and when should it be practiced as a whole? How do speed and accuracy influence skill acquisition? How are skills that must be performed with equal proficiency on both the dominant and non-dominant side best learned?

### Whole versus Part Practice

Learning a novel motor skill can be a daunting task. To simplify the learning process, instructors commonly use part practice. The **part practice method** generally involves breaking the skill down into natural parts or segments, practicing those parts separately until they are learned, and then integrating them to perform the skill in its entirety. This strategy is advantageous in that it (1) simplifies the skill, (2) allows learners to experience early success, leading to increased motivation, and (3) permits practice on problematic components without wasting time on those already mastered. However, separating the skill into parts might not be the most efficient method in all cases. In fact, under certain conditions, the whole practice method, where the learner practices the complete skill, is favored.

The decision to use whole or part practice in a given situation depends on which method is more likely to result in the greatest amount of positive transfer to the performance of the whole skill (Wightman & Lintern, 1985). To make that judgment, the practitioner must carefully assess the nature of the skill and the capability of the learner.

## Nature of the skill

As we have seen repeatedly, the nature of the skill influences the learning process. Recognizing this, Naylor and Briggs (1963) hypothesized that the effectiveness of part and whole practice depended on two inherent features of the skill. The first, *task complexity,* directly correlates with the number of subcomponents that make up the skill. It is also a function of the information processing demands imposed by the task. The more components and the greater the attention, memory, and decision-making requirements, the more complex the task. Given this description, it may seem appropriate to use the part practice method to simplify highly complex skills for the learner; however, this judgment would be premature without taking into account a second variable, task organization.

Breaking down skills that are high in task organization may change their underlying dynamics.

*Task organization* refers to the degree to which the sub-components of the skill are interdependent. In other words, how much does the performance of each part depend on the component that precedes it? If the answer is very dependent, as is the case in a cartwheel, the task is considered to be high in organization. Breaking a highly organized skill down into parts would not be effective, as this would change its natural rhythm. Similarly, for gait training using parallel bars or for running the hurdles, the performer must make continuous adjustments according to the positioning of the previous part. If an athlete clears the hurdle too high or hits it, he must make adjustments in the step pattern in order to negotiate the next hurdle successfully. The athlete can acquire this ability only by practicing over several hurdles. Finally, for actions characterized by rapid loading of the muscles, such as a slap shot in hockey, breaking the skill into parts may eliminate the stretch reflex inherent to the task and change its underlying dynamics (Schmidt & Young, 1987). Conversely, the freestyle stroke, where the kick and arm action are relatively independent, is a skill low in organization and would lend itself quite well to part practice. Figure 8.1 provides additional examples of skills classified according to their complexity and organization.

Once we know the complexity and organization of a skill, how do we determine which technique, the whole or part practice method, will be most effective for that skill? Generally, skills that are high in organization and low in complexity are best served through whole practice, whereas part practice is the preferred technique for skills low in organization and high in complexity (Naylor & Briggs, 1963). Of course, this guideline does not account for all possible combinations of complexity and organization. For example, it does not suggest the optimal method for a skill that is high in both complexity and organization. In these situations, remember that the objective is to maximize learning. Select the technique that will be most efficient in achieving the desired outcome.

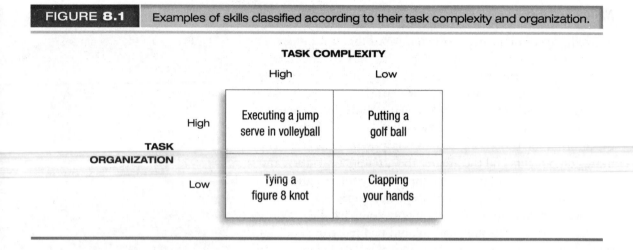

FIGURE **8.1**    Examples of skills classified according to their task complexity and organization.

**TASK COMPLEXITY**

|  |  | High | Low |
|---|---|---|---|
| **TASK ORGANIZATION** | High | Executing a jump serve in volleyball | Putting a golf ball |
|  | Low | Tying a figure 8 knot | Clapping your hands |

C E R E B R A L   **challenge**   8.1

Using the worksheet below (Coker & Hunfalvay, 2004), conduct a basic task analysis to determine the level of complexity and organization of the following skills:

Fielding a ground ball               Heading a soccer ball

Slalom ski racing                    Playing the piano

Transferring from a chair to a wheelchair    Balance beam routine

Grapevine (aerobics)                 Walking with crutches

Layup                                CPR

*Part A: Skill Complexity*

| List the motor actions (or steps) required in the skill | List the decisions needed when performing the skill |
|---|---|
| 1. _____ | 1. _____ |
| 2. _____ | 2. _____ |
| 3. _____ | 3. _____ |
| 4. _____ | 4. _____ |
| 5. _____ | 5. _____ |

Can these be grouped, i.e., can parts of the skill be combined to reduce the number of steps without making the skill too complex for the learner? Describe and justify which actions (or steps) could be grouped.

*Part B: Task Organization*

Does performance on one part of the skill influence the next skill component?

YES          NO

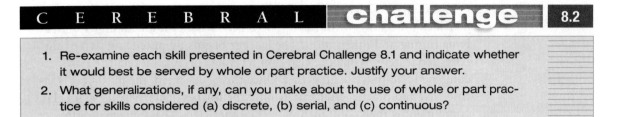

1. Re-examine each skill presented in Cerebral Challenge 8.1 and indicate whether it would best be served by whole or part practice. Justify your answer.
2. What generalizations, if any, can you make about the use of whole or part practice for skills considered (a) discrete, (b) serial, and (c) continuous?

### Capability of the learner

Although the assessment of a skill may indicate the use of either whole or part practice, the practitioner should take the capability of the learner into consideration before making a final decision about which method to employ. Learners with limited movement experiences, for example, may be overwhelmed by the demands imposed by the task if it is presented in its entirety. Similarly, if the cognitive or attentional requirements of a task exceed the learner's capacity, use of the whole practice method may hinder skill acquisition and leave the learner frustrated. That frustration—the result of a lower success rate—could, in turn, lead to a loss of motivation. In this situation, breaking the skill down into more manageable units will be more effective. Conversely, when learners are highly motivated and have had a variety of movement experiences, gains in skill acquisition can be achieved through the whole method.

### Part practice techniques

When conditions indicate the use of part practice, the practitioner has several variations from which to choose. Wightman and Lintern (1985) categorized these variations as segmentation, simplification, and fractionization. It is important to remember that when using part practice—regardless of the variation selected—learners must be taught how the parts are associated with the whole skill. Failure to do this may decrease the transfer to the whole skill. This was demonstrated in an experiment by Newell, Carlton, Fisher, and Rutter (1989), who found that providing learners with part practice in addition to information regarding the goal of the skill resulted in greater learning gains than were gained by part practice only.

**Segmentation.** In **segmentation**, a commonly used part practice technique, the skill is separated into parts according to spatial or temporal elements. The specific structure of this type of practice can take several forms.

1. *Part–whole method.* In this method, each part is practiced separately until a certain level of proficiency is demonstrated, and then the parts are combined and the skill is practiced in its entirety. For the football punt, the catch, approach, drop, and kick would each be practiced separately, and then the parts would be combined and practiced as a unit until the punt is mastered.

2. *Progressive-part method.* In addition to simplifying the skill, this method provides the learner with the opportunity to better understand its underlying timing and integration. The learner begins by practicing two of the parts separately. When the criterion level has been achieved, the parts are combined and practiced together. Once this is mastered, the third part is introduced and practiced separately until the learner achieves proficiency. This component is then combined with the other two. This pattern continues until the whole skill is being performed. For the football punt, the learners might practice the catch and approach separately, combine them, practice the drop separately, combine it with the catch and approach, and so on.

3. *Repetitive-part method.* Like the progressive-part method, this method provides the learner with a better understanding of how the parts of a skill fit into the whole. Rather than practicing the new component independently, the learner adds it to the previous part(s) and practices them together. For example, the catch would be practiced first, and then combined with the approach. Once that combination is acquired, the drop would be added, and so on.

Figure 8.2 illustrates the sequence of each part practice strategy, for the football punt.

When a skill is broken down using segmentation, the practitioner may also choose to use forward or backward chaining. In **forward chaining,** the parts are presented and practiced in a sequence progressing from the first to the final part of the skill. The examples given thus far for the football punt have employed forward chaining. In **backward chaining,** the sequence progresses in reverse order, from the final segment to the initial one. For the football punt, the kick would be practiced, then the drop, then the approach, and finally the catch. See Figure 8.3.

**Fractionization.** In **fractionization,** skill components that are normally performed simultaneously are partitioned and practiced independently. For example, tacking (changing direction by turning into the wind) on a windsurfer requires si-

---

| FIGURE 8.2 | Implementation of part practice sequences in punting. |
| --- | --- |

| PART–WHOLE METHOD | PROGRESSIVE-PART METHOD | REPETITIVE-PART METHOD |
| --- | --- | --- |
| Catch | Catch | Catch |
| Approach | Approach | Catch + Approach |
| Drop | Catch + Approach | Catch + Approach + Drop |
| Kick | Drop | Catch + Approach + Drop + Kick |
| Catch + Approach + Drop + Kick | Catch + Approach + Drop | |
| | Kick | |
| | Catch + Approach + Drop + Kick | |

Reprinted, with permission, from C.A. Coker, 2006. "To break it down or not break it down: That is the question," *Teaching Physical Education* 17(1): 26–27.

Select a skill for which segmentation would be effective. Outline how you would organize (a) progressive-part practice and (b) repetitive-part practice.

multaneous movements of the arms and legs. The learner would separate these movements, practice them in isolation until they are mastered, and then reassemble them to perform the whole skill. Other examples of fractionization are practicing the movements of each hand separately in keyboarding or drumming, and practicing the kicking and arm stroke of the breaststroke independently. The effectiveness of this part practice technique remains in question. For rhythmic skills that require bimanual coordination (simultaneous use of the arms) or upper and lower limb coordination (simultaneous use of arms and legs), such as playing a musical instrument, fractionization

| FIGURE 8.3 |
| --- |
| Forward and backward chaining combined with the part–whole method for the punt. |

| FORWARD CHAINING | BACKWARD CHAINING |
| --- | --- |
| 1. Catch | 1. Kick |
| 2. Approach | 2. Drop |
| 3. Drop | 3. Approach |
| 4. Kick | 4. Catch |

Reprinted, with permission, from C.A. Coker, 2006. "To break it down or not break it down: That is the question," *Teaching Physical Education* 17(1): 26–27.

appears to transfer poorly to the whole skill (Klapp, Nelson & Jagacinski, 1998; Lee, Chamberlin & Hodges, 2001). Such tasks are high in organization, and whole practice is recommended. When the spatial or temporal movement characteristics of each limb are different, fractionization may be a viable technique. Further research is needed to determine its effectiveness in such situations.

**Simplification.** Another part practice technique, **simplification**, reduces the level of difficulty of the task or some aspect of the task. Practitioners can implement this strategy in several ways.

1. *Modify the equipment.* According to Rink (2002), modifying equipment is "one of the most useful ways to reduce the difficulty or complexity of performance in learning skills" (p. 114). (Table 8.1 presents examples of modification strategies.) Oversized striking implements (e.g., larger racket heads, bat barrels, and lacrosse baskets) provide a greater contact surface area. Bigger balls are easier to catch. Shorter or lighter implements are easier

| TABLE 8.1 |
| --- |
| Equipment modification strategies. |

| MODIFICATION | EXAMPLE | RATIONALE |
| --- | --- | --- |
| Size | Larger bat | Easier to contact |
| | Bigger ball | Easier to catch |
| Length | Shorter racket | Easier to swing |
| Weight | Lighter bat | Easier to swing |
| Grip | Foam grip bat | Easier to hold |
| | Gator skin ball | |
| Rigidity | Spongy ball | Easier to grasp |

Reprinted, with permission, from C.A. Coker, 2006. "To break it down or not break it down: That is the question," *Teaching Physical Education* 17(1): 26–27.

| FIGURE **8.4** | Examples of occupational training and daily living aids. |
| --- | --- |

The nosey cup is designed to eliminate the need to tilt the head back while drinking.

The rocking-T knife, which requires less strength and dexterity, is designed to simplify cutting for individuals with either a weak grip or the use of only one hand.

Training stairs, designed for mobility training, present different step configurations.

to swing. Softer balls with anti-slip surfaces are easier to grasp and catch and have lower bounce heights. Countless rehabilitative and daily living aids, such as those pictured in Figure 8.4, are available, including magnetic jewelry clasps, dressing sticks, weighted utensils, nosey cups, rocking-T knives, doorknob grippers, training stairs, and ramp and curb training sets.

2. *Reduce the coordination requirements.* The practitioner can reduce task difficulty by manipulating task complexity. It may be possible to reduce or eliminate the learners' need to change location when performing a skill by having them throw, dribble, or kick from a stationary position. When teaching how to receive an object, toss, throw, or roll it directly to the learner. You may be able to manipulate balance, force, speed, and accuracy, provided that the underlying dynamics of the skill (e.g., relative timing) remain intact. For example, training wheels on a bicycle and parallel bars in gait training assist learners in maintaining balance. When teaching Swiss ball exercises, practice basic positioning initially and make exercises progressively more difficult by decreasing the areas of support, increasing the lever arm length on the ball, and increasing the range of motion (Hoglblum, 2001). Reduce accuracy requirements by increasing the target size. Have learners serve from half court rather than the baseline to reduce the amount of force necessary to get the ball over the net. Permit swimmers with weak kicks to use fins on occasion, so that they can generate enough propulsion to allow them to focus on other aspects of the stroke, such as the arm movement and breathing. Finally, the tempo at which a movement is performed may be decreased by slowing down the overall movement or changing the object being manipulated, such as when juggling scarves are substituted for balls.

3. *Change the complexity of the environment.* The practitioner may manipulate the complexity of the environment to decrease the attentional demands

imposed by the task. This can be accomplished by changing the environmental characteristics of an open skill to make it more closed. For example, hitting in baseball or softball may be initially taught as a closed skill, with the ball stationary (placed on a batting tee). Once learners have acquired the basic striking pattern, the skill can be made progressively more open through use of, first, a pitching machine that consistently delivers the ball to a specific location and then a live pitcher who delivers a variety of pitches.

4. *Use skill-building activities and lead-up games.* These activities are a form of simplification, as they allow learners to apply newly acquired skills in a controlled environment. Kickball, one-bounce volleyball, keep away in soccer, and twenty-one in basketball are examples.

## C  E  R  E  B  R  A  L  challenge   8.4

1. Using the Internet or product catalogs, survey the companies that manufacture equipment for physical education/rehab and list products that are specifically designed for simplification.

2. Read the following progression for the overhead pass and rearrange the items in sequential order from simple to complex by numbering from 1 to 9.

   _____ a. Randomly toss the ball so that the learner is forced to move forward, backward, and side to side. The learner should set the ball back to the individual who tossed it.

   _____ b. Toss the ball to a stationary learner. The learner should catch the ball above the head in the correct position and be facing the individual who tossed it.

   _____ c. The learner sets the ball continuously with a partner.

   _____ d. The learner assumes the correct ready position for the set.

   _____ e. Toss the ball so that the learner is forced to move forward, backward, and side to side. The learner should catch the ball in the correct setting position and be facing the individual who tossed it. Prior to tossing the ball, indicate to the learner the direction of the toss.

   _____ f. Toss the ball to a stationary learner. The learner should set the ball back to the individual who tossed it.

   _____ g. Toss the ball to the learner. The learner then sets it to a spiker.

   _____ h. Toss the ball so that the learner is forced to move forward, backward, and side to side. The learner should set the ball back to the individual who tossed it. Prior to tossing the ball, indicate to the learner the direction of the toss.

   _____ i. The learner assumes the correct ready position for the set, with the ball placed in the hands just above the head. The learner then pushes the ball away using the correct setting motion.

To gain a further understanding of the influence of task progressions, Hebert, Landin and Solmon (2000) examined their influence on students' practice quality and task-related cognition. Eighty-one students enrolled in university beginning tennis classes learned and practiced the serve under one of three conditions. The Criterion group practiced the criterion task, serving using the complete motion from behind the baseline. The remaining two conditions, Part to Whole and Extension, practiced using a simple to complex 4-step progression that ended with the criterion task. Within this progression, the Part to Whole group practiced using segmen-

tation where the skill was broken down into the toss, tossing and hitting from back scratch position, tossing and hitting from hip and full serve. Learners in the Extension group, on the other hand, were engaged in a simplification practice strategy. Here, the full serve was performed from four different distances on the court starting at the net and ending at the baseline. Although performance changes were not measured, data revealed that those instructional conditions that involved easy to difficult progressions (Part to Whole and Extension groups) resulted in more successful and appropriate practice trials and enhanced student self-efficacy and motivation.

5. *Sequence from simple to complex.* Tasks may be sequenced to become progressively more difficult. For example, patients may first learn to reach and grasp for a can that is directly in front of them, eventually developing the ability to select a particular can from many. Sanders (2003) provides another example, a progression of aquatic balance training exercises that can be viewed online at the website noted at left. For assistance with designing progressions, refer to Gentile's taxonomy in Chapter 1.

www.

**Aquatic Balance
Training Exercises**

www.icaa.cc/Journal%20on%20
Active%20Aging/Journalarticles/
Journalarticles11/splash11.pdf

### Attention cueing

A practice option that combines the benefits of both part and whole practice is attention cueing. In **attention cueing,** the learner directs attention to a specific aspect of the skill during its performance as a whole. Examples are focusing on a high elbow recovery while swimming the freestyle or on the placement of an assisted walking device while traversing a room. This strategy allows the learner to concentrate on one particular task component or movement problem without disrupting the skill's underlying temporal and spatial characteristics.

## SPEED–ACCURACY TRADEOFF

**M**ovements that require both speed and accuracy in their execution are governed by a basic motor behavior tenet known as the **speed–accuracy tradeoff.** As the name implies, a tradeoff exists between speed and accuracy such that an emphasis on speed negatively affects accuracy and vice versa. Through a series of experiments with a rapid aiming task, Fitts (1954) found that performers had to slow their movements as the distance to be moved increased or the size of the target decreased, if they were to perform the task accurately. Try Exploration Activity 8.5 to experience this tradeoff for yourself.

Whereas spatial accuracy is governed by the speed–accuracy tradeoff, it appears that temporal accuracy is not. Temporal accuracy, or timing accuracy, concerns *when* a movement should be executed. For example, a tennis player must decide when to swing in order to intercept the ball. Interestingly, research has found that when temporal accuracy is a determining factor in successful skill performance, increasing movement speed decreases timing errors (Schmidt et al., 1979). In other words, timing accuracy *improves* when the performer swings faster, violating the speed–accuracy tradeoff. Similar results have been found for the production of very forceful movements (Schmidt & Sherwood, 1982).

The speed–accuracy tradeoff has several implications for motor skill performance. First, if spatial accuracy is the goal of the task, such as when a patient

# exploration A C T I V I T Y 8.5

## Speed–Accuracy Tradeoff

**EQUIPMENT:**

Piece of paper                           Pen

Timer or watch with second hand          Someone to keep time

**PROCEDURE:**

On a piece of paper, draw a circle about the size of a half dollar coin two inches from the top edge of the paper and a second circle, the same size, two inches from the bottom edge. Draw a second set of circles, about the size of a dime, near the right edge. Your paper should be a full-size version of this one.

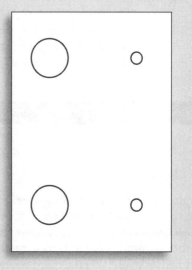

Now, place the tip of your pen in the large top-left circle. Your objective is to move the pen back and forth for 10 seconds between the two large circles as fast as possible, placing a dot inside each one with each pass. (*Note:* Lift the pen off the paper during the movement.) Then repeat the exercise, keeping in mind the objective of moving as fast as possible, using the smaller circles.

What changes did you note between the two tasks? Do your results support the speed–accuracy tradeoff?

reaches for an object or when a computer user moves the mouse to click on an icon, accuracy will suffer if the task is attempted with too much velocity. If, on the other hand, the goal of the skill is temporal accuracy or the production of a very forceful movement, such as a smash in table tennis, speed should be emphasized.

Although these guidelines are useful, they are somewhat limited in applicability for the practitioner. First, they are the product of experiments that employed laboratory tasks. In actual performance, complex motor skills usually involve a combination of spatial and temporal accuracy, as well as the production of forceful movements (Belkin & Eliot, 1997). Second, these experiments examined issues of control rather than skill acquisition. Studies examining the influence of the speed–accuracy tradeoff on the development of complex motor skills found that an emphasis on accuracy during the initial stages of skill acquisition may impede the development of efficient motor patterns. When learners sacrificed velocity to increase accuracy, a constrained movement pattern emerged. Conversely, an emphasis on speed facilitated skill development (Belkin & Eliot, 1997; Southard, 1982).

These results suggest that during the initial stages of skill acquisition, accuracy should be de-emphasized. Many traditional practice techniques, however, are not structured this way. For example, a technique often used to practice the in-step kick in soccer is to have learners pair up and kick the ball back and forth. Rather than focusing on technique, the goal of the task is for the learner to get the ball to the partner. Because this practice strategy establishes an accuracy goal, learners may adopt a less efficient kicking pattern in order to get the ball successfully to the partner. Instead, practitioners should either eliminate targets or make them much larger and instruct learners to emphasize speed. Examples include throwing a ball as far across the gymnasium as possible, throwing lacrosse balls into a soccer goal instead of a lacrosse goal, and hitting tennis balls against a backstop rather than into the tennis court (Ciapponi, 2001). To investigate the influence of the speed–accuracy tradeoff in an applied setting, try Exploration Activity 8.7.

## C E R E B R A L  challenge  8.6

The relationship between speed and accuracy is described mathematically by Fitts' Law:

$$MT = a + b[\log2(2A/W)]$$

The law states that movement time (MT) for rapid aiming tasks is linearly related to the distance to be moved (A) and the width of the target (W). Perform the experiments at http://fww.few.vu.nl/hci/interactive/fitts/. Based on what you learned through the Fitts' Law demonstration, explain how it influences the functions you perform with your computer. How might you redesign your desktop to maximize efficiency?

## exploration    A C T I V I T Y    8.7

### Speed–Accuracy Tradeoff II

**EQUIPMENT:**

2 partners                    1 tennis ball

**PROCEDURE:**

Position the partners so that they are facing one another at a distance of approximately 5 feet. Have them throw the tennis ball back and forth 10 times. Assess their throwing technique using the characteristics of a mature throwing pattern provided. Next, have them repeat the task from a distance of 25 feet. Again, observe and assess the technique used to accomplish the task. Finally, have one of the two individuals perform hard throws into an open field, and assess the throwing technique.

Reflect on your assessments of the three different situations. Which situation led to the use of a technique that most resembles a mature throwing pattern? What influence did the speed–accuracy tradeoff have in each condition? Based on your observations, speculate as to the optimal practice conditions to elicit a mature throwing pattern. How might you apply this information when teaching a class of 25 students?

*Characteristics of a Mature Throwing Pattern*

1. Side/shoulder toward the target
2. Throwing arm back behind the head
3. Step with the opposite foot toward the target
4. Rotate trunk to face target
5. Follow through

## BILATERAL TRANSFER

The ability to use both limbs with equal proficiency is advantageous in many sport and daily living skills. The question facing the practitioner is how to design practice to best achieve this proficiency. To answer that question, the practitioner must understand a phenomenon known as **bilateral transfer.** In Chapter 6 we examined the transfer of learning between tasks. Transfer may also occur between limbs, when practice with one limb enhances the rate of skill acquisition with the opposite limb on the same task.

Two explanations have been offered to explain the existence of bilateral transfer. The first explanation derives from a motor control perspective. Theoretically, the non-practiced limb would utilize the same generalized motor program as the practiced limb, because the specification of muscles or limbs to perform the movement is considered a parameter (see Chapter 3 for a review). When a

Liu and Wrisberg (2005) examined the effect of limb prefer-ence, age, and gender on the bilateral transfer of throwing accuracy. One hundred sixty children aged 6, 8, 10, and 12 years were randomly assigned to either an experimental or a control group. The task consisted of projecting a Koosh ball to a target on the floor using a basketball hook shot. Participants performed a 10-trial pretest with either the preferred or non-preferred hand. Hand use was counterbalanced, with half the participants throwing with the preferred hand and the other half with the non-preferred hand.

Following the pretest, those participants assigned to the experimental group practiced the task with the hand not used during the pretest until a designated criterion performance was obtained. The control group performed a balancing ac-tivity. Participants then performed an immediate (10 minutes later) and delayed (24 hours later) transfer test under the same conditions as the pretest. Results revealed significantly higher throwing accuracy for the experimental group on both transfer tests, supporting the phenomenon of bilateral transfer.

movement is performed with one limb, electromyography (EMG) evidence in-dicates the presence of subthreshold electrical activity in the other limb (Hicks, Gualtieri & Schroeder, 1983).

The second explanation suggests that when a skill is practiced with one limb, the learner acquires important cognitive information about the movement problem, such as the goal of the skill and how to achieve it. When the learn-er later practices the same skill with the untrained limb, these same cognitive elements apply and are immediately incorporated, and performance with the previously unpracticed limb is enhanced. Kohl and Roenker (1983) have pro-vided support for this cognitive explanation, finding that the degree of bilateral transfer was about the same regardless of whether practice was performed physi-cally or mentally. Kohl and Roenker surmise that an interaction between motor and cognitive components likely accounts for the bilateral transfer phenomenon (Chamberlin & Lee, 1993).

Since the training of one limb has been shown to enhance the rate of skill ac-quisition on the opposite limb, the question of how to sequence practice with the preferred versus non-preferred limb is relevant for the practitioner. The general consensus, according to Magill (2007), is that a greater degree of transfer occurs from the preferred to the non-preferred limb. Consequently, to achieve maxi-mum transfer effects when training bilateral manipulative skills or, for example, teaching a volleyball player to spike with both hands, the skill should first be practiced with the preferred limb. Once the task can be skillfully performed, it should then be introduced to the non-preferred limb.

Bilateral transfer can also be capitalized upon when a learner has sustained an injury to the preferred limb. In this situation, practicing with the non-preferred limb may facilitate performance with the injured limb after its rehabilitation (Christina & Corcos, 1988).

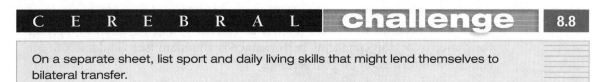

On a separate sheet, list sport and daily living skills that might lend themselves to bilateral transfer.

## PSYCHOLOGICAL STRATEGIES

**P**hysical rehearsal is not the only method by which skills may be practiced; learners can also mentally rehearse skills. Because neither physical nor mental practice will be effective unless the learner is motivated, the following section will discuss motivation and introduce various psychological strategies that can be incorporated into practice to maximize skill acquisition and performance.

### Motivation and Practice

Motivation is a powerful force. Learners who are motivated not only devote time and energy to practice but do so with great effort. Those who lack motivation may never realize their potential.

Two factors that can lead to a loss of motivation are boredom and frustration. Proficiency often requires countless repetitions of a task or its components, and at higher levels change comes slowly. By making practices fun and introducing variety, the practitioner can reduce the monotony of this repetition. In addition, the instructor should design each practice period to provide every learner with the opportunity to experience some degree of success. This will lead to feelings of achievement that will further motivate the learner to practice. Since mistakes are an integral part of the learning process, the practitioner should establish a positive practice environment where learners are not afraid to make them (Stratton, 1996). Providing reinforcement to learners plays a major role in creating such an environment and will be discussed in detail in Chapter 11.

### Goal Setting

Perhaps one of the most powerful motivational strategies is goal setting. Goals help to focus learners' attention, encourage learners to develop new skills and

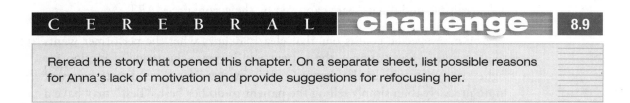

Reread the story that opened this chapter. On a separate sheet, list possible reasons for Anna's lack of motivation and provide suggestions for refocusing her.

strategies to improve performance (Stratton, 1997), and provide a means of monitoring progress or success (Harris & Harris, 1984). Research supporting their effectiveness in enhancing performance is abundant (see Gould, 2006, for additional information on goal setting).

### Types of goals

Based on the nature of the performer's objective, we can divide goals into three categories:

1. **Outcome goals** are concerned with the final result of a competition relative to one's opponent. Examples are beating the defending champion and performing a skill before a fellow patient performs it. The use of such goals can be problematic. Because the performance of the opposition cannot be controlled, a learner can achieve peak performance but still lose a contest and fail to accomplish the goal. Conversely, a learner can perform poorly yet still be victorious.

2. **Performance goals** are concerned with self-improvement. They focus on improvements in performance based on one's own previous results, such as increasing distance in the long jump or the number of steps that can be taken unassisted. Performance goals tend to be more effective than outcome goals, because they focus on self-improvement, which is under the direct control of the performer.

3. **Process goals,** which direct the performer's focus to achieving some technical element during skill execution, may be used to help learners achieve their outcome and performance goals. Examples are maintaining a pelvic tilt position throughout an exercise and pulling the arms in quickly when performing a triple axel. Like performance goals, process goals are favored over outcome goals, as their self-improvement nature tends to enhance motivation.

Research has shown that employing multiple strategies (a combination of outcome, performance, and process goals) leads to superior performance (Filby, Maynard & Graydon, 1999).

### Elements of a well-constructed goal

The benefits of goal setting can be realized only if goals are carefully constructed in accordance to several criteria. These criteria—specific, measurable, achievable, realistic, and timely—are captured by the acronym SMART.

**Specific.** A specific goal is one that clearly defines what the performer wants to accomplish. For example, the patient will increase the range of motion for right knee extension by 10 percent within two weeks. This directs behavior more precisely than simply telling the patient to do her best. "Best" may have a clear meaning in some situations, but in others, such as driving a golf ball or pitching, the concept is somewhat elusive, as "best" has yet to be achieved. When goals are specific, the performer is able to evaluate progress toward achieving them.

**Measurable.** Goals should be measureable. The goal of increasing range of motion by 10 percent provides a quantifiable means of tracking progress.

**Achievable.** An achievable goal is one that is attainable given the learner's current skills and abilities. Note that while a goal may be considered attainable, it may not be realistic. For example, the patient working on increasing range of motion for right knee extension may set another goal of completing a round-trip hike from the rim to the base of the Grand Canyon. Although she may have the skill and fitness level to achieve this goal eventually (hence, it is attainable) accomplishing it within a month of sustaining her injury may not be realistic.

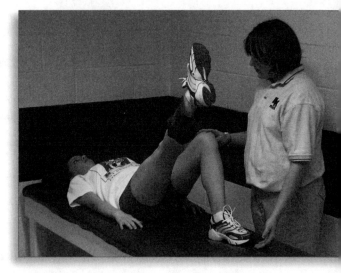

Goal setting can motivate a patient to use correct technique when performing rehabilitative exercises.

**Realistic.** Unless a goal is set at an appropriate level of difficulty—one that requires the learner to strive for its attainment—the goal will have little value. Be careful not to exceed the learner's capabilities. This will only result in failure, which will negatively affect learning and performance. A good rule of thumb is to set a goal at a level slightly beyond the learner's reach based on the current level of performance. Basing goals on the existing level of performance allows them to be adjusted according to changing conditions. For example, if the learner progresses faster than expected, the goal can be raised. When an athlete returns to play following an injury, goals may have to be lowered to be realistic.

**Timely.** Each goal should specify the time for completion, providing a clear target. Without a definite time frame for accomplishment, a learner may lose interest and motivation.

### Goal-setting guidelines

When setting goals, establish both short- and long-term goals. Long-term goals may identify the ultimate objective, such as winning a certain championship, but their remoteness makes them less effective. That is not to say that they are inappropriate, but they should be used in conjunction with short-term goals. Short-term goals, because they are more immediate, increase motivation, as they

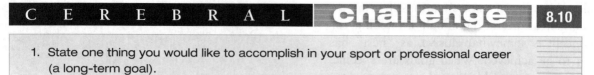

C E R E B R A L **challenge** 8.10

1. State one thing you would like to accomplish in your sport or professional career (a long-term goal).
2. Identify three short-term goals that will assist you in achieving your long-term goal.
3. Analyze your short- and long-term goals to determine whether they are based on outcome, performance, or process.
4. Analyze your goals to determine whether they meet the SMART criteria.

allow learners to see performance improvements and serve as stepping-stones for long-term goal achievement.

Goals are most meaningful when they account for individual differences and when learners are involved in the goal-setting process and encouraged to evaluate their progress frequently.

Finally, practitioners should support learners throughout the process by providing positive reinforcement.

## Mental Practice

Skill acquisition and performance can benefit from mental practice as well as physical practice. One technique in particular—that of imagery—has received much attention and boasts a variety of applications. **Imagery** involves the visualization or cognitive rehearsal of a movement in the absence of any physical execution. Repeated demonstrations of its effectiveness make it a worthy performance enhancement strategy. In Exploration Activity 8.11 you will practice several imagery tasks.

**exploration** A C T I V I T Y 8.11

### Mental Imagery

*Exercise 1*

Select any object in the room for this exercise. Look at its shape and color. Examine it thoroughly, concentrating on every detail. Close your eyes and visualize the object. Then open your eyes and compare your mental image to the actual object.

*Exercise 2*

Close your eyes and imagine that you are in your living room and your roommate is cooking dinner in the kitchen. Can you see your furniture? What color is it? Is the

*(continued)*

television on? Can you hear it? Are there any other noises? What can you smell? What other details do you notice? (Modified from Weinberg & Gould, 2007)

*Exercise 3*

Close your eyes and mentally recreate your journey to school today. Did you walk, ride your bike, drive, or take the bus? See and feel yourself performing the movements associated with your mode of transportation. Visualize the people, environment, and scenery. Are you hot or cold? What are you thinking about? What do you smell?

When you performed this exercise, did you see the image through your own eyes or vantage point, or did it seem as if you were watching a movie of yourself? If you felt you were seeing through your own eyes, then you were using internal imagery. If, on the other hand, your perspective was that of an observer, you were using external imagery. The preference for internal or external imagery will vary among individuals, and many will switch back and forth depending on the situation. Try Exercise 3 again, but this time use the other perspective.

While everyone has the capacity to perform imagery, not everyone will be equally proficient in its use. Initially, you may have difficulty in creating vivid, controlled images that incorporate all their senses. Practice will help you develop your imagery capability. Start with objects or situations that are familiar, as in these exercises.

## Applications and evidence

Although it is not a substitute for physical practice, mental practice has been shown to be more effective than no practice at all (Feltz & Landers, 1983; Hird, Landers, Thomas & Horan, 1991). Furthermore, the combination of physical practice and imagery has been found to be superior to physical practice alone. The implication of these findings is that practitioners should include imagery in the practice routine to assist in the learning or re-learning of a skill or part of a skill.

Imagery can be useful as a preparatory strategy to enhance performance (Vealey & Greenleaf, 2006). Athletes commonly mentally rehearse their performance prior to actually executing it. For example, a figure skater might rehearse a routine just before taking to the ice, or a golfer might visualize the successful performance of a strategically placed shot prior to actually hitting the ball. This quote from a successful Olympic diver describes his frequent use of detailed imagery:

> I did my dives in my head all the time. At night, before going to sleep, I always did my dives. Ten dives. I started with a front dive, the first one that I had to do at the Olympics, and I did everything as if I was actually there. I saw myself on the board with the same bathing suit. Everything was the same. I saw myself in the pool at the Olympics doing my dives. If the dive was wrong, I went back and

## R E S E A R C H   N O T E S

To explore the effect of mental imagery on skill acquisition, Millard, Mahoney, and Wardrop (2001) randomly assigned 60 competent female swimmers between the ages of 11 and 16 to one of four experimental groups: mental practice, physical practice, combined mental and physical practice, and no practice. The task to be learned was a kayak wet exit. Participants in the mental practice group completed one 30-minute mental practice session daily for three consecutive days. The physical practice group practiced three drills for three consecutive days. The combined group performed the same practice routine as the mental practice group for the first three days and then engaged in the same physical practice as the physical practice group for the next three days. Participants in these three groups were asked to main-

tain a diary following their practice attempts, where they recorded information such as confidence level and perceived progress. Finally, the no practice group received neither instructions nor practice.

Diary findings indicated that the mental practice and combined groups were confident in their mental ability of the wet exit drill. The mental practice group had higher wet exit ratings than the no practice group. The researchers assert that "the results provide evidence that a combination of mental practice and physical practice are more effective than any single practice type investigated" (p. 982), supporting the notion that novices can benefit from mental and physical practice for skill acquisition.

started over again. It takes a good hour to do perfect imagery of all of my dives, but for me it was better than a good workout. I felt like I was on the board. (Orlick & Partington, 1988, p. 112)

Research has shown that imagery can also assist in reducing or controlling pre-competitive anxiety (e.g., Ryska, 1998; Savoy, 1997), increasing self-confidence (e.g., Callow, Hardy & Hall, 2001; Garza & Feltz, 1998; Mamassis & Doganis, 2004), enhancing motivation (e.g., Beauchamp, Halliwell, Fournier & Koestner, 1996), and improving selective attention (Calmels, Berthoumieux & d'Arripe-Longueville, 2004).

**www.**

**Using the Mind to Heal the Body: Imagery for Injury Rehabilitation**

http://appliedsportpsych.org/resource-center/injury-&-rehabilitation/articles/imagery

Imagery may also be a useful strategy in rehabilitation (e.g., Driediger, Hall & Callow, 2006; Milne, Hall & Forwell, 2005). In addition to helping athletes "stay in the game" by rehearsing sport-specific skills and strategies, mental imagery can help patients focus on aspects of injury recovery, including pain management and healing. Check out the adjoining website to learn more.

### Theoretical explanations

Two major explanations have been offered to account for the performance-enhancing effects of mental imagery. Before reading about them, try Exploration Activity 8.12.

## exploration A C T I V I T Y    8.12

### Mental Imagery II*

**EQUIPMENT:**

10-inch piece of string                    1 key

**PROCEDURE:**

Attach the key to the end of the string. Next, place your elbow on a table while holding the other end of the string between your forefinger and thumb so that the key hangs freely. Once the string is still, focus on the key and visualize it moving back and forth like a pendulum.

Were you able to move the key? How do you explain this result?

*Modified from Vealey and Greenleaf, 2006.

**Neuromuscular theory.** The neuromuscular theory postulates that the act of visualizing oneself executing a movement results in the activation of the same motor pathways that would have activated had the movement been physically performed, yet at a subthreshold level. Research supporting this notion has found that muscle activity during imagery, as measured by EMG, was indeed comparable to that during the actual movement, though at a lesser magnitude (Harris & Robinson, 1986; Jacobson, 1931; Jowdy & Harris, 1990; Suinn, 1980). It appears that by rehearsing a skill through imagery, one can strengthen the neural pathways used to perform the actual movement.

**Cognitive theory.** According to the cognitive theory, imagery facilitates the acquisition of the cognitive elements of a skill by allowing learners to develop an understanding of a movement's requirements, test solutions to movement problems, and develop performance strategies (Hird et al., 1991; Sackett, 1934). The efficiency of imagery lies in the fact that the learner can practice a skill repeatedly without the risk of injury and without becoming physically fatigued.

### Imagery guidelines

To maximize the effectiveness of imagery, follow these guidelines. First, because good imagery skills must be developed, learners should practice imagery every day. Those who are new to the technique, should practice in a distraction-free setting and should focus on familiar situations and skills. As learners become more proficient, they should strive to create positive, vivid, and controllable images of the skill or parts of a skill they wish to refine. This rehearsal should be done in real time and focus on successful performance and goal attainment. Finally, learners should try to incorporate all of their senses in imagery, to replicate the actual situation or environment of performance: smell the freshly cut grass, hear the roar of the crowd when they score, and focus on how the movement feels.

Additional suggestions for designing an effective imagery-training program may be found in Vealey and Greenleaf (2006) or Weinberg and Gould (2007).

## ▶ a look ahead

Skill acquisition and performance enhancement result from carefully designed practice opportunities. In this chapter, we have examined several strategies, including sequencing and psychological strategies, that will help practitioners maximize gains in skill proficiency. We will continue to focus on factors that influence practice effectiveness in the next chapter, as we turn our attention to practice organization and scheduling.

## ● focus points

After reading this chapter, you should know that . . .

- Skills that are high in task complexity and low in task organization are generally best served through part practice, whereas whole practice is preferred for skills low in complexity and high in organization.

- Several part practice methods are available to the practitioner:

  - Segmentation means separating the skill into parts according to spatial or temporal elements. It can be implemented through the part–whole, progressive-part, or repetitive-part methods, and the parts may progress either from the first to the final part (forward chaining) or in reverse order (backward chaining).

  - Fractionization is a part practice technique where skill components that are normally performed simultaneously are partitioned and practiced independently.

  - Simplification reduces the level of difficulty of the task or some aspect of the task. It can be accomplished by modifying equipment, reducing the coordination requirements of a task, making open skills more closed.

- Attention cueing directs the learner's attention to a specific aspect of the skill during its performance as a whole, allowing the learner to concentrate on one particular task component or movement problem without disrupting the skill's underlying temporal and spatial characteristics.

- Spatial accuracy is governed by the speed–accuracy tradeoff, where an emphasis on speed negatively affects accuracy and vice versa.

- Bilateral transfer occurs when practice with one limb enhances the rate of skill acquisition with the opposite limb on the same task.
- A combination of outcome goals, performance goals, and process goals leads to superior performance.
- A well-constructed goal is specific, measurable, achievable, realistic, and timely (SMART).
- The combination of physical practice and imagery (the visualization or cognitive rehearsal of a movement) is superior to physical practice alone.

## ? review questions

1. What two task characteristics must you consider when deciding whether to break a skill into parts?
2. Explain the difference between segmentation and fractionization. Illustrate your explanation with an example, using a skill of your choice.
3. What advantage do the progressive-part and repetitive-part practice techniques provide over the part–whole method?
4. Give an example of backward and forward chaining, with a skill of your choice.
5. Define simplification. List and explain three different simplification strategies for skills of your choice.
6. What is attention cueing? Why is it included in a discussion about whole versus part practice?
7. What condition violates the speed–accuracy principle?
8. What is bilateral transfer? Explain how an athlete who has been injured might be able to capitalize on this phenomenon.
9. What does the acronym SMART stand for?
10. Define imagery. How could imagery be incorporated into a rehabilitation program?

## R E F E R E N C E S

Anderson, A. (1997). Learning strategies in physical education: self-talk, imagery and goal setting. *Journal of Physical Education, Recreation and Dance, 68*(1), 30–35.

Beauchamp, P.H., Halliwell, W.R., Fournier, J.F. & Koestner, R. (1996). Effects of cognitive-behavioral psychological skills training on the motivation, preparation and putting performance of novice golfers. *The Sport Psychologist, 10,* 157–70.

Belkin, D.S. & Eliot, J.F. (1997). Motor skill acquisition and the speed-accuracy trade-off in a field based task. *Journal of Sport Behavior, 20*(1), 16–28.

Callow, N., Hardy, L. & Hall, C. (2001). The effects of motivational general-mastery imagery intervention on the sport confidence of high-level badminton players. *Research Quarterly for Exercise and Sport, 72,* 389–400.

Calmels, C., Berthoumieux, C. & d'Arripe-Longueville, F. (2004). Effects of an imagery training program on selective attention of national softball players. *The Sport Psychologist, 18,* 272–96.

Chamberlin, C.J. & Lee, T.D. (1993). Arranging practice conditions and designing instruction. In R.N. Singer, M. Murphy, and L.K. Tennant (Eds.), *Handbook of research on sport psychology* (pp. 213–41). New York: MacMillan.

Christina, R.W. & Corcos, D.M. (1988). *Coaches guide to teaching sport skills.* Champaign, IL: Human Kinetics.

Ciapponi, T. (2001, April). *Speed-accuracy tradeoff in sport skills.* Paper presented at the meeting of the American Alliance for Health, Physical Education, Recreation and Dance. Cincinnati, OH.

Coker, C.A. (2006). To break it down or not break it down: that is the question. *Teaching Elementary Physical Education, 17,* 26–27.

Coker, C.A. (2005). Teaching tips for simplification. *Teaching Elementary Physical Education, 16,* 8–9.

Coker, C.A. & Hunfalvay, M. (2004). *Progressions and practice.* Paper presented at the annual meeting of the American Alliance for Health, Physical Education, Recreation and Dance. New Orleans, LA.

Driediger, M., Hall, C. & Callow, N. (2006). Imagery use by injured athletes: a qualitative analysis. *Journal of Sports Sciences, 24,* 261–71.

Feltz, D.L. & Landers, D.M. (1983). The effects of mental practice on motor skill learning and performance: a meta analysis. *Journal of Sport Psychology, 5,* 1–8.

Filby, W.C.D., Maynard, I.W. & Graydon, J.K. (1999). The effect of multiple-goal strategies on performance outcomes in training and competing. *Journal of Applied Sport Psychology, 11,* 230–46.

Fitts, P.M. (1954). The information capacity of the human motor system in controlling the amplitude of movement. *Journal of Experimental Psychology, 47,* 381–91.

Garza, D.L. & Feltz, D.L. (1998). Effects of selected mental practice on performance, self-efficacy and competitive confidence of figure skaters. *The Sport Psychologist, 12,* 1–15.

Gould, D. (2006). Goal setting for peak performance. In J. Williams (Ed.), *Applied sport psychology:*

*personal growth to peak performance* (pp. 240–59). New York: McGraw-Hill.

Harris, D.V. & Harris, B.L. (1984). *The athlete's guide to sport psychology: mental skills for physical people.* Champaign, IL: Human Kinetics.

Harris, D.V. & Robinson, W.J. (1986). The effects of skill level on EMG activity during internal and external imagery. *Journal of Sport Psychology, 8,* 105–11.

Hebert, E.P., Landin, D. & Solmon, M.A. (2000). The impact of task progressions on students' practice quality and task-related thoughts. *Journal of Teaching in Physical Education, 19,* 338–54.

Hicks, R.E., Gaultieri, C.T. & Schroeder, S.R. (1983). Cognitive and motor components of bilateral transfer. *American Journal of Psychology, 96,* 223–28.

Hird, J.S., Landers, D.M., Thomas, J.R. & Horan, J.J. (1991). Physical practice is superior to mental practice in enhancing cognitive and motor task performance. *Journal of Sport and Exercise Psychology, 13,* 281–93.

Hoglblum, P. (2001). *Therapeutic exercise for athletic injuries.* Champaign, IL: Human Kinetics.

Jacobson, E. (1931). Electrical measurements of neuromuscular states during mental activities. *American Journal of Physiology, 96,* 115–21.

Jowdy, D.P. & Harris, D.V. (1990). Muscular responses during mental imagery as a function of motor skill level. *Journal of Sport and Exercise Psychology, 12,* 191–201.

Klapp, S.T., Nelson, J.M. & Jagacinski, R.J. (1998). Can people tap concurrent bimanual rhythms independently? *Journal of Motor Behavior, 30,* 301–22.

Kohl, R.M. & Roenker, D.L. (1983). Mechanism involvement during skill imagery. *Journal of Motor Behavior, 15,* 197–206.

Lee, T.D., Chamberlin, C.J. & Hodges, N.J. (2001). Practice. In R.N. Singer, H.A. Hausenblas, and C.M. Janelle (Eds.), *Handbook of sport psychology* (pp. 115–43). New York: MacMillan.

Liu, J. & Wrisberg, C.A. (2005). Immediate and delayed bilateral transfer of throwing accuracy in male and female children. *Research Quarterly for Exercise and Sport, 76,* 20–28.

Magill, R.A. (2007). *Motor learning: concepts and applications* (8th ed.). New York: McGraw-Hill.

Mamassis, G. & Doganis, G. (2004). The effects of a mental training program on juniors precompetitive anxiety, self-confidence, and tennis performance. *Journal of Applied Sport Psychology, 16,* 118–37.

Millard, M., Mahoney, C. & Wardrop, J. (2001). A preliminary study of mental and physical practice on the kayak wet exit skill. *Perceptual and Motor Skills, 92,* 977–84.

Milne, M., Hall, C. & Forwell, L. (2005). Self-efficacy, imagery use, and adherence to rehabilitation by injured athletes. *Journal of Sport Rehabilitation, 14*(2), 150.

Naylor, J.C. & Briggs, G.E. (1963). Effects of task complexity and task organization on the relative efficiency of part and whole training methods. *Journal of Experimental Psychology, 65,* 217–24.

Newell, K.M., Carlton, M.J., Fisher, A.T. & Rutter, B.G. (1989). Whole-part training strategies for learning the response dynamics of microprocessor driven simulators. *Acta Psychologica, 71,* 197–216.

Orlick, T. & Partington, J. (1988). Mental links to excellence. *The Sport Psychologist, 2,* 105–30.

Rink, J.E. (2002). *Teaching physical education for learning.* St. Louis, MO: McGraw-Hill.

Ryska, T.A. (1998). Cognitive-behavioral strategies and precompetitive anxiety among recreational athletes. *Psychological Record, 48,* 697–708.

Sackett, R.S. (1934). The influences of symbolic rehearsal upon the retention of a maze habit. *Journal of General Psychology, 13,* 113–28.

Sanders, M. (2003). Splash! Catch a wave for better balance on land. *The Journal on Active Aging,* Sept/Oct, 51–54.

Savoy, C. (1997). Two individual mental training programs for a team sport. *International Journal of Sport Psychology, 28,* 259–70.

Schmidt, R.A. & Sherwood, D.E. (1982). An inverted-U relation between spatial error and force requirements in rapid limb movements: further evidence for the impulse variability model. *Journal of Experimental Psychology: Human Perception and Performance, 8,* 158–70.

Schmidt, R.A. & Young, D.E. (1987). Transfer of motor control in motor skill learning. In S.M. Cormier and J.D. Hagman (Eds.), *Transfer of learning* (pp. 47–79). Orlando, FL: Academic Press.

Schmidt, R.A., Zelaznik, H.N., Hawkins, B., Frank, J.S. & Quinn, J.T. (1979). Motor-output variability: a theory for the accuracy of rapid motor tasks. *Psychological Review, 86,* 415–51.

Stratton, R. (1996). Motivating your athletes and yourself. *Coaching Youth Sports.* http://www.tandl. vt.edu/rstratto/CYSarchive/CoachSept96.html.

Stratton, R. (1997). Goal setting: the concept. *Coaching Youth Sports.* http://www.tandl.vt.edu/rstratto/CYSarchive/FeatureMay97.html.

Suinn, R.M. (1980). Psychology and sport performance: principles and applications. In R.M. Suinn (Ed.), *Psychology in sports: methods and applications* (pp. 26–36). Minneapolis: Burgess.

Vealey, R.S. & Greenleaf, C.A. (2006). Seeing is believing: understanding and using imagery in sport. In J. Williams (Ed.), *Applied sport psychology: personal growth to peak performance* (pp. 306–48). New York: McGraw-Hill.

Weinberg, R.S. & Gould, D.M. (2007). *Foundations of sport and exercise psychology.* Champaign, IL: Human Kinetics.

Wightman, D.C. & Lintern, G. (1985). Part-task training for tracking and manual control. *Human Factors, 27*(3), 267–83.

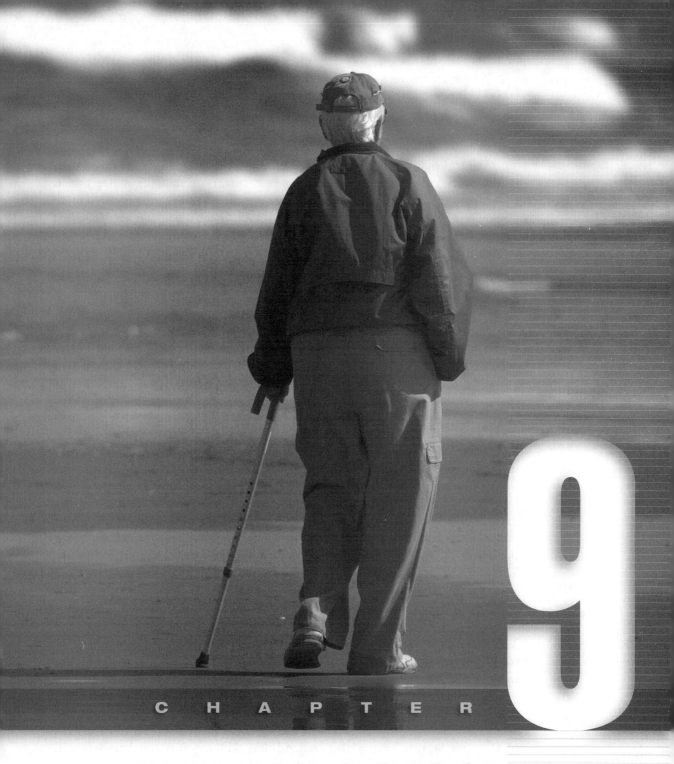

9

Practice Schedules

M r. Green has had hip replacement surgery, and now he is waiting for his first physical therapy appointment. He needs to relearn how to walk using his "new hip." He has been warned that it will involve a lot of hard work and practice, but he is up for the challenge. After all, he has a goal. He wants to be able to dance with his granddaughter at her wedding.

The fact that practice is a critical component in the learning or re-learning of a motor skill is not surprising. Nor is it surprising that the mastery of a skill takes time. To make the most of practice time, practice attempts should be not only maximized but also optimized. If Mr. Green's physical therapist has developed a thorough understanding of how practice context and distribution influence learning, his dream of dancing with his granddaughter at her wedding may become a reality.

## PRACTICE CONTEXT

A common belief in the sports arena is that athletes must master the fundamentals. Coaches who subscribe to this philosophy typically believe that practicing under constant conditions—for example, throwing the same pass or taking the same shot over and over again—will lead to superior learning, as the movement pattern will become engrained in memory. What this approach fails to consider is the importance of being able to generalize a skill to a variety of performance situations, including ones that may not have been experienced in the past. A shortstop, for example, will not field ground balls with the exact same specifications (speed, trajectory, location on the field) repeatedly in a game. Nor will a carpal tunnel patient training to regain hand function button the same shirt every day. Since buttons come in an assortment of shapes, textures, and sizes and are used with an array of fabrics, to accomplish the goal of being able to button her shirt independently, the learner will have to manipulate a variety of buttons under numerous conditions. This inherent variability should, therefore, be the focus of practice.

### Support for Variable Practice

The notion that variability in movement and context is a necessary ingredient for skill development and generalizability has strong theoretical underpinnings. In fact, a fundamental prediction of Schmidt's schema theory is that **variable practice** will enhance the development of the learner's schema. This schema, in turn, will enhance the performer's capability to select the appropriate response specifications or parameter values to accomplish a movement goal. Proponents of Dynamic System Theory also contend that skill acquisition is best achieved through the modification of constraints, forcing learners to engage in a continuous search for task solutions (Newell & McDonald, 1992).

The theoretical prediction that variable practice benefits learning has received support from several studies. Shea and Kohl (1991) found that throughout

Douvis (2005) examined the effect of variable practice on the forehand drive in tennis by children and adolescents. Forty male children aged 9 to 10 years and 40 male students aged 18 to 19 years participated in a common instructional program three times a week for six weeks, differing only in practice condition. In the practice phase of each session, participants executed 100 forehand drives from a fixed execution point on the court to no specific target, one target, four targets, or five targets. Following the completion of the training program and a 72-hour rest period, all participants performed 60 transfer trials to a single target point on the court. Deviations in accuracy were recorded. Results revealed that the adolescents executed the shots with greater accuracy than did the children. In addition, children who practiced with four or five targets (variable practice) were significantly more accurate than those who practiced with one or no specific target, and for adolescents variable practice resulted in greater accuracy than practice with no specific target. The variability of practice hypothesis was supported, as practicing with four or five targets resulted in greater performance consistency regardless of age group.

the practice trials of their study, the constant practice groups, who practiced the same skill variation repeatedly, clearly outperformed the variable practice group, who practiced multiple variations of a single skill, in a force-producing task. The results of the retention test, however, revealed the opposite effect, indicating that greater learning gains were actually achieved by the variable practice group.

To fully understand the significance of these findings, we must revisit the distinction between learning and performance. Recall that learning is defined as a relatively permanent change in a person's capability to execute a motor skill, as a result of practice or experience. Performance, on the other hand, is a temporary expression of a skill. Although constant practice has been found to have a greater influence on performance, variable practice has a greater influence on learning. Similar findings have been reported for free throw shooting (Memmert, 2006; Shoenfelt et al., 2002), an obstacle avoidance task (Cohen, Bloomberg & Mulavara, 2005), and the forehand drive in tennis (Douvis, 2005).

## Variable Practice Guidelines

To maximize the potential benefits of variable practice, the practitioner must carefully consider how and when to implement variability into the practice session.

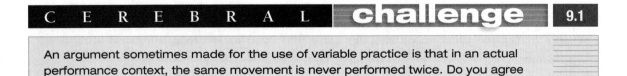

C E R E B R A L    **challenge**    9.1

An argument sometimes made for the use of variable practice is that in an actual performance context, the same movement is never performed twice. Do you agree or disagree with this statement? Develop an argument to support your position.

For open skills, variations in both regulatory and non-regulatory conditions should be systematically introduced into practice.

### How to implement variability

According to Gentile (2000), to determine how to implement practice variability, one must first assess the nature of the skill being learned and the environment in which it will be performed. Then, depending on that assessment, the practitioner should systematically introduce variations in the regulatory conditions, non-regulatory conditions, or both. For example, in open skills, such as fielding a ground ball, one's response must conform to the demands of an ever-changing environment. For this skill, practice should present variations in both the regulatory (e.g., learner's position on the field, speed and trajectory of the ball) and non-regulatory conditions (e.g., performer's level of fatigue, heckling from fans) that might occur in the applied setting. The same approach applies to closed skills that involve inter-trial variability. Variable practice for the sit-to-stand task, for example, might include different chair heights, chairs with and without armrests, variations in seat padding, and various floor surfaces (tile, carpet, linoleum, etc.).

But what about those skills, such as performing a balance beam routine, where the objective of the performance is to replicate a movement pattern consistently and accurately? In such cases, practice should be designed so that the regulatory conditions remain constant (e.g., height and width of the beam) while the learner is subjected to a variety of potential non-regulatory conditions (e.g., distractions).

### When to implement variability

Gentile's stages of learning model provides the practitioner with guidelines regarding when to implement variable practice. According to Gentile, the goal of the learner when introduced to a new motor skill is to develop an understanding of the requirements of the task. Practice during this initial stage of learning should, therefore, facilitate the learner's development of a basic movement pattern. The practice

## CEREBRAL challenge 9.2

1. Your patient is Mr. Green, the gentleman in the opening story who is re-learning how to walk after hip replacement surgery. His goal, you will recall, is to dance with his granddaughter at her wedding. Explain how you will incorporate variable practice into his therapeutic program. Describe the variables that you will manipulate and give your reasons for doing so.

2. For a skill of your choice, explain how you would implement variable practice.

C  E  R  E  B  R  A  L    **challenge**    9.3

> A practitioner may decide to continue to utilize constant practice rather than switch to variable practice once the learner develops an understanding of the basic movement pattern because the learner will experience greater success during practice. You learned earlier that experiencing success in practice leads to greater motivation. What strategies might you employ to maintain a learner's motivation while incorporating a variable practice schedule?

should be conducted in such a manner as not to overwhelm the novice learner, while providing opportunities for success to enhance the learner's confidence. These goals are best achieved through constant practice. Once the learner has acquired the basic movement pattern, variable practice strategies should be introduced.

## Organizing the Practice Session: Contextual Interference

Having determined that practice variability is desirable, the practitioner must next decide how to organize the practice session. Whether the learner is learning multiple variations within a single skill (e.g., performing a jump shot from different areas on the court both with and without defenders) or working to acquire a variety of skills (e.g., set shot, lay-up, jump shot, and free throw), the practitioner must decide on an optimum practice sequence. Useful implications can be drawn from a practice phenomenon known as contextual interference.

**common** *myth*

Long-term retention of a motor skill is best achieved by practicing a skill repeatedly before moving to either a different version of the task or a different task altogether.

**Contextual interference** is the interference that results from switching from one skill to another or changing the context in which a task is practiced from trial to trial. Although the term "interference" usually carries a negative connotation, contextual interference has been shown to facilitate learning (Battig, 1972, 1979). How much contextual interference occurs is a function of how the tasks are integrated within a practice session. On one end of a range of possibilities, low contextual interference results when practice trials are organized in a blocked schedule. In **blocked practice,** the learner practices one skill or skill variation repeatedly and then moves to another skill or skill variation. For example, in a 30-minute practice, a hockey coach might have his players work on passing for 10 minutes, move on to wrist shots for the next 10 minutes, and dedicate the final 10 minutes to slap shots. High contextual interference results when multiple tasks or task variations are performed in a random order. In **random practice,** the hockey coach might have his players perform the same number of repetitions during the 30-minute practice, but the skills would be organized so that no variation (pass, slap shot, wrist shot) was rehearsed twice in a row.

## The contextual interference effect

Studies examining the effectiveness of random versus blocked practice for skill acquisition have demonstrated the relatively consistent finding that low contextual interference (blocked practice) often produces superior short-term performance during practice, but practicing multiple skills or skill variations in a random order (high contextual interference) leads to greater long-term learning gains (e.g., Shea & Morgan, 1979). This reversal of results for random practice has been labeled the **contextual interference effect.**

Researchers have offered two explanations to account for the contextual interference effect. The first, the elaboration hypothesis, contends that when random practice is used, multiple tasks are simultaneously housed in working memory, allowing distinctions between them to be more readily formulated (Shea & Morgan, 1979). These distinctions strengthen the memory representation of each skill, making it more readily available to the learner.

A second proposal, offered by Lee and Magill (1985) and known as the action plan reconstruction hypothesis, suggests that random practice facilitates learning by causing temporary between-trials forgetting of task solutions. Consequently, the learner is required to regenerate a task solution each time a particular skill variation is attempted. In blocked practice, this regeneration would occur only on the first trial of each block. Hence, blocked practice encourages passive learning rather than engaging the learner in processing activities that strengthen the motor plan and its retrieval from memory (Patterson & Lee, 2008).

## Contextual interference in applied settings

Although the contextual interference effect has been shown to be relatively robust in laboratory settings (e.g., Lee & Magill, 1983; Li & Wright, 2000; Maslovat, Chua, Lee & Franks, 2004; Shea & Morgan, 1979; Simon, 2007; Tsutsui, Lee & Hodges, 1998; Wood & Ging, 1991), studies examining its generalizability to applied settings have been less persuasive (see Barreiros, Figueiredo & Godinho, 2007; Brady 1998, 2004, 2008 for reviews). Although superior retention results have been found for random practice in studies using badminton serves (Goode & Magill, 1986; Wrisberg & Liu, 1991), baseball batting (Hall, Domingues & Cavasos, 1994), forehand and backhand ground strokes in tennis (Hebert, Landin & Solomon, 1996), kayak rolling (Smith & Davies, 1995), rifle shooting (Boyce & Del Rey, 1990), and snowboarding skills (Smith, 2002), other investigations have shown no difference between blocked and random practice schedules (e.g., Jones & French, 2007; Smith, Gregory & Davies, 2003; Zetou, Michalopoulou, Giazitzi & Kioumourtzoglou, 2007).

These equivocal findings for random practice benefits in applied settings have been attributed to a number of factors. First, the nature of the task appears to influence the contextual interference effect. This notion is based on Magill and Hall's (1990) hypothesis that the probability of eliciting a contex-

To determine whether the contextual interference effect holds true for skilled performers, Hall, Domingues, and Cavasos (1994) examined the influence of different batting practice schedules on the hitting performance of collegiate baseball players. Players participated in two additional batting practice sessions for six weeks, during which they received 15 fastballs, 15 curveballs, and 15 change-ups. The order of pitch presentation depended on group assign-ment. Players in the blocked group received 15 consecutive pitches of each type in repetitive blocks, and the random group received the same pitches but in random order. When tested under game-like conditions, the players in the random group outperformed those in the blocked group. These results demonstrated that random practice not only benefits beginners but facilitates performance improvement for skilled performers.

tual interference effect depends on whether the task variations implemented are governed by the same generalized motor program. Magill and Hall suggest that practicing tasks controlled by different motor programs requires the learner to engage in more cognitive processing, which, in turn, leads to greater interference and enhanced learning. On the other hand, intra-task variations, which only require parameter modifications of the same program, are less likely to generate the critical level of interference to elicit the same effect. Magill and Hall further contend that practicing more dissimilar skills than similar ones would result in greater learning gains. However, several studies have shown that parameter-only modifications can elicit the contextual interference effect (Keller, Li, Weiss & Relyea, 2006; Landin & Hebert, 1997; Sekiya, Magill, Sidaway & Anderson, 1994). Further research is needed to resolve this debate.

Learner characteristics, such as age and skill level, are also thought to influence the contextual interference effect. Though limited in number, studies exploring contextual interference and age have found that blocked practice (low contextual interference) generally promotes greater learning for children (Brady, 1998; Hall & Boyle, 1993). Similarly, blocked practice advantages have been found for novice learners during the early stages of skill acquisition (Del Rey, Whitehurst & Wood, 1983; Hebert et al., 1996; Landin & Hebert, 1997). Given that the initial stage of learning is characterized by a high degree of cognitive processing to develop an understanding of the movement, it is likely that the elevated level of interference created by random practice conditions simply overwhelms the learner (Magill & Hall, 1990). Conditions of high interference may, therefore, be effective only after a certain degree of proficiency is achieved (Del Rey, 1989; Del Rey et al., 1983; Hebert et al., 1996).

These results suggest that initial learning should be organized with blocked practice followed by random practice once the learner has acquired some degree of proficiency. However, Landin and Hebert (1997) suggest that in an applied setting, moderate levels of contextual interference might be superior. To create moderate contextual interference, the practitioner can use a repeated-blocked schedule of practice. For example, instead of 10 successive shots at each of four positions (blocked) or one shot from each position over 10 rotations (random), taking five successive shots at each of the four positions, with this rotation repeated twice, would create moderate contextual interference. Because the applied setting is typically characterized by the presence of a wide range of skill levels (Landin & Hebert, 1997), repeated-blocked practice, which combines the advantages of blocked and random practice (Proteau, Blandin, Alain & Dorion, 1994), seems advantageous because it would theoretically accommodate more learners. Although additional research is needed to explore fully the potential of moderate contextual interference in applied settings, support for its use has been reported by Keller and colleagues (2006).

Moderate levels of contextual interference appear to align with ideas forwarded by Guadagnoli and Lee's (2004) challenge point framework (Brady, 2008). According to this framework, for learning to occur, an optimal amount of information must be available. That amount is a function of the skill level of the learner and the difficulty of the task being learned (Guadagnoli & Lee, 2004). Accordingly, practitioners should consider the relationship between skill level and task complexity to determine the level of contextual interference that may best facilitate learning.

Figure 9.1 illustrates how the three practice variations might be applied to hockey skills.

| FIGURE 9.1 | Examples of practice variations (blocked, repeated-blocked, and random) for practicing three different hockey skills (pass, slap shot, and wrist shot) in a session. |

| TYPE OF PRACTICE | IMPLEMENTATION |
| --- | --- |
| Blocked practice | pass x 20<br>slap shot x 20<br>wrist shot x 20 |
| Repeated-blocked practice | pass x 5<br>slap shot x 5  } x 4<br>wrist shot x 5 |
| Random practice | pass, slap shot, wrist shot, slap shot, pass, wrist shot, pass, slap shot, pass, wrist shot, slap shot, wrist shot, pass, wrist shot, slap shot, pass, slap shot, pass, wrist shot, slap shot, wrist shot, slap shot, pass, wrist shot, slap shot, wrist shot, pass, slap shot, pass, wrist shot, pass, slap shot, pass, wrist shot, slap shot, wrist shot, slap shot, pass, slap shot, wrist shot, pass, wrist shot, slap shot, wrist shot, slap shot, pass, wrist shot, pass, slap shot, wrist shot, slap shot, pass, wrist shot, pass, slap shot, pass, wrist shot, pass, wrist shot, slap shot |

## *Implications of contextual interference for practice organization*

Although further investigations in a variety of sport and movement settings are needed, the available research should encourage practitioners to reconsider deeply rooted traditional practice methods (Coker & Fischman, 2010). Blocked practice appears to be beneficial during early skill acquisition and should be used until learners get the idea of the movement. Once basic proficiency has been achieved, moderate or high levels of contextual interference should be introduced in order to engage the learner in the higher cognitive processing activities that facilitate learning. Practice should be organized using repeated-blocked and random schedules that combine multiple skills and multiple skill variations. For example, rather than having the learner serve to the same spot on each practice attempt, place colored cones in different positions around the court to vary serve placement. In tennis, practice the forehand and backhand in the same practice session, and vary the type of ball feed or the area of the court from which the learner hits the ball (Jackson, 2001). In a clinic, design stations where patients can practice different manipulative skills. For patients re-learning to walk, vary the incline, direction, and speed. To teach catching, use multiple objects of various sizes and textures, including balls, rings, beanbags, and rubber chickens. Figure 9.2 gives steps for designing a practice session for contextual interference.

---

Designing practice sessions for contextual interference.    **FIGURE 9.2**

To design practice sessions that incorporate high levels of contextual interference:

1. Identify the skills to be practiced.
2. Identify possible skill and performance context variations that will influence how the skill is executed.
3. Design practice where the learner is confronted with different variations and contexts in a randomized schedule.

### EXAMPLE: HOCKEY SHOOTING ON GOAL

**Shots to be practiced:** wrist shot, slap shot, backhand shot

**Variations:** distance and angle to the net, with or without defenders, target location on the net, off of a pass or possession

**Practice drill:** A hockey player skates with the puck to 1 and executes a slap shot. Next, player skates to 2, where a pass is received and a wrist shot is performed. The player then skates to target 3, where a puck is waiting. The player shoots this puck using a backhand shot. The player then receives a pass from the corner and then skates to the center face-off circle and back to target 4, where another slap shot is executed. As the player is traveling to each shooting location, the coach yells out which corner of the net to shoot to. The drill may be modified by including a defender.

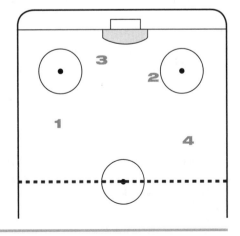

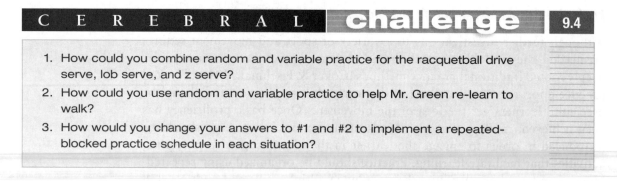

1. How could you combine random and variable practice for the racquetball drive serve, lob serve, and z serve?

2. How could you use random and variable practice to help Mr. Green re-learn to walk?

3. How would you change your answers to #1 and #2 to implement a repeated-blocked practice schedule in each situation?

When implementing higher levels of contextual interference, remember that performance during practice may decline. However, a complete break-down in movement pattern should not be allowed to occur. Practitioners must be vigilant in determining if the demands of the practice structure are adversely affecting learning and, if necessary, revert to lower levels of con-textual interference.

The poorer performance associated with higher levels of contextual inter-ference may lead to decreased motivation. This notion is supported by studies examining learners' estimates of their progress under different levels of con-textual interference. When asked to predict how they would do on a retention

Station work is an excellent way to implement repeated-blocked or random practice. For example, in soccer, six stations could be set up around the field to practice the instep kick, trapping, dribbling, volleying, throw-ins, and heading the ball. At each station, a task card, like the example provided below, would describe the activity to be performed and the number of trials to be taken before the learner rotates to the next station.

Station 1

Starting on the inside of the first cone, dribble the ball through the cones, using the inside of your foot going up and the outside of your foot coming back. Repeat 10 times and then move to Station 2.

1. Using a skill or skills of your choice, design a station practice. For each station, specify the rotation to be used, equipment needed, how you will label the station for easy visibility, and what the task card will say.

2. Speculate as to the potential weaknesses of this particular type of practice.

test, learners who practiced under random conditions underestimated their score, although they more accurately predicted their performance than did their blocked-practice counterparts, who were overconfident in their assessment of how much they had learned (Simon, 2007; Simon and Bjork, 2001). Consequently, "the mistaken impression that learning has proceeded worse than it has" could lead to the cessation of practice (Lee & Wishart, 2005; p. 74). When moving from blocked practice to increased levels of contextual interference, learners should be educated about the benefits of practicing under higher contextual interference conditions.

## PRACTICE DISTRIBUTION

T hus far, our discussion about practice organization has focused on the scheduling of tasks and variations of tasks within a practice session. Practice organization also includes decisions regarding the duration and frequency of the practice sessions themselves, as well as the allocation of time within a single session. How should these decisions be made to optimize learning?

### Massed versus Distributed Practice

Practice distribution, defined in terms of the ratio of time that the learner is physically engaged in practice versus rest, can easily be manipulated by the practitioner. Consequently, whether massed or distributed practice schedules are more beneficial for skill acquisition is a vital question. **Massed practice** is defined as practice where the amount of time allocated to rest between sessions or practice attempts is comparatively less than the time that the learner is engaged in practice. In **distributed practice,** the rest component between sessions or practice attempts is equal to or greater than the practice component.

Researchers have examined the influence of massed versus distributed practice schedules on skill acquisition both across and within practice sessions (see Figure 9.3). With respect to the duration and frequency of practice sessions themselves, research indicates a learning advantage for shorter, more frequent meetings (Baddeley & Longman, 1978). Spacing practice sessions across days relative to holding practice sessions within a day has been shown to enhance both performance and learning (Dail & Christina, 2004; Shea, Lai, Black & Park, 2001). Therefore, unless the decision as to how often to practice and for how long is out of the practitioner's control, distributed practice is preferred.

The optimal practice distribution within a single session remains controversial. Following a review of the practice distribution literature, Lee and Genovese (1988) proposed that distributed practice is beneficial to both performance and learning but more so to performance. Furthermore, optimal practice distribution appears to depend on the task (Lee & Genovese, 1988,

---

| FIGURE **9.3** | (a) Example of distribution across practice sessions. (b) Example of distribution of activity and rest within a practice session. |
|---|---|

**(a)**

| DAY | PRACTICE TIMES | TYPE OF PRACTICE |
|---|---|---|
| Mon. | 11:00 a.m. | Technique development |
| | 4:30 p.m. | Lifting |
| Tues. | 6:00 a.m. | Conditioning |
| | 2:00 p.m. | Throwing |
| Wed. | 11:00 a.m. | Technique development |
| | 4:30 p.m. | Lifting |
| Thurs. | No Practice | Active rest |
| Fri. | 11:00 a.m. | Technique development |
| | 4:30 p.m. | **Lifting** |
| Sat. | 10:00 a.m. | Throwing |

**(b) Lifting Workout**

| | |
|---|---|
| Snatch | 5 x 70, 75, 80, 85, 90 |
| Bench | 5 x 90, 100, 105, 110, 120 |
| Squat | 5 x 150, 160, 175, 185, 195 |
| Split jerks | 3 x 12 x 75 |
| Pullovers | 3 x 15 x 45 |
| Ab twists | 3 x 15 x 25 |

3-minute rest interval between sets

---

1989). For continuous skills, such as cycling or swimming, it seems that distributed schedules pose a greater learning advantage than massed practice (Lee & Genovese, 1988). Conversely, discrete skills, such as pitching, punting, or catching, appear best served by massed practice (Carron, 1969; Lee & Genovese, 1988, 1989).

## Practical Implications for Practice Distribution

Research on massed versus distributed practice offers the practitioner several guidelines for the scheduling of practice, training, or rehabilitation sessions. First, learning is enhanced when shorter, more frequent practice sessions are scheduled (distributed practice). It is better to practice three times a week for 30 minutes than once a week for 90 minutes.

Distributed practice should be used to avoid problems associated with high levels of fatigue. Prolonged fatigue can cause the learner to practice incorrect motor patterns, which will have an adverse effect on learning if the boundaries of the generalized motor program are exceeded. In addition, heightened levels of fatigue leave the learner more susceptible to injury. Therefore, shorter, more frequent work periods embedded with adequate rest intervals are recommended for new and complex skills, continuous tasks, tasks that inherently have high-energy requirements, and tasks whose performance involves some degree of risk. Examples of such tasks include figure skating and rock climbing. This schedule is also recommended for skills practiced in a therapy setting when a fall could occur due to fatigue, such as balancing on a wobble board,

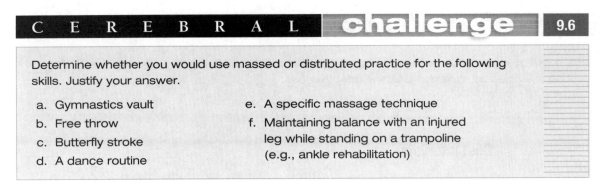

Determine whether you would use massed or distributed practice for the following skills. Justify your answer.

a. Gymnastics vault

b. Free throw

c. Butterfly stroke

d. A dance routine

e. A specific massage technique

f. Maintaining balance with an injured leg while standing on a trampoline (e.g., ankle rehabilitation)

and for learners who lack the physical conditioning needed to sustain activity over extended periods of time. Practice should be scheduled so that new skills or those that are highly technical are taught and practiced at the beginning of the session, while the learner is still fresh, and conditioning is done toward the end of practice (Jones, Wells, Peters & Johnson, 1993).

For massed practice of discrete skills, such as archery, punting a football, and a sit-to-stand transfer, practitioners should schedule short rest intervals between trials in order to maximize repetitions and enhance learning. Massed practice can also be effective when used with learners who have acquired basic skills, are motivated, are in good physical condition, and have long attention spans (Christina & Corcos, 1988; Jones et al., 1993). Finally, the fatigue often present during competition can be replicated through massed practice. Provided that the level of fatigue remains light to moderate, this strategy could enhance physical conditioning and performance in a game situation (Christina & Corcos, 1988). However, practicing when highly fatigued, as was discussed earlier, can have detrimental effects on learners and should be avoided.

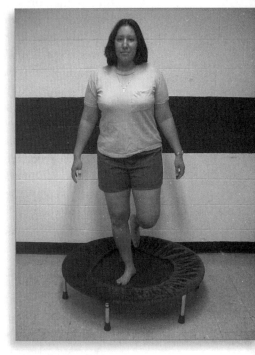

The inherent fatigue from balancing exercises dictates the use of distributed practice.

## MAXIMIZING TIME ON TASK

When a learner is resting, waiting in line, or participating in a poorly designed drill, precious practice time is wasted. Given the amount of practice needed to become proficient at a skill, and the fact that the time available for such practice is usually limited, wasted time prevents learners from maximizing their learning potential. Fortunately, certain strategies can reduce downtime and maximize time on task.

C  E  R  E  B  R  A  L  **challenge**  9.7

For a skill of your choice, suggest possible activities that could fill the rest intervals during practice and maximize practice effectiveness.

## Rest Intervals

Obviously, given the potentially harmful effects of high levels of fatigue (Arnett, DeLuccia & Gilmartin, 2000; Godwin & Schmidt, 1971), learners cannot be denied adequate rest. To maximize the utility of rest time, the practitioner can often fill the rest interval with another activity. This technique is commonly used in weight training, where the rest interval for a fatigued muscle group is filled with an activity using a different muscle group. For example, if an athlete's workout regime calls for three sets of 10 repetitions of bicep curls and triceps extensions, the athlete can alternate continuously between the two exercises. This strategy allows adequate recovery time for the biceps brachii muscle while the triceps are being conditioned. Similar results can be achieved through the use of contextual interference. In repeated-blocked or random practice, recovery is often "built in" to the program, and learners do not have to stop activity completely. For example, in volleyball, a rotation could be used where a player spikes, then moves to the setting position, then goes to the other side of the net to block, then provides coverage behind the block, and finally finishes by shagging a ball.

## Equipment Substitutions

Research shows that approximately 20 percent of a high school physical education student's time is spent waiting (Beauchamp, Darst & Thompson, 1990). One reason is the limitation imposed by an insufficient amount of equipment. A youth soccer coach, for example, may have 20 team members but only eight soccer balls. Similarly, a physical educator teaching putting in a golf unit may have only seven holes on a putting green to which 35 learners must be assigned. The impact on wait time is obvious. However, this problem can be remedied

C  E  R  E  B  R  A  L  **challenge**  9.8

For a skill of your choice, list possible alternatives that you could use when an insufficient amount of equipment is available.

Often, as is the case with the shot put, lack of facilities limits practice as learners must wait their turn. One strategy to reduce wait time is to modify the performance setting. To examine the influence of performance setting modifications on skill acquisition, Coker (2005) compared a modified practice schedule, where learners practiced 50 percent of the time in a natural performance setting and 50 percent of the time in a modified setting, to practicing in a natural performance setting 100 percent of the time. Twenty-two college students volunteered to learn the soccer throw-in. They were randomly divided into two groups. Both groups viewed the same instructional video demonstration of a correct throw and performed four blocks of 15 practice throws. The Natural Setting Practice group (NSP) practiced all 60 throws into an open gym where they could see the ball's flight and landing.

The Modified Practice Setting group (MPS) alternated each block between the full-view condition and throwing into a tarp that was mounted in front of the gym wall (50 percent natural setting and 50 percent modified setting). Feedback on throwing technique was provided. Results indicated that participants in both groups significantly improved their throwing distance. Also, throwing form significantly improved for both groups, according to kinematic analysis. Consequently, participants who spent half of their practice trials performing in the modified setting learned equally well as those who practiced in the natural performance setting 100 percent of the time. The author concluded that alternating between a natural and a modified setting appeared to be a viable strategy for reducing wait time in physical education.

through the use of alternative equipment. In addition to the eight soccer balls, the coach could use playground balls of a comparable size to teach dribbling and kicking skills. The physical educator could give each student a tee to serve as a target. Surely a student who can putt the ball to a tee will be able to get it into the hole. Softballs can serve as substitutes for shot puts, plastic grocery bags for juggling scarves, sand-filled tennis ball canisters for weights, and bicycle inner tubes for surgical tubing. The possibilities are limited only by the practitioner's imagination. Be careful that the alternative equipment does not cause the learner to execute a pattern of movement that exceeds the boundaries of the generalized motor program being developed. If distinct movement pattern changes manifest as a result of the alternative equipment being used, the equipment should be modified or withdrawn.

## Drill Design

To maximize time on task, the practitioner should design drills to ensure the active participation of all learners. In addition, effective drills directly target the learning goal. Many traditional drills and activities fail to meet these criteria. For example, in volleyball, once a basic movement pattern for bumping and setting has been developed, a common drill is to break the class into two or three large groups (six to eight people) and challenge the learners to see how many times they can hit the ball before it touches the floor. Although this drill provides learners with the opportunity to practice newly learned skills, promotes random practice, and enhances motivation, given the size of the groups, each learner will not have many contacts with the ball. Moreover, the learners' goal orientation will be on not letting the ball hit the ground, rather than on form. Consequently, the effectiveness of this activity is questionable. Use Exploration Activity 9.9 to examine the influence of drill design on time on task.

## exploration  A C T I V I T Y  9.9

### Time on Task

**EQUIPMENT NEEDED**

10 people                3 soccer balls

Open area                Stopwatch

**PROCEDURE**

Form one large circle of nine people, with one person standing in the middle. The person in the middle is to try to get the ball while those forming the circle try to keep it away from him or her by passing it around.

1. Perform the drill for 60 seconds, noting the number of ball contacts. How many times did each individual touch the ball, on average? How motivated were the participants?

2. Have two additional people go into the middle. There should now be three people in the middle and seven in the circle. Repeat the drill for 60 seconds. This time, how many times did each person touch the ball, on average? How motivated were the participants? How did the intensity of the drill change?

3. Add two balls to the drill. Again, perform for a 60-second period. How many times did each person touch the ball? How motivated were the participants? How did the intensity of the drill change?

4. Can you suggest other strategies that could be implemented to increase time on task?

## C E R E B R A L  challenge  9.10

1. Redesign the volleyball drill presented in the section titled "Drill Design." Explain why your drill would be more effective.

2. What is the purpose of learning the weave in basketball? Do you think this is an effective drill? Justify your answer.

## ▶ a look ahead

When planning practices and rehabilitative experiences, the practitioner must decide how to organize practice trials and distribute those trials across and within practice sessions to optimize learning. The practitioner must determine whether random or blocked practice should be implemented, when the use of a massed or distributed schedule is beneficial, and how to maximize time on task. Once the learner begins to practice the skill, the practitioner's focus turns to error correction—and before an error can be corrected, its cause must be determined. Error detection will be discussed in the following chapter.

## ● focus points

After reading this chapter, you should know . . .

■ When learners are first introduced to a new motor skill, they should engage in constant practice, practicing only a single variation of the task. Once they have acquired the basic movement pattern, they should engage in variable practice strategies, rehearsing multiple variations of the task.

■ For open skills and closed skills that involve inter-trial variability, the practitioner should systematically introduce variations in both regulatory and non-regulatory conditions that could be present in an applied setting. For closed skills that do not involve inter-trial variability, learners should be exposed to a variety of potential non-regulatory conditions, while the regulatory conditions of the skill should remain constant.

■ Increasing contextual interference—the interference that results from switching from one skill to another or changing the context in which a task is practiced from trial to trial—has been shown to facilitate learning.

■ Low contextual interference occurs during blocked practice, when the learner practices one skill or skill variation repeatedly before attempting another skill or skill variation, whereas high contextual interference results when multiple tasks or task variations are performed in random order.

■ Initial learning should be organized through blocked practice, and random practice should follow once learners have acquired some degree of proficiency.

■ Repeated-blocked practice combines the advantages of blocked and random practice.

■ Learning is enhanced when practice sessions are shorter and more frequent.

■ Distributed practice is recommended for novel and complex skills, continuous tasks, tasks that inherently have high-energy requirements, and tasks whose performance involves some degree of risk. Massed practice can be effective for learners who have acquired basic skills, are highly motivated, are in good physical condition, and have long attention spans.

- To maximize time on task, the practitioner should carefully consider rest intervals, equipment substitutions, and drill design.

# ? review questions

1. Explain the concept and significance of practice variability. Why is it important to make a distinction between learning and performance when answering this question?

2. What variables should the practitioner assess to determine how and when to implement practice variability?

3. Compare and contrast random and blocked practice.

4. What is the contextual interference effect?

5. Describe the two hypotheses that have been proposed to account for the contextual interference effect.

6. What limiting factors have been found to influence the contextual interference effect?

7. What practice strategy has been used to create moderate contextual interference?

8. Compare and contrast massed and distributed practice.

9. Why should prolonged high levels of fatigue be avoided?

10. List and explain three factors that can adversely affect time on task.

# REFERENCES

Arnett, M.G., DeLuccia, D. & Gilmartin, K. (2000). Male and female differences and the specificity of fatigue on skill acquisition and transfer performance. *Research Quarterly for Exercise and Sport, 71,* 201–05.

Baddeley, A.D. & Longman, D.J.A. (1978). The influence of length and frequency of training session on the rate of learning to type. *Ergonomics, 21,* 627–35.

Barreiros, J., Figueiredo, T. & Godinho, M., (2007). The contextual interference effect in applied settings. *European Physical Education Review, 13,* 195–208.

Battig, W.F. (1972). Intra-task interference as a source of facilitation in transfer and retention. In R.F. Thompson and J.F. Voss (Eds.), *Topics in learning and performance* (pp. 131–59). New York: Academic Press.

Battig, W.F. (1979). The flexibility of human memory. In. L.S. Cermak and F.I.M. Craik (Eds.), *Level of processing in human memory* (pp. 23–44). Hillsdale, NJ: Erlbaum.

Beauchamp, L., Darst, P.W. & Thompson, L.P. (1990). Academic learning time as an indication of quality high school physical education. *Journal of Physical Education, Recreation and Dance, 61*(1), 92–95.

Boyce, B.A. & Del Rey, P. (1990). Designing applied research in a naturalistic setting using a contextual interference paradigm. *Journal of Human Movement Studies, 18,* 189–200.

Brady, F. (1998). The theoretical and empirical review of the contextual interference effect and the learning of motor skills. *Quest, 50,* 266–93.

Brady, F. (2004). Contextual interference: a meta-analytic study. *Perceptual and Motor Skills, 99,* 116–26.

Brady, F. (2008). The contextual interference effect in sport skills. *Perceptual and Motor Skills, 106,* 461–72.

Carron, A.V. (1969). Performance and learning in a discrete motor task under massed vs. distributed practice. *Research Quarterly, 40,* 481–89.

Christina, R.W. & Corcos, D.M. (1988). *Coaches guide to teaching sport skills.* Champaign, IL: Human Kinetics.

Cohen, H.S., Bloomberg, J.J. & Mulavara, A.P. (2005). Obstacle avoidance in novel visual environments improved by variable practice training. *Perceptual and Motor Skills, 101,* 853–61.

Coker, C.A. (2005). Practice setting modification and skill acquisition. *The Physical Educator, 62,* 26–31.

Coker, C.A. & Fischman, M.G. (2010). Motor skill learning for effective coaching and performance. In J.M. Williams (Ed.), *Applied sport psychology: personal growth to peak performance* (6th ed., pp. 21–41). New York: McGraw-Hill.

Dail, T.K. & Christina, R.W. (2004). Distribution of practice and metacognition in learning and long-term retention. *Research Quarterly for Exercise and Sport, 75,* 148–55.

Del Rey, P. (1989). Training and contextual interference effects on memory and transfer. *Research Quarterly for Exercise and Sport, 60,* 342–47.

Del Rey, P., Whitehurst, M. & Wood, J.M. (1983). Effects of experience and contextual interference on learning and transfer by boys and girls. *Perceptual Motor Skills, 56,* 581–82.

Douvis, S. (2005). Variable practice in learning the forehand drive in tennis. *Perceptual and Motor Skills, 101,* 531–45.

Gentile, A.M. (2000). Skill acquisition: action, movement, and the neuromotor processes. In J.H. Carr and R.B. Shepard (Eds.), *Movement science: foundations for physical therapy in rehabilitation* (2nd ed., pp. 111–80). Rockville, MD: Aspen.

Godwin, M.A. & Schmidt, R.A. (1971). Muscular fatigue and discrete motor learning. *Research Quarterly for Exercise and Sport, 42,* 374–83.

Goode, S. & Magill, R.A. (1986).Contextual interference effects in learning three badminton serves. *Research Quarterly for Exercise and Sport, 57,* 308–14.

Guadagnoli, M.A. & Lee, T.D. (2004). Challenge point: a framework for conceptualizing the effects of various practice conditions in motor learning. *Journal of Motor Behavior, 36,* 212–24.

Hall, K.G. & Boyle, M. (1993). The effects of contextual interference on shuffleboard skill in children. *Research Quarterly for Exercise and Sport, Abstracts, 64,* A-74.

Hall, K.G., Domingues, D.A. & Cavasos, R. (1994). Contextual interference effects with skilled baseball players. *Perceptual and Motor Skills, 78,* 835–41.

Hebert, E.P., Landin, D. & Solomon, M.A. (1996). Practice schedule effects on the performance and learning of low- and high-skilled students: an applied study. *Research Quarterly for Exercise and Sport, 67,* 52–58.

Jackson, B. (2001, April). *Mixing and matching your repetitions: contextual interference as a learning opportunity.* Paper presented at the meeting of the American Alliance for Health, Physical Education, Recreation and Dance. Cincinnati, OH.

Jones, B.J., Wells, L.J., Peters, R.E. & Johnson, D.J. (1993). *Guide to effective coaching: principles and practice.* Madison, WI: WCB Brown and Benchmark.

Jones, L. & French, K.E. (2007). Effects of contextual interference on acquisition and retention of three volleyball skills. *Perceptual and Motor Skills, 105,* 883–90.

Keller, G., Li, Y., Weiss, L.W. & Relyea, G.E. (2006). Contextual interference effect on acquisition and retention of pistol shooting skills. *Perceptual and Motor Skills, 103,* 241–52.

Landin, D. & Hebert, E.P. (1997). A comparison of three practice schedules along the contextual interference continuum. *Research Quarterly for Exercise and Sport, 68,* 357–61.

Lee, T.D. & Genovese, E.D. (1988). Distribution of practice in motor skill acquisition: learning and performance effects reconsidered. *Research Quarterly for Exercise and Sport, 59,* 277–87.

Lee, T.D. & Genovese, E.D. (1989). Distribution of practice in motor skill acquisition: different effects for discrete and continuous tasks. *Research Quarterly for Exercise and Sport, 60,* 59–65.

Lee, T.D. & Magill, R.A. (1983). The locus of contextual interference in motor-skill acquisition. *Journal of Experimental Psychology: Learning, Memory, and Cognition, 9,* 730–46.

Lee, T.D. & Magill, R.A. (1985). Can forgetting facilitate skill acquisition? In D. Goodman, R.B. Wilberg, and I.M. Franks (Eds.), *Differing perspectives in motor learning, memory and control* (pp. 3–22). Amsterdam: North Holland.

Lee, T.D. & Wishart, L.R. (2005). Motor learning conundrums (and possible solutions). *Quest, 57,* 67–78.

Li, Y. & Wright, D.L. (2000). An assessment of the attention demands of random and blocked practice. *Quarterly Journal of Experimental Psychology, 53A,* 591–606.

Magill, R.A. & Hall, K.G. (1990). A review of the contextual interference effect in motor skill acquisition. *Human Movement Science, 9,* 241–89.

Maslovat, D., Chua, R., Lee, T.D. & Franks, I.M. (2004). Contextual interference: single task versus multi-task learning. *Motor Control, 8,* 213–33.

Memmert, D. (2006). Long-term effects of type of practice on the learning and transfer of a complex skill. *Perceptual and Motor Skills, 103,* 912–16.

Newell, K.M. & McDonald, P.V. (1992). Practice: a search for task solutions. In R.W. Christina and H.M. Eckert (Eds.), The Academy Papers, No. 25, Enhancing human performance in sport: new concepts and developments. *Proceedings of the American Academy of Physical Education* (pp. 51–59).

Patterson, J.T. & Lee, T.D. (2008). Organizing practice: the interaction of repetition and cognitive effort for skilled performance. In D. Farrow, J. Baker, and C. MacMahon (Eds.), *Developing sport expertise: researchers and coaches put theory into practice* (pp. 119–34). London: Routledge.

Proteau, L., Blandin, Y., Alain, C. & Dorion, A. (1994). The effects of the amount and variability of practice on the learning of a multisegmented motor task. *Acta Psychologica, 85,* 61–74.

Sekiya, H., Magill, R.A., Sidaway, B. & Anderson, D.I. (1994). The contextual interference effect for skill variations from the same and different generalized motor programs. *Research Quarterly for Exercise and Sport, 65,* 330–38.

Shea, C.H. & Kohl, R.M. (1991). Composition of practice: influence on the retention of motor skills. *Research Quarterly for Exercise and Sport, 62,* 187–95.

Shea, C.H., Lai, Q., Black, C. & Park, J.H. (2001). Spacing practice sessions across days benefits the learning of motor skills. *Human Movement Science, 19,* 737–60.

Shea, C.H. & Morgan, R.L. (1979). Contextual interference effects on the acquisition, retention and transfer of a motor skill. *Journal of Experimental Psychology, Human Learning and Memory, 5,* 179–87.

Shoenfelt, E.L., Snyder, L.A., Maue, A.E., McDowell, C.P. & Woolard, C.D. (2002). Comparison of constant and variable practice conditions on free throw shooting. *Perceptual and Motor Skills, 94,* 1113–1123.

Simon, D.A. (2007). Contextual interference effects with two tasks. *Perceptual and Motor Skills, 105,* 177–83.

Simon, D.A. & Bjork, R.A. (2001). Metacognition in motor learning. *Journal of Experimental Psychology: Learning, Memory, and Cognition, 2,* 907–12.

Smith, P.J.K. (2002). Applying contextual interference to snowboarding skills. *Perceptual and Motor Skills, 95,* 999–1005.

Smith, P.J.K. & Davies, M. (1995). Applying contextual interference to the Pawlata roll. *Journal of Sports Sciences, 13,* 455–62.

Smith, P.J.K., Gregory, S.K. & Davies, M. (2003). Alternating versus blocked practice in learning a cartwheel. *Perceptual and Motor Skills, 96,* 1255–1264.

Tsutsui, S., Lee, T.D. & Hodges, N.J. (1998). Contextual interference in learning new patterns of bimanual coordination. *Journal of Motor Behavior, 30,* 151–57.

Wood, C.A. & Ging, C.A. (1991). The role of interference and task similarity on the acquisition, retention and transfer of simple motor skills. *Research Quarterly for Exercise and Sport, 62,* 18–26.

Wrisberg, C.A. & Liu, Z. (1991). The effects of contextual interference on the practice retention and transfer of an applied motor skill. *Research Quarterly for Exercise and Sport, 62,* 406–12.

Zetou, E., Michalopoulou, M., Giazitzi, K. & Kioumourtzoglou, E. (2007). Contextual interference effect in learning volleyball skills. *Perceptual and Motor Skills, 104,* 995–1004.

# 10

## Diagnosing Errors

**S**ally is frustrated. She has spent hours with her coach working on her backhand. Her technique is flawless. But in competition, she consistently contacts the ball too late. Her coach tells her that her technique looks good and that she just needs to swing faster. But no matter how hard she tries, she just can't fix the problem. She doesn't know what else to do, and her coach has offered no other suggestions.

## SKILL ANALYSIS

**P**ractitioners must provide learners with information about the correctness of their performance and prescribe modifications for its improvement. Before they can provide this information, practitioners must be able to analyze performance accurately and determine not only whether an error exists but also the cause of that error and how to fix it. To determine the correctness of a response, the most common approach is simply observation of the performance. For this form of assessment, the practitioner typically compares the learner's technique to technique that is representative of a highly skilled individual. Unfortunately, three potential limitations are inherent in this approach.

First, although it may be natural to try to copy or adopt the technique of a champion athlete, that technique is not necessarily best suited for every learner. A technique may be performed in many ways, and athletes often adopt their own idiosyncrasies. Practitioners must, therefore, develop a thorough understanding of biomechanics in order to determine the fundamental components of proper technique. In addition, learners may not share the same underlying abilities and attributes as the athlete whom they are trying to emulate. Consequently, certain techniques may be inappropriate due to individual differences.

A second limitation is that an observed flaw may result from a variety of underlying causes. For example, a practitioner may observe that a volleyball player is hitting the ball into the net on the serve and try to fix the player's arm swing or the amount of force generated. However, if the athlete tosses the ball too far out in front of the hitting arm, this too would cause the player to hit the ball with too low an angle to clear the net. In this situation, the toss, not the arm swing, should be corrected. Similarly, a right-handed hitter in baseball may be consistently fouling off to the right. One explanation for the error could be a slow swing speed resulting from the athlete taking the bat off the shoulder and implementing a long, swooping swing. However, a second possibility is that the athlete is having difficulty identifying the pitch and delaying the initiation of the swing.

The last example suggests the third limitation and the focus of this chapter: errors are not always the result of poor technique. Many errors can be attributed to deficits in the area of motor learning. However, since we can only see the output of a learner's performance, practitioners tend to focus on the outcome of the movement and to provide feedback only about those technical aspects of the skill that can be observed (Rothstein, 1986). As a result, the underlying processes that lead to the performance are often overlooked, as they are not directly observable. The purpose of this chapter is to identify potential errors that may manifest not because of poor technique but because of problems related to motor learning and control.

## PLANNING AN OBSERVATION

**A**ccurate skill analysis begins with good observational skills. After all, you cannot fix an error unless you first detect it and determine its cause. Observational and analytical skills do not come naturally to most human movement practitioners (Rink, 2006), but with practice and the understanding of how to conduct a systematic observation, any practitioner can develop these skills. Test your observational skills in Exploration Activity 10.1, then use the videos found at the adjoining online reference to improve skill analysis competency.

**www.**

**Videos designed to develop skill analysis competency**

www.pevideo.org/

## exploration A C T I V I T Y 10.1

### Diagnosing Errors

**EQUIPMENT**

Stopwatch or digital watch          Partner

**PROCEDURE**

After reading this paragraph, examine the diagram below. Three differences exist between the two pictures. Time how long it takes you to find them. Then, time someone executing a vertical jump. Be sure to note the time needed to complete each task.

**QUESTIONS**

1. What was the difference in time between how long it took you to find the three flaws in the diagram and the performance of the vertical jump?

2. List the differences in observing a static picture versus a dynamic movement for the detection of performance flaws.

Unlike the still pictures presented in the activity, human movement occurs both dynamically and quickly, so that the observer has only fractions of a second to assess a performance. Hence, good observations start with a plan (Hall, 2007).

## Identify the Skill's Purpose and Key Elements

Prior to conducting an observation, the practitioner should identify both the purpose of the skill to be observed and its key elements. **Key elements,** also known as **critical features,** are specific body movements that are observable and that affect the performance of the skill (Coaching Association of Canada, 1993) (see Figure 10.1, for example). Their identification requires a thorough understanding of both the skill itself and biomechanics. Numerous textbooks, sport-specific books, web pages, and journals, as well as other movement practitioners, may be of assistance. Once the key elements of the skill have been identified, the practitioner can determine those that will be the focus of the observation.

## Determine the Viewing Perspective

The second step in developing the observational plan is to determine the optimal viewing perspective from which to observe the skill and, more specifically, the key elements chosen as the focus. In order to see all of the critical aspects of the skill, it may be necessary to watch the skill from several different positions. In

---

**FIGURE 10.1**    Key elements of fielding a ground ball.

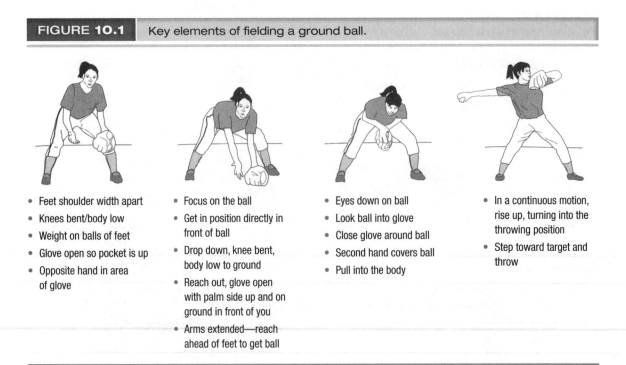

- Feet shoulder width apart
- Knees bent/body low
- Weight on balls of feet
- Glove open so pocket is up
- Opposite hand in area of glove

- Focus on the ball
- Get in position directly in front of ball
- Drop down, knee bent, body low to ground
- Reach out, glove open with palm side up and on ground in front of you
- Arms extended—reach ahead of feet to get ball

- Eyes down on ball
- Look ball into glove
- Close glove around ball
- Second hand covers ball
- Pull into the body

- In a continuous motion, rise up, turning into the throwing position
- Step toward target and throw

addition, the distance from which you observe will vary depending on the focus of the observation. To focus on the entire movement, for example, the observer will need to be positioned farther away from the learner, whereas if the practitioner needs to observe the performer's eye movements to determine where the athlete's visual focus is directed, a close-up view may be necessary. The observer should select a position that permits a good view without distractions.

## Decide on the Number of Observations

How many trials should be observed prior to making a judgment as to the quality of the performance? No concrete number exists, but analysis based on a single performance attempt should be avoided. Practitioners with limited observational experience will need to view additional trials to determine the underlying cause of an error. Also, as the complexity of the task increases, so too will the number of observations needed to accurately assess performance. Finally, as we have noted, a characteristic of beginning learners is inconsistency in performance. Determining the consistent and/or critical error may therefore require repeated observations.

## Consider Using Video

The final decision is whether or not to capture the performance on video. Video is useful, as it permits repetitive viewing by both the practitioner and the learner, it can be slowed, paused, and advanced frame by frame, and it captures movements that occur too rapidly (less than a quarter of a second) for the human eye to see (Hall, 2007). Video does have a few disadvantages. Learners who are not used to being videoed may be intimidated and alter their performance. Also, a TV set or computer is often needed for viewing, since it is difficult to see intricate performance details when viewing the replay through the camera.

---

### C E R E B R A L  challenge  10.2

For a skill of your choice, list the key elements and determine the optimal viewing perspective from which to observe each.

Skill: _____

| KEY ELEMENTS | OBSERVATION PLAN |
|---|---|
|  |  |
|  |  |
|  |  |
|  |  |

## DETERMINING THE CAUSE OF AN ERROR AND ITS RESOLUTION

nce the practitioner has observed the performance and detected the existence of one or more movement errors, he or she must determine their underlying cause. The practitioner should start by asking why a certain behavior is observed. Why is the backhand late? Why is the patient losing balance? Remember, as was noted earlier, the answer may not be related to technique. Consequently, the practitioner must be aware of the variety of potential sources of error in order to ensure that corrections offered are both accurate and effective. Sources of error can be grouped into the five major categories depicted in Figure 10.2: (1) errors due to constraints, (2) comprehension errors, (3) errors in selection, (4) execution errors, and (5) sensory errors.

### Errors Due to Constraints

Constraints shape behavior. Accordingly, errors may emerge as a result of the task or environment relative to the performer's personal developmental level. For example, a common error displayed by young learners executing a free throw is the projection of the ball in a shot put–type manner. This unorthodox pat-

| FIGURE 10.2 | Possible causes of error related to motor learning and control. |
| --- | --- |

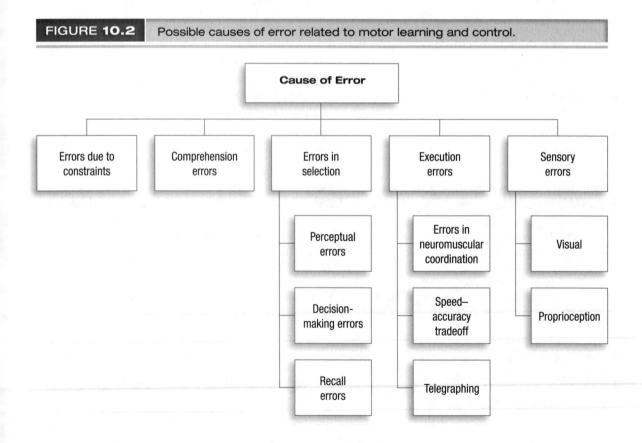

tern emerges not because the learner doesn't understand the correct technique but because it is the only way the learner can generate enough force to get the ball to a basket that is positioned too high. When the practitioner lowers the basket to accommodate the learner's developmental level, the error will likely be corrected.

Equipment may also create unwanted movement errors. A bat that is too heavy will alter a learner's swing pattern, crutches that are not properly fitted will cause problems with a patient's locomotion, and the speed of a treadmill can dictate the user's stride length and frequency.

Errors may also result from the structure of a task or drill. For example, by 5 or 6 years of age, the visual system develops to the point that objects moving in the horizontal plane can be efficiently tracked (Payne & Isaacs, 2008). However, it is not until between the ages of 8 and 9 that a child can track a ball traveling in an arc (Morris, 1980). The common practice of tossing a ball with a high arc to give a youngster more time to get under it actually makes the task much more difficult and reduces the learner's chances of catching successfully. Instead, until the age of 8 to 9, the ball should be thrown straight toward the learner horizontally in order to accommodate the child's visual development and increase the chances of success.

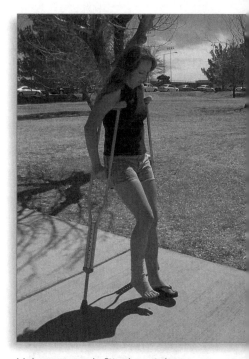

Unless properly fitted, crutches may cause errors in locomotion.

Other errors will arise when the environment changes from one that is closed, such as hitting off a tee, to one that is more open, such as hitting a pitch. Practitioners should expect to see a decline in performance as learners adapt to the new demands imposed upon them. Prolonged recurrence of errors without signs of adaptation, however, could, of course, indicate that the demands of the new task are exceeding the learner's current capacity. In such instances, the practitioner may have to revert to having the learner practice the skill in a more closed environment for a period of time.

Fear may also be a source of error. Beginning swimmers are often afraid of the water. Fear of the ball plays a role in catching and striking. Fear of heights will have to be overcome before learners can correctly rappel, ski jump, or rock climb.

**common** *myth*

When teaching a youngster how to catch, you should toss the ball with a high arc to give the child enough time to follow it and get underneath it for a successful catch.

C E R E B R A L **challenge** 10.3

List movement errors that could occur in sport or rehab as a result of incorrect sizing of equipment, objects, or implements.

The fear of falling can interfere with a rock climber's performance.

Furthermore, performers may alter their technique because of a fear of re-injuring a recently rehabilitated limb. Finally, a different type of fear, the fear of failure, may have a negative impact on performance. To counter the fear of failure, practitioners should incorporate goal setting, provide opportunities for all learners to experience success in practice, and create an environment where learners are not afraid to make mistakes.

## Comprehension Errors

A comprehension error occurs when the learner does not understand the requirements of the skill or what is expected. These errors develop when learners do not fully understand the instructions given, have a short attention span or limited attentional capacity, or lack motivation. In this instance, simply explain the skill again. Be sure to use terminology that is appropriate for the age and skill level of the learner and avoid overloading the learner with too much information. Finally, check for understanding.

Errors in comprehension may also occur when learners are trying to correct and refine their skills. Although a practitioner may have made a learner aware of the existence of a problem, the learner may not fully understand what the error is or how it is being created. A useful strategy in this situation is to video the performance and show the learner what he or she is doing wrong. In addition, learners must be taught to pay attention to the sensory consequences of their movements in order to develop their error detection and correction capabilities. Questioning strategies that encourage learners to evaluate their own performance prior to being given feedback are effective in accomplishing this and will be discussed in detail in the next chapter. On the other hand, it may be the case that the learner understands the error but is uncertain how to implement a change to correct the behavior. In addition to continued demonstrations and feedback, manual guidance or a simulator may prove useful in this situation.

## Errors in Selection

The successful performance of many motor skills, such as a tennis backhand, depends not only on how the skill is executed but also on how quickly and accurately the performer assesses the situation and decides how best to respond. Any delays in the processes that lead to response selection influence not only the timing of the response but its quality as well. Practitioners must, therefore, be able to differentiate between slow movement execution and slow initiation of movement. Slow movement execution most often results from a problem with technique. On the other hand, if the movement is initiated slowly, the error can likely be attributed to a perceptual or decision-making problem. This distinction, had it been considered, would have assisted Sally's coach in diagnosing her error. Since her technique was correct and speeding up the overall movement was ineffective, the next step would be to examine Sally's response selection strategies.

### Perceptual errors

Good decision-making begins with good assessment. Unless the learner can quickly and accurately distinguish what is task relevant from the abundance of stimuli present in the environment, response selection will be delayed or incorrect. Movement errors often result when a learner does not know what cues to look for in the environment, cannot distinguish between task-relevant and irrelevant stimuli, or focuses attention on the wrong cues. For example, a basketball player who focuses attention on an opponent's head movements rather than the mid torso will likely be drawn into a fake. In some instances, the learner may understand what cues are relevant but fail to look at the information-rich areas in the environment where those critical cues occur (Magill, 1998; Rothstein, 1986). This can equally hamper the learner's decision-making capabilities.

To determine if any of these causes are the source of Sally's timing error, her coach must establish whether Sally can correctly read game situations. First, does Sally know what critical cues to look for? Second, is she able to detect that information during a game? If not, intervention strategies would focus on

1. teaching the critical cues

2. prompting Sally to prepare her response sooner (e.g., beginning preparation as soon as the ball leaves the opponent's racket and getting the racket into the backswing position by the time the ball bounces)

3. directing her attention to where in the environment cues occur

4. providing extensive practice opportunities in a variety of situations that contain common task-relevant cues.

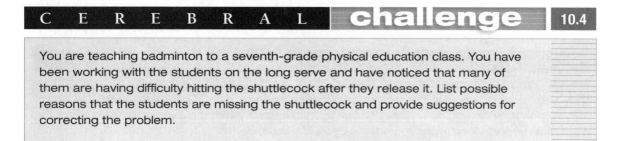

CEREBRAL **challenge** 10.4

You are teaching badminton to a seventh-grade physical education class. You have been working with the students on the long serve and have noticed that many of them are having difficulty hitting the shuttlecock after they release it. List possible reasons that the students are missing the shuttlecock and provide suggestions for correcting the problem.

Level of arousal may lead to a perceptual error, as it influences a learner's assessment proficiency. As we noted in Chapter 2, when arousal levels are too low, attentional focus becomes too broad and learners are unable to focus solely on task-relevant cues. On the other hand, when arousal levels are elevated to the point where the learner becomes over-aroused, attentional focus becomes so narrow that the learner may no longer be capable of effectively scanning the environment, leaving potentially significant stimuli undetected. Both situations may lead to inaccurate responses, as the performer lacks the necessary information for appropriate decision-making.

### Decision-making errors

Many errors result from problems in decision-making. A learner who misjudges velocity, direction, height, weight, distance, trajectory of an object, or position of opponents or teammates could select the wrong motor program or select the appropriate motor program but apply erroneous parameters for the situation. Paying attention to task-irrelevant stimuli, such as being tricked by a head fake, may also lead to momentary delays in responding. Furthermore, mispredicting the arrival of an object, person, or musical cue can cause learners to mistime the initiation of their movement and respond either too early or too late. Again, these decision-making errors can be resolved by increasing the performer's ability to identify and locate critical cues and helping the performer develop a stronger cause-and-effect relationship between a specific cue and the appropriate response.

Response delays may occur if the learner fails to reduce the number of response alternatives. According to Hick's Law, the higher the degree of uncertainty in a given situation, the longer it will take the learner to decide which response to make. Many decision-making problems can be resolved by reducing the number of possible response alternatives. Learners should be taught how to look systematically for key

C E R E B R A L **challenge** 10.5

Throughout a rehearsal, one dancer is consistently out of sync with the rest of the dancers. Suggest reasons why this may be occurring and provide suggestions to correct the problem.

C E R E B R A L **challenge** 10.6

An athlete is constantly being beaten when playing person-to-person defense. What will you look at to determine why this learner is unable to stay with the assignment? What recommendations might you offer to correct the problem?

performance characteristics in a situation, as a quarterback does during an option play. Increasing the learner's capability to identify potential predictors, such as opponent or situational tendencies, can also help reduce uncertainty. For example, if Sally knows that whenever her opponent gets into trouble during the game, she hits a shot to Sally's backhand, Sally can better prepare her upcoming shot.

### Recall errors

A common cause of movement errors is forgetting. Learners often have difficulty remembering movements and strategies because of the passage of time between practice sessions. Some learners will even forget what the instructor has just told them to try to incorporate into their next attempt.

At times, learners will be unable to recall what to do in a given situation. For example, in soccer, young learners are taught to play their positions, but in their excitement for the game many forget about positioning and follow the ball. Frequently, the learner is capable of performing the correct movement but simply forgets to do it at the appropriate time. Reminders and attention-focusing questioning strategies, such as "What are you going to focus on this time?" are usually sufficient to correct errors due to forgetting.

## Execution Errors

Sometimes the learner selects the appropriate response to a situation but cannot execute that response correctly. For example, a racquetball player might correctly choose a kill shot in a given situation but mishit the ball. Execution errors occur for a number of reasons, including insufficient practice and performing the movement too quickly.

### Errors in neuromuscular coordination

Practitioners must be able to distinguish between what learners can do and what they know (Christina & Corcos, 1988). Often, movement errors occur not because of a lack of understanding but because the learner has not yet had enough practice time to establish the proper neuromuscular coordination (Wang & Griffin, 1998). In such cases, the error will likely resolve with additional opportunities to practice. However, in some cases, the learner does not possess the underlying abilities necessary to develop a high degree of skill proficiency or lacks the physical prerequisites to accomplish the task or a component of the task. If the problem stems from a physical deficit, such as inadequate strength levels or poor range of motion, the deficit must first be addressed. In other words, the learner will have to improve his or her strength levels or range of motion before the correct performance of the skill will be possible. If the problem stems from a physical quality that is genetically determined, then additional practice will not bring a solution.

Problems in neuromuscular coordination will arise when a learner is trying to replace an established movement pattern with a new one. Throughout this process, negative transfer will occur, in that the previously learned pattern will interfere with the acquisition of the new movement. Errors will result not from a lack of understanding or ability but because negative transfer must be overcome. This, of course, takes time and practice. Negative transfer may also occur between two skills that are similar in nature, such as the golf swing and the baseball swing. Coordination errors will arise when an individual who has experience in one skill tries to resolve the similarities and differences with another.

Finally, neuromuscular coordination can be compromised when a learner consciously attends to the specifics of a skill normally performed automatically. Attending to movement components that are otherwise performed automatically causes the normal flow of the movement to be interrupted. This can be seen when first-time users of a treadmill are told to walk the way they normally would. Their gait pattern will exhibit changes until they become comfortable using the equipment and are no longer thinking about how they normally walk.

### Speed–accuracy tradeoff

Performance outcome may be influenced by the speed–accuracy tradeoff. For example, if the windmill pitch is executed too fast, the pitcher will lose accuracy and have difficulty getting the ball in the strike zone. Similarly, movement patterns will not be performed accurately if patients perform their rehabilitation exercises too quickly. Simply by slowing down the execution of the movement, the learner can remedy the error.

In cases involving temporal accuracy, however, speeding up the movement can reduce errors. Sally's coach's suggestion to speed up her swing was, therefore, a good one. However, when increasing her speed did not fix the error, the coach should have continued to explore other potential causes.

### Telegraphing

In competition, success can depend on the performer's ability to gain an advantage over an opponent. One method for gaining advantage is to increase the

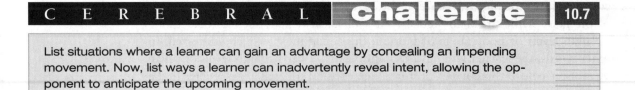

RESEARCH NOTES

Several researchers have proposed that a relationship exists between the type of footwear worn and gait and balance for elders (Sudarsky, 1990; Wasson, Gall, McDonald & Liang, 1990). According to Waked, Robbins, and McClaran (1997), this relationship results from the shoe's effect on proprioception. Thirteen elderly male volunteers walked along a balance beam (height 3.9 cm, width 7.8 cm, length 9 m) barefoot and in six pairs of shoes that were identical with the exception of midsole thickness and hardness. Measures included balance failure frequency, foot position error, and foot position awareness. Results showed that (1) stability and foot position awareness are related, (2) as midsole thickness increased, so did foot position error, and (3) harder midsoles resulted in lower foot position errors. Based on these results, the researchers concluded that footwear midsole thickness and hardness influence foot position awareness, which in turn affects stability. Interestingly, the elderly tend to prefer soft, thick running shoes. Consequently, stability problems in the elderly may be the result of their shoe preference.

uncertainty in the situation for the opponent, causing a delay in the opponent's response. This advantage can be lost if the opponent is able to guess correctly what event will occur and when. For example, the reason a learner's serve is always easily returned could be that the learner is somehow revealing his or her intent, thereby allowing the opponent to prepare for it in advance. The learner must be taught how to conceal his or her intentions.

## Sensory Errors

Errors may result from limitations of the sensory mechanisms of motor performance. Given the importance of vision and proprioception in both perception and the feedback, interference with their contributions can hinder learning and performance.

### Visual errors

According to Knudson and Kluka (1997), movement errors can result from the visual demands of the sport exceeding what is physically possible. For example, a learner could fail to see important cues because she was in mid-blink or because the event occurred too quickly. Shadows can play havoc with the visual system and affect performance. An improper vantage point may obstruct a learner's field of view. Obstructions can also be intentionally set, such as in hockey when one teammate attempts to block the vision of the goalie as another teammate shoots the puck.

### Proprioception errors

Inaccurate sensory feedback stemming from musculoskeletal pain or injury to joint, muscle, or cutaneous receptors may lead to impaired coordination and control during voluntary movement, as well as faulty error detection and correction (Hodges, 2007). A patient with a proprioceptive deficit, for example, may lack control when performing everyday tasks. In this instance, equipment may be altered, such as enlarging the handles of kitchen utensils to enhance their "feel" and make them easier to control.

Proprioceptive deficits can also cause "delayed reflex responses as a result of increased time to reach the threshold for movement detection" (Hodges, 2007, p. 121). This delay will not only affect performance but may also increase the risk of injury or re-injury, as when a cross-country runner has an impaired ability to make the constant minor adjustments needed to maintain balance when running on an uneven surface.

## SHOULD THE ERROR BE CORRECTED?

Christina and Corcos (1988) suggest that once the nature of the error has been identified, three questions be considered prior to correcting it. These questions concern the learner's capability, time, and the learner's motivation (see Figure 10.3).

### Is the Learner Capable?

The first question to ask is whether the learner is capable of making the correction. Successful performance of the corrected technique will depend on whether the learner possesses the necessary underlying abilities. In addition, if the learner does not have the physical prerequisites (strength level, range of motion, etc.) and intellectual capacity to perform the correction, changing the technique will be unsuccessful.

### How Much Time is Needed?

The second question to consider is how much time will be needed for the learner to make the correction. This will depend on the type of correction necessary.

---

**FIGURE 10.3**    Decisions to be made to determine whether to correct an error.

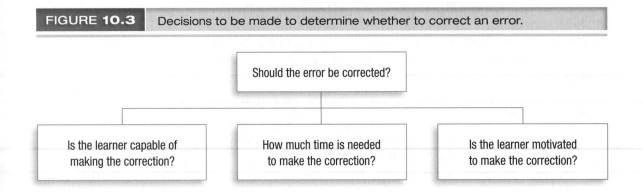

| | Categories of corrections. | **TABLE 10.1** |
|---|---|---|
| **RETRY** | **REFINE** | **REBUILD** |
| Simple modification of established pattern | Improvement of established pattern | New pattern |
| Easy to correct | Moderate effort to correct | Difficult to correct |
| Little or no learning required | Reasonable amount of learning required | Extensive learning required |
| Can be changed quickly | Varying amounts of time | Substantial amount of time |
| Little or no adverse effect on performance | Initial performance decrement | Negative impact on performance initially |
| | | Negative transfer |
| | | Frustrating |

Reprinted, with permission, from C.A. Coker, 2005. "Teaching tips for simplification," *Teaching Physical Education* 16(6): 8–9

Corrections may be classified into three general categories, summarized in Table 10.1: (1) retry, (2) refine, or (3) rebuild (Coker, 2005).

In cases where the motor program is correct and the change merely involves a modification in execution, the learner may simply need to *retry* the skill. Errors that occur because of forgetting, for example, can easily be rectified through reminders. Similarly, parameter changes, such as increasing the speed at which the movement is performed, are relatively easy to implement. A racquetball player may simply need to snap her wrist faster at contact to improve her kill shot's effectiveness, or a patient may have to adjust his cane placement during gait. Through attention cueing, these errors can be resolved relatively quickly and with little or no adverse effect on performance.

Other corrections involve *refining* a developing coordination pattern or motor program. For example, a common error in the freestyle swimming stroke is dropping the elbows during the recovery, which is often the result of overextending the arms before they enter the water. To correct this error, the learner must further develop the existing movement pattern. Performance will be somewhat inconsistent initially as the swimmer learns to refine the timing and coordination of the skill. This type of correction can take weeks, months, or in some cases even longer (Melville, 1988).

Corrections involving fundamental changes to a well-learned technique are the most time consuming. Not only will the learner have to revert back to the cognitive stage of learning, but negative transfer will occur between the previously learned technique and the corrected technique. Consequently, the motor program or pattern of coordination will have to be *rebuilt,* a process requiring substantial practice. Timing is everything. If such a correction is attempted two weeks prior to a major competition, the results could be disastrous.

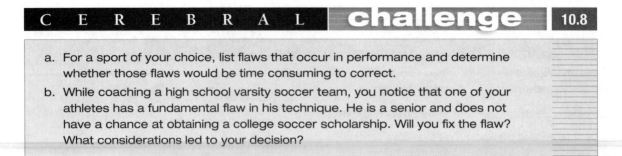

**C E R E B R A L challenge** 10.8

a. For a sport of your choice, list flaws that occur in performance and determine whether those flaws would be time consuming to correct.

b. While coaching a high school varsity soccer team, you notice that one of your athletes has a fundamental flaw in his technique. He is a senior and does not have a chance at obtaining a college soccer scholarship. Will you fix the flaw? What considerations led to your decision?

### Is the Learner Motivated?

The final question that must be addressed is whether the learner is motivated to make the correction. In some instances, the learner will not be convinced that making the correction is the right decision. Also, if the correction involves the development of a new motor program, performance will deteriorate before it gets better, and the learner will have to invest a considerable amount of time and practice to see the change through. The practitioner must be certain that the learner is prepared and willing to accept this challenge.

## ▶ a look ahead

Once an error (or errors) has been detected, the cause identified, and the determination made to correct the error(s), the next step is to provide the learner with the necessary information to make the correction. The practitioner should structure feedback to convey information that will both assist the learner in improving skill proficiency and reinforce and motivate the learner. Principles and guidelines for accomplishing this will be explored in the next chapter.

## ● focus points

After reading this chapter, you should know . . .

- When diagnosing errors, practitioners tend to focus on the outcome of the movement and provide feedback only about technical aspects of the skill that can be observed, although many errors can be attributed to deficits in motor learning.

- When conducting an observation, the practitioner should identify the purpose and key elements of the skill, determine the optimal viewing perspective, decide how many trials to observe prior to making a judgment regarding performance quality, and choose whether to record.

- Errors may occur as a result of organismic, task, or environmental constraints.

- Comprehension errors occur when a learner does not understand the requirements of the skill or what is expected.

- Errors in selection may result from problems in assessing the environment for task-relevant cues, faulty decision-making, or forgetting.

- Execution errors may occur when the learner has not had enough time to establish proper neuromuscular coordination, when movements are performed too quickly, or when the learner reveals intent, thereby allowing the opponent to anticipate the learner's movements.

- Errors in decision-making and motor control can result from difficulties with vision and proprioception.

- Whether an error should be corrected depends on the learner's capability to make the correction, the amount of time available, and the learner's motivation.

## ? review questions

1. List and explain three possible limitations to using observations to assess performance.

2. What four decisions should be made when planning an observation?

3. When would you use a video camera to capture a learner's performance?

4. Once an error has been detected, the practitioner should always ask what question?

5. When working with children, why might it be useful to modify equipment size? Provide an example to support your answer.

6. What strategies might be useful in assisting a learner who is making a comprehension error? Fully explain your answer.

7. Errors related to response selection fall into three categories. List and explain each.

8. What should a practitioner consider in order to decide whether to correct a movement error?

9. What amount of time may be needed to incorporate a "rebuild" correction?

# REFERENCES

Christina, R.W. & Corcos, D.M. (1988). *Coaches guide to teaching sport skills*. Champaign, IL: Human Kinetics.

Coaching Association of Canada. (1993). *Coaching theory level I: National Coaching Certification Program*. Gloucester, Ontario: Coaching Association of Canada.

Coker, C.A. (2005). Correcting faulty mechanics: to fix or not to fix? *Strategies, 19*(1), 29–31.

Hall, S.J. (2007). *Basic biomechanics*. New York: McGraw-Hill.

Hodges, P.W. (2007). Motor control. In G. Kolt and L. Snyder-Mackler (Eds.), *Physical therapies in sport and exercise* (pp. 115–32). Edinburgh: Churchill Livingstone.

Knudson, D. & Kluka, D. (1997). The impact of vision training on sport performance. *Journal of Physical Education, Recreation and Dance, 68*(4), 17–24.

Magill, R.A. (1998). Knowledge is more than we can talk about: implicit learning in motor skill acquisition. *Research Quarterly for Exercise and Sport, 69*(2), 104–10.

Melville, D.S. (1988). When to teach new techniques. In J.K. Groppel, J.E. Loehr, D.S. Melville, and A.M. Quinn (Eds.), *Science of coaching tennis* (pp. 73–81). Champaign, IL: Leisure.

Morris, G.S. (1980). *Elementary physical education: toward inclusion*. Salt Lake City: Brighton.

Payne, V.G. & Isaacs, L.D. (2008). *Human motor development: a lifespan approach*. New York: McGraw-Hill.

Rink, J.E. (2006). *Teaching physical education for learning*. New York: McGraw-Hill.

Robbins, S., Waked, E. & McClaran, J. (1995). Proprioception and stability: foot position sense as a function of age and footwear. *Age and Aging, 24,* 67–72.

Rothstein, A.L. (1986). The perceptual process, vision and motor skills. In L.D. Zaichkowsky and C.Z. Fuchs (Eds.), *The psychology of motor behavior: development, control, learning and performance* (pp. 191–214). Ithaca, NY: Mouvement.

Sudarsky, L. (1990). Geriatrics: gait disorders in the elderly. *New England Journal of Medicine, 322,* 1055–1059.

Waked, E., Robbins, S. & McClaran, J. (1997). The effect of footwear midsole hardness and thickness on proprioception and stability in older men. *Journal of Testing and Evaluation, 25*(1), 143–48.

Wang, J. & Griffin, M. (1998). Early correction of movement errors can help student performance. *Journal of Physical Education, Recreation and Dance, 69*(4), 50–52.

Wasson, J.H., Gall, V., McDonald, R & Liang, M.H. (1990). The prescription of assistive devices for the elderly: practical considerations. *Journal of General Internal Medicine, 5*(1), 46–54.

# CHAPTER 11

Correcting Errors

**H**ow did that look?" asked the dancer. "I think I was able to keep my pelvis in line that time." Such inquiries are commonplace, as learners often turn to practitioners for feedback. That feedback, according to Chen (2001), is the most critical form of guidance that a practitioner can provide a learner. To ensure that feedback is effective in facilitating learning and performance, the practitioner must carefully consider its type, content, frequency, and timing.

## TYPES OF FEEDBACK

**F**eedback is a general term used to describe the information a learner receives about his or her own performance of a movement or skill. That information can be available from both internal (intrinsic) and external (augmented) sources (see Figure 11.1). **Intrinsic feedback** is response-produced information that is available to learners through their sensory system both during and as a consequence of performance. Examples include the pitcher's seeing the ball after releasing it and the feeling a gymnast gets when he begins to lose balance. **Augmented feedback** is information received from an external source that supplements the learner's own sensory information. Examples of augmented feedback include a practitioner's comments, a video replay of the learner executing a skill, and the distance, time, or score resulting from one's performance posted by an official. Generally, augmented information is presented to the learner after the movement is completed and is therefore labeled **terminal feedback.** There are occasions when augmented feedback is provided during the execution of a skill. It is then termed **concurrent feedback.** When a coach yells out split times for an athlete during a race or a therapist reminds a patient to keep a good pelvic tilt during an exercise, this feedback is augmented and concurrent.

Feedback can be further classified as either knowledge of results or knowledge of performance. **Knowledge of results (KR)** is augmented feedback that provides the learner with information about the outcome of a response and is concerned with the success of the intended action with respect to its goal. For example, a coach might tell a long jumper that his plant foot was 4 cm over the takeoff board, a therapist could tell a patient the outcome of a functional reach test and compare it to previous results, or a personal fitness trainer might acknowledge the client's correct execution of an exercise. Information regarding the specific characteristics of the performance that led to the outcome is known as **knowledge of performance (KP).** Informing a patient that she needs to shift her weight forward more before attempting to stand, telling a student that his elbow recovery in the freestyle should be higher, and showing an athlete a video replay of a performance attempt are all examples of providing knowledge of performance.

Types of feedback.    FIGURE **11.1**

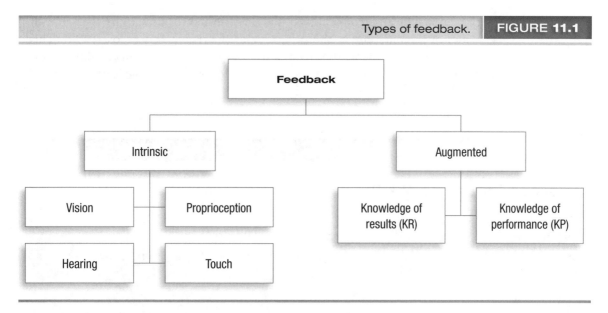

C E R E B R A L    challenge    11.1

Determine whether the following augmented feedback statements are examples of knowledge of results (KR) or knowledge of performance (KP).

_____ a. Your foot placement on the beam should be more angled.

_____ b. You have to keep your head down and your eye on the ball.

_____ c. That was great! You stayed on the wobble board for 28 seconds.

_____ d. According to the radar gun, that pitch was 92 miles per hour.

_____ e. When you swing your leg through, try to pull your toes up.

_____ f. You need to let the weight down more slowly.

_____ g. Looking at the pattern of hits, you are shooting high and to the right.

## FUNCTIONS OF AUGMENTED FEEDBACK

 ugmented feedback serves three major functions: error correction, motivation, and reinforcement.

**Error correction.** One role of augmented feedback is to provide information for the correction of performance errors. This information might include a description of the correct and/or incorrect aspects of the performance, an explanation as to why an error occurred, the prescription for how to fix the error, or specifics of the outcome of the performance (Christina & Corcos, 1988). This information guides the learner to modify subsequent movement attempts in order to enhance skill acquisition and performance. This outcome is demonstrated through Exploration Activity 11.2.

## exploration A C T I V I T Y 11.2

### Guidance Properties of KR

**EQUIPMENT**

5 paper clips

Partner

Blindfold

Pencil

Enlarged reproduction of the diagram below.

**PROCEDURE**

Blindfold one person. This person should attempt to "pin the tail" (place a paper clip) on the donkey. After each attempt, the other partner removes the paper clip and makes a pencil mark where the tip of the paper clip had been placed. This process continues for five trials. For the next five trials, the blindfolded individual is given KR specifying which ring the paper clip had been placed on and whether the paper clip was on the left or right half of the vertical line drawn through the target. (If the target is completely missed, indicate to which direction.) Using a different symbol, the

partner will place a pencil mark where the tip of the paper clip had been placed. After all 10 trials have been completed, the blindfolded partner may remove the blindfold and look at the results.

**QUESTIONS**

1. How do the results of the two KR conditions (no-KR versus KR) compare?

2. Reflect on your thoughts during the two conditions. Were there any differences?

3. In general, under what conditions do you think it would be important to provide the learner with KR? Do any conditions exist where the provision of KR may not be necessary?

Injuries from repetitive stress may result from impact forces such as those that occur in the jump–landing sequence in spiking. Cronin, Bressel, and Finn (2008) investigated whether a single session of augmented feedback regarding landing technique would reduce the impact forces of the volleyball spike. After five practice jumps to help them become familiar with protocol, 15 female Division I intercollegiate volleyball players performed five baseline spikes from a four-step approach, landing on both feet, with one foot landing on a force platform. After the performance of the baseline jumps, the researchers conducted a two-minute intervention session, where participants observed the coach demonstrating the correct landing technique—emphasizing toe–heel action, an even landing on both legs, and knee flexion close to 90 degrees to absorb landing forces. The participants were then given five practice jumps with feedback about limb kinematics from the coach. After the intervention, participants performed five additional test jumps without instruction or feedback. Augmented feedback was found to reduce vertical ground reaction force by 23.6 percent, a significant reduction. Consequently, this study demonstrated that a single session of augmented feedback had an immediate effect in reducing landing impact forces.

**QUESTION**

In this study, a post-test was used to examine the effects of augmented feedback on reducing impact forces in landing. What suggestions do you have for determining whether these results are persistent? In other words, how could you see whether the intervention had a long-term effect?

**Motivation.** Augmented feedback can play a motivational role in the learning process. When learners receive information regarding their performance, they can compare it with pre-established goals to determine their progress. If that comparison indicates improvement, the learners will be encouraged to continue trying to achieve their goals. Statements such as "You can do it!" and "Hang in there, you're on the right track" can also help learners work through tough practices, difficult challenges, and performance plateaus.

**Reinforcement.** The third function that augmented feedback can serve is to reinforce the learner. When used in this manner, augmented feedback increases the likelihood of a response recurring on future attempts under similar circumstances. Statements and gestures of praise, such as "Great effort," "Way to get after the ball," or giving the learner a high-five, can positively reinforce and, therefore, strengthen a behavior. Similarly, the satisfaction that learners derive from an acknowledgment that they have successfully executed a response may instill the desire to repeat the successful action. Eliminating a negative consequence can also reinforce behaviors. If you have learned how to drive a car with a manual transmission, you probably experienced what is known as negative reinforcement. Until new drivers learn to coordinate their movements when shifting gears, the car will jump or stall. Because the learner wants to avoid this embarrassing result, negative reinforcement serves to strengthen the desired coordinated movement.

# exploration    A C T I V I T Y    11.3

## Functions of Augmented Feedback

Observe a teacher, coach, therapist, or yourself teaching a skill. Using the tally sheet below, note whether each feedback statement provided information for the correction of performance errors, was used to motivate the learner, or served to reinforce a behavior.

| INFORMATION FOR CORRECTION | MOTIVATION | REINFORCEMENT |
|---|---|---|
|  |  |  |
|  |  |  |

**QUESTIONS**

1. Which category received the most tally marks? The fewest?
2. Speculate as to why you obtained these results.
3. Speculate as to how effective the pattern revealed will be for the learner's skill acquisition.
4. What other observations are noteworthy?

## SOURCES OF AUGMENTED FEEDBACK

Perhaps the most common source of augmented feedback is verbal descriptions and demonstrations. However, feedback can be delivered in a number of other ways.

### Auditory Sources

In many instances, augmented feedback takes an auditory form. For instance, sounds that result from skill execution can assist learners in evaluating their performance. Information about rhythm can be conveyed through clapping or a metronome. Auditory feedback also exists in the form of buzzers and warning signals. Auditory feedback devices have been shown to have positive effects in correcting foot position in a bar exercise in dance (Clarkson, James, Watkins & Foley, 1986), assisting swimmers in maintaining a desired stroke cadence and overall swimming velocity (Chollet, Micallef & Rabischong, 1988), aiding gymnasts in maintaining desired body alignment while performing a circle movement on the pommel horse (Baudry, Leroy, Thouvarecq & Choller, 2006), and improving the functional base of support in gait rehabilitation (Aruin, Hanke & Sharma, 2003).

## Biofeedback

When physiological measures are concurrently fed back to a learner through some form of instrumentation, the augmented sensory information provided is known as **biofeedback.** Shown to be effective in shaping behavior, biofeedback permits the constant monitoring of physiological conditions during a response. The auditory devices that were used in the studies listed in the previous section are examples of biofeedback. Other examples are marathon runners taking their own pulse during a workout or using a heart rate monitor to determine their level of intensity.

Using information from biofeedback, performers learn to alter and control their movements. For example, using a portable electrodermal response (EDR) feedback device, Peper and Schmid (1983/84) illustrated to the athletes of the U.S. Rhythmic Gymnastics Team how their thoughts and feelings affected their physiological state. The researchers used this information to help each athlete not only identify and stop negative thoughts and feelings but also restructure their self-talk, making it more positive.

Biofeedback is particularly useful in teaching rehabilitation patients to regulate their movements. Using a computer-assisted feedback system that provided instantaneous feedback on muscle activity and joint angular excursions, Colborne, Olney, and Griffin (1993) examined the use of biofeedback for retraining gait in stroke patients. Muscle activity and joint motion targets, along with cues regarding their specific timing during the gait cycle, were provided throughout the training period. Based on their findings, the authors concluded that computer-assisted feedback is an effective tool for retraining gait in stroke patients.

## Visual Displays

Performance feedback can be displayed visually in a number of ways. Game statistics may be charted on graphs and shot patterns revealed by inspection of targets. Frame-by-frame photographs can display important information about the execution of numerous skill components. Computer graphics are a popular means of offering feedback. In some physical education classes, children track their progress using handheld pocket electronic devices to examine data obtained from heart rate monitors.

Advances in technology have made computer-based skill analysis tools generally accessible. These programs create stick-figure representations of a movement, as shown in Figure 11.2, and can calculate and graphically depict numerous kinematic variables, including time, displacement, velocity, and angles. Studies exploring the effectiveness of kinematic feedback are limited, but the results to date have found its impact to be positive (Swinnen, Walter, Lee & Serrien, 1993; Wood, Gallagher, Martino & Ross, 1992). Developments in real-time kinematic feedback systems (e.g., Hawkins, 2000) should provide further insights into the effectiveness of this source of information for skill enhancement.

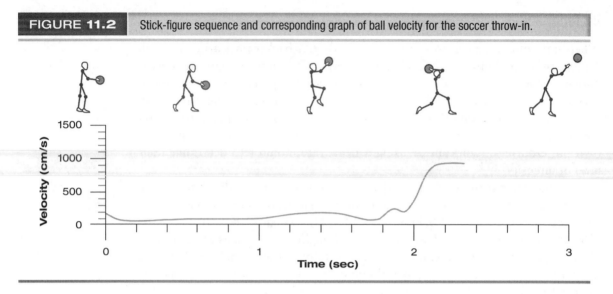

**FIGURE 11.2**    Stick-figure sequence and corresponding graph of ball velocity for the soccer throw-in.

### Video replay

Video recordings have found widespread use among movement practitioners. Guadagnoli, Holcomb, and Davis (2002) have demonstrated the effectiveness of incorporating video technology for improving performance. Video feedback (VFB) coupled with verbal feedback during practice was found to be superior for improving the shot distance and accuracy of moderately skilled golfers than verbal feedback alone or practicing without augmented feedback.

Video can capture performance attempts and store those images for repeated viewing, but for this powerful technology to be effective, learners have to understand what to look for and how to interpret what they are seeing. Whether learners develop this understanding depends on both the skill level of the learner and whether the replay is accompanied by cueing. In an extensive review of studies exploring the effectiveness of using video as a delivery mechanism of feedback, Rothstein and Arnold (1976) found that when learners were provided with cues to help direct their attention to the most important aspects of the performance replay, they were better able to utilize video as a source of information to facilitate skill acquisition, especially in the case of beginning learners. Without the benefit of attention-directing cues, the novice likely becomes overwhelmed by the magnitude of information presented (Newell & Walter, 1981). The benefits of including augmented cues with video feedback are not limited to novices. A study of highly skilled gymnasts illustrated the value of augmented cues with VFB, extending previous findings into the realm of skilled performers (Menickelli, Landin, Grisham & Hebert, 2000).

The provision of cues that direct the learner's attention to specific technical aspects of the movement prior to the learner's viewing the video replay has been shown to be effective; so, too, have cues that present information about the nature of the correction to be made. Kernodle and Carlton (1992) found that

One of the functions of augmented feedback is to motivate the learner to strive for goals. To examine how visual feedback aids in goal achievement, Hopper, Berg, Andersen, and Madan (2003) investigated the influence of VFB on power during the performance of a leg press. Sixteen elite female field hockey players were randomly assigned to two groups, both of which were tested with and without visual feedback but in reverse order. All participants were required to complete a standardized warm-up prior to testing. Two trials of three repetitions at an absolute load of 50 kg were then conducted for both conditions (with visual feedback and without visual feedback). Visual feedback was provided in the form of a computer monitor positioned to the left of the leg press machine displaying power output on a bar graph. Results revealed that the provision of visual feedback had a positive effect on performance, as power output was significantly higher than when visual feedback was not provided. The authors suggest that the provision of visual feedback in both resistance and rehabilitation training could enhance performance.

attention-focusing cues (e.g., "Focus on the left arm at the point of ball release") and cues that suggested what correction should be made (e.g. "Extend the left arm at ball release") were superior to the provision of KR (verbal information regarding outcome) and KP (video replay only) for learning the overhand throw. In addition, participants who received information about the nature of the correction to be made displayed more advanced throwing technique compared to participants in the three other conditions.

### Video feedback learning stages

Hebert, Landin, and Menickelli (1998) identified four distinct stages through which athletes progressed when introduced to video. Darden (1999) described these stages as shock, error detection, error correction, and independence and suggested a number of practical tips based on the characteristics of each stage.

1. *Shock stage.* When learners are initially introduced to viewing themselves on video, they go through a period of preoccupation with their appearance. Before they can begin to use video feedback as an instructional tool, they first have to get used to seeing themselves on screen. Until then, pointing out technical aspects of their performance will be futile.

2. *Error detection stage.* In the error detection stage, learners begin to observe their practice attempts critically and identify specific performance errors. The provision of attention-focusing cues regarding the environment or aspects of the movement itself is important in this stage to facilitate the development of error detection capabilities. As indicated earlier, learners are not always able to distinguish between task-relevant and task-irrelevant information. For example, if a projectile is involved in the performance, learners have a natural tendency to track it to see where it goes rather than

looking at their technique. Learners should be reminded to attend to the movement pattern in addition to the performance outcome (Darden, 1999).

3. *Error correction stage.* With practice and guidance, learners will begin to make associations between specific technical elements and outcome and will progress to the third stage. Here, learners not only identify their own errors but begin to understand why an error occurred. This understanding, in turn, forms the basis for decision-making with respect to the development of error correction strategies. Enhancing a learner's problem-solving skills should, therefore, be emphasized during this stage.

4. *Independence stage.* In the final stage, little, if any, dependency on teacher feedback remains. Learners can consistently identify and correct their own errors and should be encouraged to continue doing so. Self-guidance is, therefore, the focus of this final stage.

## Equipment and Drills

Drills and equipment can provide performance feedback. For example, the extended club drill is designed to provide the learner with feedback as to whether the hands were too active during a chip shot (Owens & Bunker, 1995). A second club is introduced to the learner's normal setup, creating an extension that projects above the waist. If the hands are too active during the swing, the shaft of the second club will touch the learner on the side.

Augmented feedback may also come from devices available to monitor performance, such as a radar gun, or from the equipment being used to perform the skill. For example, playing catch with a raw egg is a fun but potentially messy strategy to teach the concept of absorption. Whether the egg is broken or intact following an attempt provides augmented information to the learner regarding the performance. Many teaching aids in golf, such as the hinged golf club, are designed to provide feedback. If a flaw in swing mechanics occurs, the hinge of the club will break, folding the club. Much of the aerobic fitness equipment found in health clubs is designed to provide the learner with both concurrent and terminal feedback, such as how many steps have been climbed, calories burned, or distance rowed, ridden, or run. Similarly, heart rate monitors, pedometers, and cycle computers are popular informational sources. For pilot training, sophisticated flight simulators can capture measurements such as heartbeat, respiration rate, blood pressure, EEG, eye point of gaze, pupil size, and blink rate. After completion of the flight, these physiological variables can be correlated with recordings such as stick input and aircraft response, providing detailed performance feedback.

The extended club drill is designed to provide learners with performance feedback.

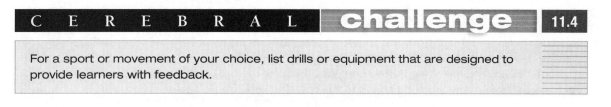

For a sport or movement of your choice, list drills or equipment that are designed to provide learners with feedback.

## CONTENT OF AUGMENTED FEEDBACK

**T**o ensure that feedback is useful, regardless of its source or delivery method, the practitioner must consider its content. Telling a learner that a shot missed when the outcome is clearly visible, for example, would be redundant. We now turn to questions concerning what information should be depicted in a feedback statement to best assist the learner. Should practitioners tell learners what was done correctly, or should they focus on performance errors? Should performance errors be described, or would an explanation of how to modify the movement be more beneficial? How precise should information be?

### Error versus Correct Feedback

An important decision regards whether to focus on the learner's performance errors or to highlight what was done correctly. Recall that augmented feedback can serve three major functions: to motivate, reinforce, or provide information regarding the correctness of a response in order to modify future attempts. When a learner is given information regarding a performance error, he or she will use that feedback to modify future performances. Consequently, if the goal of the feedback is to facilitate skill acquisition, the practitioner should provide error-based information. If, however, the goal is to confirm the learner's progress or encourage persistence, the practitioner should focus on the learner's achievements and highlight the correct features of the performance attempt. A combination of both would likely be optimal. This recommendation is supported by Coker and Fischman (2010) and Wrisberg (2007), who advocate the use of a "sandwich" approach, where error correction information is sandwiched between reinforcement and motivation. With this strategy, the practitioner first gives the learner information to reinforce correct performance, then provides the learner with information to facilitate error correction, and finally offers encouragement to motivate the learner to incorporate the error correction recommendations. An example of using the sandwich approach for the dancer in the opening story might be:

> Reinforcement: "Good! Your pelvis was in line that time."
>
> Error correction: "On this next trial, try to maintain your outward rotation while still concentrating on pelvic alignment. When you can combine both the pelvic alignment and outward rotation, your stability will improve and it will be easier to turn."
>
> Encouragement: "You almost have it."

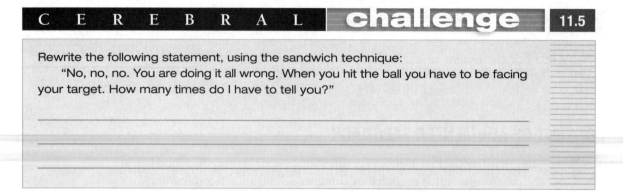

C E R E B R A L    **challenge**    11.5

Rewrite the following statement, using the sandwich technique:
    "No, no, no. You are doing it all wrong. When you hit the ball you have to be facing your target. How many times do I have to tell you?"

Interestingly, a learning advantage was demonstrated when KR was provided after relatively good trials (higher accuracy scores) versus relatively poor trials (lower accuracy scores) for a beanbag throwing task (Chiviacowsky & Wulf, 2005). Also, when learners were given the option to self-regulate when feedback was received, they showed a clear preference for requesting feedback after relatively successful trials (Chiviacowsky & Wulf, 2002). These findings support the contention that feedback serves a motivational function that can facilitate skill acquisition. Additional research is necessary to determine the generalizability of these results.

## Descriptive versus Prescriptive Feedback

The practitioner can provide knowledge of performance to a learner in two forms. In the first, **descriptive feedback,** the practitioner simply describes the nature of the performance error. If a learner's outside-of-the-foot pass in soccer is inaccurate due to excessive spin, for example, the practitioner might state, "You are putting too much spin on the ball." In **prescriptive feedback,** the practitioner offers a suggestion as to how to correct the problem. "You need to contact the ball just left or right of its midline to eliminate unwanted spin" is an example.

Whether to use descriptive or prescriptive feedback depends on the skill level of the learner. Descriptive statements can be effective only if the learner understands their implications. Recall that novice learners are trying to develop an understanding of the movement's requirements. In addition, they lack the capability to associate the cause of an error with the adjustments required to correct it. This implies that, while descriptive feedback may be adequate for learners who have obtained a degree of skill proficiency, beginners would benefit more from prescriptive statements. A combination of descriptive and prescriptive feedback, such as, "You initiated your movement too soon. Wait until you see the pitcher's back heel lift off of the ground" could assist learners in developing associations between errors and corrections.

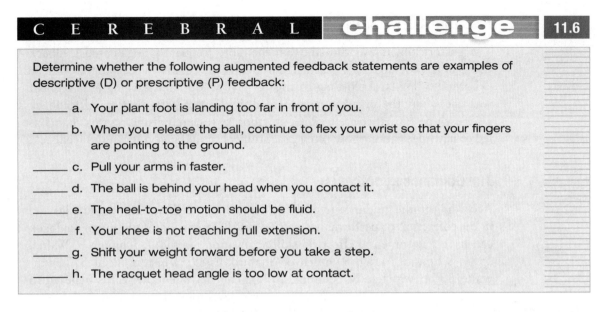

CEREBRAL **challenge** 11.6

Determine whether the following augmented feedback statements are examples of descriptive (D) or prescriptive (P) feedback:

_____ a. Your plant foot is landing too far in front of you.

_____ b. When you release the ball, continue to flex your wrist so that your fingers are pointing to the ground.

_____ c. Pull your arms in faster.

_____ d. The ball is behind your head when you contact it.

_____ e. The heel-to-toe motion should be fluid.

_____ f. Your knee is not reaching full extension.

_____ g. Shift your weight forward before you take a step.

_____ h. The racquet head angle is too low at contact.

## Precision of Augmented Feedback

The practitioner can use varying degrees of precision to convey information to a learner. "Your angle of attack was only 30 degrees" and "The tip of the javelin was too low at release" are both legitimate feedback statements describing the same error. The question is how the degree of precision in feedback affects the learner's capability to utilize the information. Again, the practitioner must consider the skill level of the learner. During the early stages of learning, as the learner is trying to develop an understanding of the movement's requirements, feedback can be quite general and still be effective (Magill & Wood, 1986). Later in the learning process, when skills are being refined, more precise information becomes useful, provided that the learner understands its meaning.

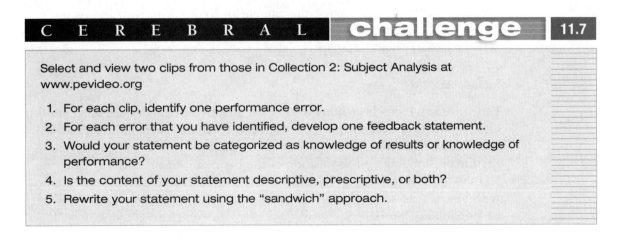

CEREBRAL **challenge** 11.7

Select and view two clips from those in Collection 2: Subject Analysis at www.pevideo.org

1. For each clip, identify one performance error.
2. For each error that you have identified, develop one feedback statement.
3. Would your statement be categorized as knowledge of results or knowledge of performance?
4. Is the content of your statement descriptive, prescriptive, or both?
5. Rewrite your statement using the "sandwich" approach.

# FREQUENCY OF AUGMENTED FEEDBACK

H istorically, it was thought that the more frequently augmented feedback was provided to a learner, the greater the gains in learning would be (Thorndike, 1931). According to this notion, an optimal learning environment was one where the practitioner provided the learner with augmented feedback after each performance attempt. Contemporary research disputing this claim has led to new ideas about how often practitioners should give augmented feedback.

## The Guidance Hypothesis

According to the guidance hypothesis, augmented feedback can guide a learner in the correction of performance errors, but the provision of too much feedback can have a detrimental effect on skill acquisition (Salmoni, Schmidt & Walter, 1984; Schmidt, Young, Swinnen & Shapiro, 1989; Winstein, Pohl & Lewthwaite, 1994; Winstein & Schmidt, 1990). This detrimental effect is believed to result from the learner's development of an overdependence on external feedback. A learner who receives augmented feedback at a high frequency, such as after every attempt, begins to rely on it and abandons the processing of other important sources of information, such as internal feedback. Rather than being actively engaged in the learning process, the learner instead may tend to become a passive listener and fail to develop valuable problem-solving skills that will be needed on future occasions when augmented feedback is not available. In contrast, the provision of augmented feedback at a lower relative frequency encourages the learner to become a reflective thinker and enhances learning. The question yet to be resolved is exactly how much augmented feedback should be given to optimize learning.

**common** *myth*

The more frequently augmented feedback is provided, the greater the gains in learning will be.

## Feedback Frequency Reduction Strategies

To avoid feedback dependency, the amount of feedback provided must be reduced. Strategies for reducing feedback frequency include faded, bandwidth, summary, average, and learner-regulated feedback approaches.

### Faded feedback

Faded feedback has been shown to be an effective frequency-reducing strategy (Winstein & Schmidt, 1990). In **faded feedback**, learners are provided with a high frequency of feedback in the initial stages of learning to facilitate their understanding and acquisition of the basic movement pattern. Once the learners achieve a basic proficiency level, augmented feedback is gradually withdrawn. The schedule for reducing feedback frequency will depend on each individual's progress.

## Bandwidth feedback

A technique that fosters important information-processing activities on the part of the learner is bandwidth feedback (Lai & Shea, 1999; Sherwood, 1988; Smith, Taylor & Withers, 1997). It, too, is based on the concept of providing more information during the early stages of learning and gradually reducing feedback as the learner improves. In **bandwidth feedback,** a range of "correctness" is predetermined, and augmented feedback is provided only on those trials where an error falls outside this range. For the volleyball serve, for example, a range of correctness for the toss might be defined as between the shoulder and 1 foot in front of the shoulder. If the learner's toss falls within this range, no feedback is provided, indicating that the toss was acceptable. If the toss falls outside the range, by being too far backward or forward, the practitioner gives the learner information for correction. The benefit of this approach is that feedback is systematically reduced according to the learner's level of proficiency. In addition, the learner receives positive reinforcement on those trials that do fall within the bandwidth, which will serve to strengthen the behavior that led to the outcome.

Vickers and colleagues (e.g., Vickers, Reeves, Chambers & Martell, 2004) identified an interesting problem with the use of bandwidth feedback. A number of coaches who were using bandwidth feedback reported that they had experienced communication problems with some of their athletes, parents, and even administrators. The coach's reduction of information was interpreted by some as a failure to assist the athletes, and some athletes felt neglected or ignored (Chambers & Vickers, 2006). In an attempt to resolve this dilemma, as well as other issues they identified, Chambers and Vickers (2006) examined the effectiveness of asking athletes questions about their performance as feedback frequency was reduced. This combined use of bandwidth feedback and questioning was shown to be effective for improving swimming technique in competitive athletes. Questioning strategies will be discussed further later in this chapter.

## Summary feedback

Summary feedback is another way to avert the potentially harmful effects of augmented feedback on learning. In **summary feedback,** the practitioner provides the learner with a summary of the performance after the completion of a certain number of trials. For example, in show jumping, a horse and rider have to negotiate numerous barriers. Augmented feedback would be withheld until the series of jumps is completed. The learner would then receive specific feedback about each jump in the series. Another example of summary feedback is showing the learner a video replay of his or her performance attempts after a certain number of trials.

Given the positive effect of summary feedback on learning (Schmidt et al., 1989), research has turned to defining the optimal number of performance trials that should be summarized. The answer may be a function of task complexity (Schmidt et al., 1990; Swinnen, 1996).

## Average feedback

Average feedback is another effective feedback-reduction strategy, similar to summary feedback. In **average feedback,** the learner receives augmented feedback after the completion of a certain number of attempts, as in summary feedback. This feedback, however, will be on the average performance error that occurred in the series. For example, to assist a patient learning how to rise from a chair using a walker, a therapist designs practice in which the patient receives feedback after every fifth attempt. Although the therapist notices several mistakes in the practice trials, the patient's most common tendency was to pull up on the walker while rising. Feedback would address only this error.

For the practitioner, average feedback offers several advantages over summary feedback. First, it eliminates the need to recount every error that is observed. Second, it forces the practitioner to focus the analysis to uncover true errors in performance and disregard occasional performance variability. Finally, it reduces the possibility of overwhelming the learner with too much information.

## Learner-regulated feedback

In **learner-regulated feedback,** the learner controls when augmented feedback is given. Rather than the practitioner determining when to offer feedback, the learner requests it and only then receives it. In addition to both reducing and individualizing feedback frequency, this strategy actively involves the learner in the learning process (Chen & Singer, 1992; Janelle, Kim & Singer, 1995). By giving the learner control over when and how much feedback is received, this strategy enhances the retention of crucial information (Chen, 2001; Hardy & Nelson, 1988; Holt, 1982; Zimmerman, 1989)—an idea supported by the findings of numerous studies that learner-regulated feedback results in superior retention than traditional practitioner-controlled feedback (Chen, Kaufman & Chung, 2001; Chen & Singer, 1992; Chiviacowsky & Wulf, 2002; Janelle et al., 1997; Janelle et al., 1995).

In an attempt to better understand the advantages of self-controlled feedback, Chiviacowsky and Wulf (2002) asked participants when and why they chose to ask for feedback. The participants demonstrated a clear preference for receiving feedback after a perceived successful (67 percent) versus unsuccessful

C E R E B R A L **challenge** 11.8

In Exploration Activity 11.2, when the performer was shown the pencil marks for each trial after the completion of all 10 trials, this was summary feedback. How would you redesign the experiment to provide bandwidth feedback? How would you redesign the experiment to provide average feedback?

(0 percent) attempt, suggesting that they requested feedback in order to confirm that their performance was on the right track. In a follow-up study, the same authors hypothesized that if learners base requests for feedback on their performance, then learning advantages would be expected for those who make the decision to ask for feedback after a trial rather than before it (Chiviacowsky & Wulf, 2005). This was indeed found to be the case.

## TIMING OF AUGMENTED FEEDBACK

**T**he presentation of augmented feedback can be broken down into three temporal intervals, illustrated in Figure 11.3. The time from the end of one performance attempt to the beginning of the next performance attempt is known as the **inter-trial interval.** That interval is further broken down into the **feedback-delay interval,** the time from the end of a performance attempt until augmented feedback is provided, and the **post-feedback interval,** the time from the provision of augmented feedback to the initiation of the next performance attempt. The following section examines these two sub-intervals, as their length and the nature of the activity that takes place within them both influence the effectiveness of performance-related feedback.

### Feedback-Delay Interval

A misconception regarding the timing of augmented feedback is that it should be provided to the learner immediately after a performance attempt. On the contrary, research has demonstrated that the instantaneous provision of augmented feedback has a negative impact on learning (Swinnen, Schmidt, Nicholson & Shapiro, 1990). When augmented feedback is provided too soon, learners are prevented from evaluating response-produced intrinsic feedback, impeding their development of error detection and correction mechanisms. In research supporting this notion, Anderson, Magill, Sekiya, and Ryan (2005) found that learners who received delayed KR used a greater number and variety

**common** *myth*

Augmented feedback should be delivered to the learner immediately after the performance attempt.

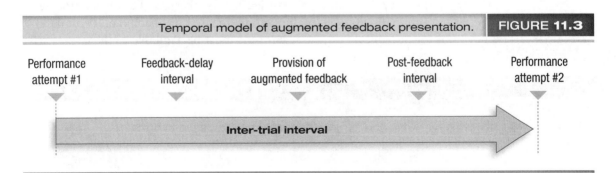

Temporal model of augmented feedback presentation.    **FIGURE 11.3**

| Performance attempt #1 | Feedback-delay interval | Provision of augmented feedback | Post-feedback interval | Performance attempt #2 |

Inter-trial interval

of intrinsic feedback sources than those who received KR immediately after each trial.

How long should the practitioner wait before giving feedback? It appears that learners simply need sufficient time, generally a few seconds, to process their own movement-produced feedback. Delaying the provision of feedback for longer periods of time does not appear to affect learning adversely, although an extended delay may cause the learner to forget the details of the practice attempt.

Prompting learners to estimate their own performance errors before the practitioner provides augmented feedback has also led to superior learning (Liu & Wrisberg, 1997; Swinnen et al., 1990). Consequently, Chen (2001) recommends that practitioners assist learners in developing their self-evaluation skills by asking them questions during practice to provoke reflective thinking regarding practice attempts. A practitioner might, for example, ask a learner, "How was your follow-through that time?" or "Why do you think the ball went off to the left?" The dancer in the opening of the chapter, who indicated that she thought her pelvis was in line, might be prompted to explain how she came to that conclusion. Chambers and Vickers (2006) provided support for this strategy, finding a positive effect on performance when bandwidth feedback and questioning strategies were utilized. They contend that "questioning provides coaches with a method of encouraging active learning through problem solving, discovery and performance awareness" (p. 187).

Initially, learners might have difficulty responding to such questioning. Self-evaluation is a capability that must be developed. Practitioners can guide learners through the process by asking more specific follow-up questions that will lead learners to the answer. For example, a secondary question about a player's follow-through might be, "Do you think your arm came straight down, or did it cross your body?" Eventually, practitioner–learner interactions will become an exchange of ideas rather than the one-way transfer of information, and the learner will develop the problem-solving capabilities needed for further skill acquisition and performance enhancement.

## Post-feedback Interval

During the post-feedback interval, the learner synthesizes the information received both internally and externally (via augmented feedback) and formulates a new movement plan. Again, sufficient time must be available to the learner to

CEREBRAL **challenge**    11.9

Make yourself a checklist for giving augmented feedback, based on the information provided in this chapter.

## RESEARCH NOTES

In a study, Liu and Wrisberg (1997) manipulated KR delay and subjective estimation of movement form to examine their effects on throwing accuracy. Forty-eight participants were randomly assigned to one of four conditions: (1) immediate KR, (2) delayed KR, (3) immediate KR plus subjective estimation of movement form, and (4) delayed KR plus subjective estimation of movement form. The task was to throw a ball at a target placed on the floor as accurately as possible, using the non-dominant hand and in the absence of vision. After the release of the ball, participants in the immediate-KR conditions were permitted to track the ball and see it land. Those in the KR-delay conditions were shown where the ball had landed after a 13-second delay interval. Participants in the subjective estimation groups were asked to rate their form in terms of force, release angle, and trajectory either 2 seconds after the ball's landing (immediate KR plus subjective estimation) or during the 13-second delay interval (delayed KR plus subjective estimation). Results indicated that while the immediate-KR groups displayed higher accuracy scores during practice, those in the delayed-KR conditions were significantly more accurate during retention. Moreover, the performance accuracy of the subjective estimation groups was significantly higher during the retention tests, where no KR was given. These findings support both the recommendation to delay the provision of feedback and the use of subjective error estimation.

process and plan. Given that these operations depend on the complexity of the skill, the length of the post-feedback interval will vary accordingly.

In some instances, learners may need to be reminded to engage in processing activities. By asking the learner what he or she is thinking about with respect to the upcoming attempt, the practitioner can both encourage active processing for movement modification and check for understanding. The practitioner can further ensure the learner's understanding by observing the degree to which augmented feedback assisted the learner in modifying the subsequent response.

## ▶ a look ahead

Through augmented feedback, practitioners can guide, motivate, and reinforce learners in order to enhance skill acquisition and performance. The effectiveness of the feedback depends on a number of variables, including the feedback's type, source, content, frequency, and timing.

This book has introduced you to the processes that govern movement acquisition and control. By understanding the concepts and principles described here, as well as their applications, you can look ahead to the challenges you will face with confidence that you will be able to make effective instructional decisions to maximize your patients', students', or athletes' potential.

# focus points

After reading this chapter, you should know . . .

- Feedback is a general term used to describe the information a learner receives about the performance of a movement or skill.
- Feedback can be intrinsic, coming from one's own sensory system, or augmented, supplied from an external source.
- Knowledge of results provides information regarding the outcome of a response and is concerned with the success of the intended action with respect to its goal.
- Knowledge of performance provides information regarding the specific characteristics of the performance that led to the outcome.
- Augmented feedback serves to provide information for error correction, motivate, and reinforce.
- Sources of augmented feedback include auditory feedback, visual displays, video replay, equipment and drills, and biofeedback.
- In the sandwich approach, the practitioner first gives the learner information to reinforce correct performance, then provides information regarding error correction, and finally offers encouragement to motivate the learner to incorporate the recommendations.
- The provision of both descriptive and prescriptive information can assist learners in developing associations between errors and corrections.
- Learners need a high frequency of feedback in the initial stage of learning. However, unless that frequency is reduced as the learner becomes more proficient, the learner may develop an overdependence on augmented feedback.
- To reduce feedback frequency, the practitioner can use faded, bandwidth, summary, average, and learner-regulated feedback.
- Learners need time to process intrinsic feedback and formulate a new movement plan for the next attempt.
- Prompting learners to estimate their own performance errors before providing them with augmented feedback results in superior learning.

# review questions

1. Define the following terms:
   a. feedback
   b. intrinsic feedback
   c. augmented feedback

  d. knowledge of results

  e. knowledge of performance

2. Compare and contrast terminal and concurrent feedback.

3. Develop a flow chart to represent all of the categories and sub-categories of feedback.

4. Compare and contrast positive and negative reinforcement.

5. What three functions can feedback serve?

6. Name the four stages of videotape feedback learning and the characteristics of each.

7. Compare and contrast:

  a. error-based and corrective feedback

  b. descriptive and prescriptive feedback

8. What is the significance of the guidance hypothesis?

9. What strategies can a practitioner use to reduce the frequency of augmented feedback?

10. The inter-trial interval can be broken down into two additional intervals. Name and define them.

## R E F E R E N C E S

Anderson, D.I., Magill, R.A., Sekiya, H. & Ryan, G. (2005). Support for an explanation of the guidance effect in motor skill learning. *Journal of Motor Behavior, 37*, 231–38.

Aruin, A.S., Hanke, T.A. & Sharma, A. (2003). Base of support feedback in gait rehabilitation. *Journal of Rehabilitation Research, 26*, 309–12.

Baudry, L., Leroy, D., Thouvarecq, R. & Choller, D. (2006). Auditory concurrent feedback benefits on the circle performed in gymnastics. *Journal of Sports Sciences, 24*, 149–56.

Chambers, K.L. & Vickers, J.N. (2006). Effects of bandwidth feedback and questioning on the performance of competitive swimmers. *The Sport Psychologist, 20*, 184–97.

Chen, D.D. (2001). Trends in augmented feedback research and tips for the practitioner. *Journal of Physical Education, Recreation and Dance, 72*(1), 32–36.

Chen, D.D., Kaufman, D. & Chung, M.W. (2001). Emergent patterns of feedback strategies in performing a closed motor skill. *Perceptual and Motor Skills, 93*, 197–204.

Chen, D.D. & Singer, R.N. (1992). Self-regulation and cognitive strategies in sport participation. *International Journal of Sport Psychology, 23*, 277–300.

Chiviacowsky, S. & Wulf, G. (2002). Self-controlled feedback: does it enhance learning because performers get feedback when they need it? *Research Quarterly for Exercise and Sport, 73*, 408–15.

Chiviacowsky, S. & Wulf, G. (2005). Self-controlled feedback is effective if it is based on the learner's performance. *Research Quarterly for Exercise and Sport, 76*, 42–48.

Chiviacowsky, S. & Wulf, G. (2007). Feedback after good trials enhances learning. *Research Quarterly for Exercise and Sport, 78*, 40–47.

Chollet, D., Micallef, J.P. & Rabischong, P. (1988). Biomechanical signals for external biofeedback to improve swimming techniques. In B.E. Ungerechts, K. Wilke, and K. Reischle (Eds.), *Swimming V* (pp. 389–96). Champaign, IL: Human Kinetics.

Christina, R.W. & Corcos, D.M. (1988) *Coaches guide to teaching sport skills.* Champaign, IL: Human Kinetics.

Clarkson, P.M., James, R., Watkins, A. & Foley, P. (1986). The effect of augmented feedback on foot pronation during bar exercise in dance. *Research Quarterly for Exercise and Sport, 57,* 33–40.

Coker, C.A. & Fischman, M.G. (2010). Motor skill learning for effective coaching and performance. In J.M. Williams (Ed.), *Applied sport psychology: personal growth to peak performance* (6th ed., pp. 21–41). New York: McGraw-Hill.

Colborne, G.R., Olney, S.J. & Griffin, M.P. (1993). Feedback of ankle joint angle and soleus electromyography in the rehabilitation of hemiplegic gait. *Archives of Physical Medicine and Rehabilitation,* 74(10), 1100–1106.

Cronin, J.B., Bressel, E. & Finn, L. (2008). Augmented feedback reduces ground reaction forces in the landing phase of the volleyball spike jump. *Journal of Sport Rehabilitation, 17,* 148–59.

Darden, G.F. (1999). Videotape feedback for student learning and performance: a learning stages approach. *Journal of Physical Education, Recreation and Dance,* 70(9), 40–45, 62.

Guadagnoli, M., Holcomb, W. & Davis, M. (2002). The efficacy of video feedback for learning the golf swing. *Journal of Sports Sciences, 20,* 615–22.

Hardy, L. & Nelson, D. (1988). Self-regulation training in sport and work. *Ergonomics, 31,* 1573–1583.

Hawkins, D. (2000). A new instrumentation system for training rowers. *Journal of Biomechanics,* 33(2), 241–46.

Hebert, E., Landin, D. & Menickelli, J. (1998). Videotape feedback: what learners see and how they use it. *Journal of Sport Pedagogy, 4,* 12–28.

Holt, J. (1982). *How children fail.* New York: Delacorte.

Hopper, D., Berg, M., Andersen, H. & Madan, R. (2003). The influence of visual feedback on power during leg press on elite women field hockey players. *Physical Therapy in Sport, 4,* 182–86.

Janelle, C.M., Barba, D.A., Frehlich, S.G., Tennant, L.K. & Cauraugh, J.H. (1997). Maximizing performance feedback effectiveness through videotape replay and a self-controlled learning environment. *Research Quarterly for Exercise and Sport,* 68(4), 269–79.

Janelle, C.M., Kim, J. & Singer, R.N. (1995). Subject-controlled feedback and learning of a closed motor skill. *Perceptual and Motor Skills, 81,* 627–34.

Kernodle, M.W. & Carlton, L.G. (1992). Information feedback and the learning of multiple-degree-of-freedom activities. *Journal of Motor Behavior,* 24(2), 187–96.

Lai, Q. & Shea, C.H. (1999). Bandwidth knowledge of results enhances generalized motor program learning. *Research Quarterly for Exercise and Sport, 70,* 79–83.

Liu, J. & Wrisberg, C.A. (1997). The effect of knowledge of results delay and the subjective estimation of movement form on the acquisition and retention of a motor skill. *Research Quarterly for Exercise and Sport,* 68(2), 145–51.

Magill, R.A. & Wood, C.A. (1986). Knowledge of results precision as a learning variable in motor skill acquisition. *Research Quarterly for Exercise and Sport, 57,* 170–73.

Menickelli, J., Landin, D., Grisham, W. & Hebert, E.P. (2000). The effects of videotape feedback with augmented cues on the performances and thought processes of skilled gymnasts. *Journal of Sport Pedagogy,* 6(1), 56–72.

Newell, K.M. & Walter, C.B. (1981). Kinematic and kinetic parameters as information feedback in motor skill acquisition. *Journal of Human Movement Studies, 7,* 235–54.

Owens, D. & Bunker, L.K. (1995). *Golf: steps to success.* Champaign, IL: Human Kinetics.

Peper, E. & Schmid, A.B. (1983/84). The use of electrodermal biofeedback for peak performance training. *Somatics IV, 3,* 16–18.

Rothstein, A.L. & Arnold, R.K. (1976). Bridging the gap: application of research on videotape feedback and bowling. *Motor Skills: Theory into Practice, 1,* 36–61.

Salmoni, A.W., Schmidt, R.A. & Walter, C.B. (1984). Knowledge of results and motor learning: a review and critical appraisal. *Psychological Bulletin, 95,* 355–86.

Schmidt, R.A., Lange, C.A. & Young, D.E. (1990). Optimizing summary knowledge of results for skill learning. *Human Movement Science, 9,* 325–48.

Schmidt, R.A., Young, D.E., Swinnen, S. & Shapiro, D.E. (1989). Summary knowledge of results for skill acquisition: support for the guidance hypothesis. *Journal of Experimental Psychology: Learning, Memory and Cognition, 15*, 352–59.

Sherwood, D.E. (1988). Effect of bandwidth knowledge of results on movement consistency. *Perceptual and Motor Skills, 66*, 535–42.

Smith, P., Taylor, S. & Withers, K. (1997). Applying bandwidth feedback scheduling to a golf shot. *Research Quarterly for Exercise and Sport, 68*, 215–21.

Swinnen, P.S. (1996). Information feedback for motor skill learning: a review. In H.N. Zelaznik (Ed.), *Advances in motor learning and control* (pp. 37–66). Champaign, IL: Human Kinetics.

Swinnen, P.S., Schmidt, R.A., Nicholson, D.E. & Shapiro, D.C. (1990). Information feedback for skill acquisition: instantaneous knowledge of results degrades learning. *Journal of Experimental Psychology: Learning, Memory and Cognition, 16*, 706–16.

Swinnen, P.S., Walter, C.B., Lee, T.D. & Serrien, D.J. (1993). Acquiring bimanual skills: contrasting forms of information feedback for interlimb decoupling. *Journal of Experimental Psychology: Learning, Memory and Cognition, 19*, 1321–1344.

Thorndike, E.L. (1931). *Human learning.* New York: Century.

Vickers, J.N., Reeves, M., Chambers, K.L. & Martell, S. (2004). Decision training: cognitive strategies for enhancing motor performance. In A.M. Williams and N.J. Hodges (Eds.), *Skill acquisition in sport: research, theory and practice* (pp. 103–20). New York: Routledge.

Winstein, C.J., Pohl, P.S. & Lewthwaite, R. (1994). Effects of physical guidance and knowledge of results on motor learning: support for the guidance hypothesis. *Research Quarterly for Exercise and Sport, 65*, 316–23.

Winstein, C.J. & Schmidt, R.A. (1990). Reduced frequency of knowledge of results enhances motor skill learning. *Journal of Experimental Psychology: Learning, Memory and Cognition, 16*, 677–91.

Wood, C.A., Gallagher, J.D., Martino, P.V. & Ross, M. (1992). Alternate forms of knowledge of results: interaction of augmented feedback on modality in learning. *Journal of Human Movement Studies, 22*, 213–30.

Wrisberg, C.A. (2007). *Sport skill instruction for coaches.* Champaign, IL: Human Kinetics.

Young, D.E. & Schmidt, R.A. (1992). Augmented kinematic feedback and motor learning. *Journal of Motor Behavior, 24*, 261–73.

Zimmerman, B.J. (1989). Models of self-regulated learning and academic achievement. In B.J. Zimmerman and D.H. Schunk (Eds.), *Self-regulated learning and academic achievement theory, research and practice: progress in cognitive development research* (pp. 1–26). New York: Springer-Verlag.

# Teaching Scenarios

Y our effectiveness as a practitioner will depend on your ability to integrate multiple motor learning and motor control concepts and principles. Following are two scenarios and corresponding questions designed to provide you with the opportunity to apply what you have learned in this book. Remember to consider the learner, the task, and the environment in which the task is performed in all cases.

## SCENARIOS

### 1. Physical Education

As part of your teacher preparation, you have to complete several observations of a physical education class at the local junior high school. You decide to observe an eighth-grade coeducational class that has just started a unit on soccer. There are 30 students in the class, including Chris and Morgan. Chris's movement experiences have been limited and were predominantly acquired through physical education. Morgan, on the other hand, is very active, and has played baseball, softball, and basketball and runs track.

**Question 1.1** During your first observation, the teacher introduces dribbling. Following the *initial* description and demonstration, the students are paired up for a drill. In this drill, one student is to dribble the ball to the other side of the gym while the partner tries to take it away. The goal of the drill, the teacher emphasizes, is to dribble without looking at the ball. As the drill progresses, the teacher notices that all of the students are either losing the ball or totally focusing their vision on it.

   a. Explain why this is not an effective drill.

   b. Suggest an alternative drill that would be more effective for this group of learners, and provide a comprehensive rationale for your suggestion.

**Q 1.2** When you arrive for your observation the following day, you notice that there are not enough soccer balls for everyone. Apparently the soccer coach borrowed some of the balls and has not yet returned them. In order for everyone to have a ball for the lesson on passing, the teacher has decided to replace the missing soccer balls with playground balls that are similar in size.

   a. Assess the potential advantages and disadvantages of this strategy.

   b. Based on your assessment, would you agree or disagree with using the playground balls in this situation? Justify your answer.

**Q 1.3** The next skill to be introduced to the class is trapping.

   a. Which method, part or whole, would you use if you were going to teach this skill?

   b. What factors did you take into consideration when making your decision? Fully explain your answer.

**Q 1.4** When teaching trapping, the teacher makes a reference to cushioning or absorbing the ball like you would when fielding a softball or baseball.

   a. What strategy is the teacher using to try to facilitate learners' understanding of the concept?

   b. Will this cue be equally effective for Chris and Morgan? Why or why not?

**Q 1.5** a. Which method, segmentation or simplification, would you suggest using to teach learners the skill of heading a soccer ball? Defend your selection.

   b. Outline how you would design the learning experience, using the method that you selected.

**Q 1.6** a. Design a drill that incorporates both random practice and variable practice to assist your learners in refining their dribbling, trapping, and passing skills.

   b. Would incorporating random and variable practice be equally effective for Chris and Morgan? Explain.

**Q 1.7** Chris is having a tough time passing the ball, and the teacher goes over to help. Having analyzed Chris's attempts, the teacher provides the following extrinsic feedback: "No, that's not it. You are too tense. Why are you so uptight? Your head isn't straight and you aren't kicking through the center of the ball—no wonder it doesn't go straight! Can't you do better than that?"

   a. Rewrite this statement to provide Chris with more effective feedback.

   b. Explain why your version is more effective.

**Q 1.8** Chris has come a long way in practice and has become quite proficient in shooting. However, every time the ball is passed near the goal, the defender steals it before Chris can get the shot off. The teacher decides that Chris's shooting technique is okay, but Chris is taking too long to react to the ball.

   a. List potential reasons for Chris's inability to respond quickly in this situation.

   b. Provide suggestions for each reason given to correct the problem.

## 2. Rehabilitation

You have just started working at a rehabilitation clinic. One of your first cases is a patient who has had a below-the-knee amputation (BKA) of the left leg. The patient has been fitted with a prosthetic and is ready to start balance training, transfers training (e.g., to the car), and gait training.

**Question 2.1** The psychological effects that accompany the amputation of a limb are a significant factor to consider during the patient's rehabilitation.

The patient's level of motivation, for example, will directly influence the learning process. When patients are not progressing as fast as they anticipated, frustration can lead to a loss of motivation. What strategies will you employ to motivate the patient during the rehabilitation process?

**Q 2.2** A major concern for the patient, common for those learning to use a lower limb prosthesis, is the fear of falling.

   a. What arousal level might you expect to be associated with the fear of falling?

   b. How might that influence the patient's training? The performance of activities of daily living?

   c. What strategies will you incorporate into the patient's rehabilitation program to reduce the fear of falling?

**Q 2.3** Describe how you could incorporate goal-setting into the rehabilitative process for this patient. Include an example of a goal that might be appropriate in this situation.

**Q 2.4** Given the loss of proprioception, patients with BKA will have difficulty learning to equalize stride length. What alternative feedback mechanisms could you use to compensate for the patient's lost proprioception?

**Q 2.5** In order to design effective variable practice experiences, the practitioner must assess the nature of the skill and the contexts in which it will be performed. List variations that should be incorporated into prosthetic training for

   a. learning to fall safely

   b. transfers (e.g., to the car)

   c. gait (both indoors and outdoors)

## ANSWERS

## 1. Physical Education Scenario

*Question 1.1*

This is not an effective drill for several reasons. First, the learning goal expressed by the teacher, to dribble the ball without looking at it, is too advanced. Given that the students have received only an initial explanation and demonstration, most of them would be in the cognitive stage of learning. Consequently, they should be given the opportunity to practice the skill in order to develop a basic under-standing of the movement. Once the learners have developed some proficiency in dribbling, the next step would be to learn to do so without looking at the ball.

Second, the drill does not target the learning goal. According to the teach-er's instructions, the goal of the drill is to dribble to the opposite side of the gym without looking at the ball. With a defender in front of the dribbler, the goal of the drill for the learner becomes protecting the ball.

Third, with a defender in front of the learner whose task is to try to take away the ball, the context in which the skill is being performed becomes open and, as a result, more complex. Given that the learners are in the cognitive stage, the attentional demands of movement production are high. The additional demand imposed by the defender exceeds the learner's attentional capacity, causing interference to occur. The result is either a decline in the level of performance or a disregard for one of the tasks. This was evident in that the learners were either losing control of the ball or totally focusing their vision on it.

## Question 1.2

Two factors should be considered here. The advantage to utilizing the playground balls is that it will increase the amount of time on task. The question the practitioner must ask prior to implementing this strategy is whether use of the playground balls will cause the learners to execute a pattern of movement that exceeds the boundaries of the generalized motor program being developed. Provided that distinct movement pattern changes would not manifest as a result of using the alternative equipment, this is a good strategy.

## Question 1.3

Given that the skill is high in task organization and low in task complexity, whole practice would be recommended.

## Question 1.4

The teacher's reference to cushioning the ball like you would when fielding a softball or baseball is an example of attempting to capitalize on positive transfer. Anytime you attempt to capitalize on transfer, it is important to be sure that the skill or concept you refer to has been well learned. Given Morgan's past experiences with baseball and softball, the reference will likely be effective. For Chris, who has limited movement experiences, the reference will not be meaningful and the idea the teacher is trying to convey will not be communicated effectively.

## Question 1.5

Again, the practitioner must assess task organization and task complexity to determine which method, segmentation or simplification, should be used. First, the skill would be considered relatively high in task organization. Second, given that heading requires the learner to time his or her actions to an oncoming ball, the movement is somewhat complex. That complexity can easily be reduced, however. Practice could start with each learner placing a small piece of masking tape on the middle of his or her forehead. Then, using lighter balls, such as beach balls, learners could throw their balls up into the air and try to hit them with the masking-tape spot on their foreheads. As they become proficient at this, they could progress to slightly harder balls, such as volleyballs or playground balls, and finally to soccer balls. In addition, the practice could progress from self-toss to partner toss. Tosses should initially be predictable and from close range, progressing gradually to farther away and unpredictable.

### Question 1.6

One partner would dribble the ball down the field and then pass it to the other partner, who would trap it and dribble it down the field before passing it back to the first partner. Variations in distance, speed, foot used, type of pass, type of trap, and so forth would be incorporated.

High levels of contextual interference can be overwhelming if the learner is still trying to develop an understanding of the movement. Given the past experiences of Morgan and Chris, it is possible that Morgan will progress through the learning process faster and be ready to handle a drill of this nature, while Chris may not. The answer depends on the learner's degree of proficiency when the drill is introduced.

### Question 1.7

The sandwich approach would be more effective in this situation. Using this strategy, a more effective version would be:

"Good! Your contact with the ball is much stronger. On this next trial, focus on kicking through the center of the ball. That will make the ball go straight. Let's try again. You almost have it."

This version is more effective because it confirms the learner's progress, encourages continued persistence, and offers prescriptive feedback, which is more beneficial for novice learners.

### Question 1.8

The error in this situation is a delay in responding. Multiple reasons could be the cause of this delay. First, the practitioner must establish whether Chris can correctly read game situations. Does Chris know what critical cues to look for? Can Chris detect that information during a game? If not, intervention strategies should focus on teaching Chris what the critical cues are, prompting Chris to prepare a response sooner, directing Chris's attention to where in the environment the cues occur, and providing extensive practice opportunities in a variety of situations that contain common task-relevant cues. Second, Chris's attentional focus may be either too broad or too narrow, depending on levels of arousal. Third, delay in responding may result from problems with decision-making. Reducing the number of response alternatives and increasing Chris's ability to identify potential predictors, such as opponent or situational tendencies, could resolve the problem.

## 2. Rehabilitation Scenario

### Question 2.1

Throughout the learning process, the patient must have opportunities to experience some degree of success. This will lead to feelings of achievement that will further motivate the learner to practice. The patient must also be taught that challenges are an integral part of the learning process. Positive feedback and the provision of encouragement and reinforcement are critical. The monotony of repeated training can be reduced if the therapist makes practice fun and introduces variety into the training protocol when possible. Another powerful motivational technique is goal-setting. It will be discussed in detail in the answer to Question 3.

### Question 2.2

One would expect the fear of falling to result in a high level of anxiety, leading to high levels of arousal. Fear of falling will obviously influence the patient's motivation to perform various activities. Furthermore, the patient is likely to demonstrate an overdependence on the uninvolved limb. As the patient progresses, high arousal will influence her attentional focus, and the performance of activities in more open environments will likely be compromised (e.g., walking through a crowd). To reduce the patient's fear and subsequent anxiety, the practitioner must not only teach her how to fall safely (in a way to minimize the risk of injury) but also what to do in the event of a fall. Balance and coordination exercises that reinforce good posture should be incorporated in the initial stages of the rehabilitation protocol.

### Question 2.3

The practitioner should take several steps to incorporate goal-setting into the rehabilitative process. First, the practitioner and patient should set a combination of short-term, long-term, performance, and process goals. Those goals should be SMART: specific, measurable, achievable, realistic, and timely. The patient should be included in the goal-setting process and encouraged to evaluate progress frequently. Finally, the practitioner must be supportive and provide positive reinforcement throughout the rehabilitative process.

An example of a goal that might be appropriate in this situation is: "Perform an independent and safe transfer to a bed, while being spotted by the therapist, eight out of 10 times, by the end of week two."

### Question 2.4

To assist the patient in developing a frame of reference for various activities, the practitioner should provide the opportunity to experience a variety of positions and movements across a broad assortment of environments. The practitioner should focus the patient's attention on the feelings associated with a movement to help the patient recognize and interpret the proprioceptive cues received from other sources. In addition, the practitioner should assist the patient in developing self-evaluation skills by asking questions during practice to provoke the patient's reflective thinking regarding practice attempts. Information regarding movement and body position is also available through visual feedback. Other alternative feedback mechanisms might include the use of biofeedback (e.g., a load-monitoring device), mirrors, and video replay.

## Question 2.5

a. Manipulate height and position. (*Note:* Safety is a priority.)

b. Manipulate the location to which the transfer occurs. Examples include bed, wheelchair, toilet, tub, shower, floor, car, and a variety of furniture.

c. Manipulate the surface (smooth, rough, carpeted, uneven); train on stairs, ramps, curbs, elevators, and escalators; ambulate and maneuver in narrow places and in crowds; practice managing doors, stepping over obstacles, and so forth.

**Ability** A genetic trait that is prerequisite to the development of skill proficiency

**Abstract targeting task** A task with a target that is fixed in space but with an optimal aiming location that is more difficult to detect

**Afferent** Literally, carrying to; describes the part of the PNS that detects changes in the environment and conducts nerve impulses from the sensory receptors to the CNS

**Affordances** Action possibilities of the environment and task in relation to the perceiver's own capabilities

**Ambient system** Visual system that functions at a subconscious level and is thought to be responsible for spatial localization and orientation

**Amplitude** Size of a movement

**Analytical learner** Learner who prefers to have new information presented in a sequential manner building toward the main concept

**Anticipation** Prediction of what event will occur or when an event will occur

**Anxiety** An emotion resulting from an individual's perception of a situation as threatening

**Arousal** "A general physiological and psychological activation of the organism that varies on a continuum from deep sleep to intense excitement" (Gould & Krane, 1992)

**Associative stage** The intermediate stage of learning in Fitts and Posner's model

**Attention cueing** A practice technique in which the learner directs attention to a specific aspect of the skill during its performance as a whole

**Attentional focus** The process of selectively attending to specific environmental information

**Attractor state** Preferred state of stability or pattern toward which a system spontaneously shifts

**Augmented feedback** Information received from an external source that supplements the learner's own sensory information

**Automaticity** A capacity to perform a skill with little or no conscious control

**Autonomous stage** The advanced or final stage of learning in Fitts and Posner's model

**Average feedback** Augmented feedback, provided after a certain number of attempts are completed, regarding the average performance error

**Backward chaining** Part practice technique in which the parts of a skill are presented and practiced in a sequence that progresses from the final skill component to the initial one

**Bandwidth feedback** Augmented feedback in which feedback is provided only on trials where an error falls outside a predetermined range of correctness

**Bilateral transfer** Practice with one limb enhances the rate of skill acquisition with the opposite limb on the same task

**Biofeedback** A form of augmented feedback in which physiological information is concurrently available to the learner

**Blocked practice** Practice schedule in which the learner practices one variation of a skill repeatedly and then moves on to another variation

**Cerebral cortex** The outermost layer of the cerebrum

**Choice RT** Reaction time resulting from a situation that involves a choice as to how to respond

**Closed skill** Skills performed within a stable and predictable environment, allowing the performer to control the performance situation

**Closed-loop control** Mode of control in which feedback aids error detection and correction

**Cognitive stage** The initial or beginning stage of learning in Fitts and Posner's model

**Concurrent feedback** Augmented feedback provided during the execution of a skill

**Constraint** A boundary that has a bearing on the movement capabilities of an individual

**Constraint-led approach** Model of skill learning in which the instructor is a facilitator who identifies and manipulates constraints in order to facilitate skill acquisition

**Contextual interference** Interference that results from switching from one skill to another or changing the context in which a task is practiced from trial to trial

**Contextual interference effect** Low contextual interference often produces superior short-term performance during practice, but high contextual interference leads to greater long-term learning gains

**Continuous skill** A skill whose beginning and ending points are either arbitrary or determined by some environmental factor rather than by the task itself

**Control** The manipulation of variables within a movement to meet the demands of a given situation

**Control parameters** Variables that move a system into new attractor states

**Coordination** The process of organizing a system's available degrees of freedom into an efficient movement pattern that will effectively achieve a goal

**Critical features** Specific body movements that are observable and that affect the performance of a skill

**Cue utilization hypothesis** A paradigm in which changes in attentional focus occur according to arousal levels

**Declarative knowledge** Information used to decide what to do in a given situation

**Degrees of freedom** Independent elements of movement that must be organized to produce a controlled movement pattern

**Degrees of freedom problem** Problem of how we coordinate and control the available degrees of freedom to produce a particular movement

**Descriptive feedback** Augmented feedback in which the practitioner describes the nature of the performance error

**Discovery learning** Teaching strategy in which the instructor creates a learning environment that engages the learner in attempts to solve a movement problem by exploring a variety of possible task solutions

**Discrete skill** A skill whose beginning and end points are clearly defined

**Distributed practice** Practice schedule in which the rest component between sessions or practice attempts is equal to or greater than the practice component

**Ecological approach** Model of perception in which the perceiver interprets the environment and tasks directly in terms of affordances

**Efferent** Literally, carrying away from; describes the part of the PNS that transmits impulses away from the CNS to the effectors

**Episodic memory** The memory of personal experiences and events that are associated with a specific time and context

**Event anticipation** Prediction of what event will occur

**Explicit learning** Knowledge acquired through explicit verbal explanations

**External focus** Focusing attention on the effects of one's actions

**Exteroceptors** Receptors located at or near the body's surface that detect stimuli outside the body and provide information about the environment

**Faded feedback** Feedback technique in which learners are provided with a high frequency of feedback initially and then the feedback is gradually withdrawn

**Feedback-delay interval** Time from the end of one performance attempt until augmented feedback is provided

**Feedforward** Describes the sending of information ahead of a movement, for advance preparation or adjustments of the movement

**Fine motor skill** A motor skill involving very precise movements normally accomplished using smaller musculature

**Fixation** Focusing visual attention on a specific object

**Fixation/diversification** The second and final stage of learning in Gentile's model

**Fixed target** A target that is stable and predictable in position and requires a performer to fixate on a specific location prior to executing a response

**Focal system** Visual system that functions to identify objects primarily located in the central region of the visual field

**Foreperiod** Time interval between the presentation of a warning signal and the stimulus it warns of

**Forward chaining** Part practice technique in which the parts of a skill are presented and practiced in a sequence that progresses from the initial skill component to the final one

**Fractionization** Part practice technique in which skill components that are normally performed simultaneously are partitioned and practiced independently

**Freezing the degrees of freedom** Strategy in which a learner freezes or fixes the movement possibilities of a joint, causing the limb(s) to function as a single unit or segment, in order to accomplish the goal of a task

**Functional movement pattern** a movement pattern that will accomplish a specific task goal

**Generalized motor program** An abstract representation of a class of actions or pattern of movement that can be modified to yield various response outcomes

**Getting the idea of the movement stage** The first stage of learning in Gentile's model, characterized by the learner trying to develop an understanding of the movement's requirements

**Global learner** Learner who learns more easily when first presented with the big picture and then asked to concentrate on details

**Golgi tendon organs** Proprioceptors located at the junction of a tendon with a muscle that indicate the level of tension development in a tendon

**Gross motor skill** A motor skill that places less emphasis on precision and is typically the result of multi-limb movements

**Guided discovery** Learning technique where the practitioner asks a sequence of questions, each of which elicits a single correct response discovered by the learner

**Hick's Law** The higher the degree of uncertainty in a given situation, the longer the time needed to decide which response to make; choice RT is logarithmically related to the number of response choice alternatives

**Imagery** The visualization or cognitive rehearsal of a movement in the absence of any physical execution

**Implicit learning** Knowledge acquired without conscious awareness

**Individual differences** Relatively stable and enduring characteristics that make each of us unique

**Information processing** Model of perception in which a performer receives an abundance of information, focuses on pertinent stimuli, selects a response, and receives intrinsic feedback about the results of the response

**Internal focus** Focusing attention on one's own body movements

**Interneuron** Nerve cell that lies between a sensory and a motor neuron in a reflex arc

**Interoceptors** Receptors that detect stimuli from the internal viscera and provide information about the internal environment

**Inter-trial interval** The time from the end of one performance attempt to the beginning of the next performance attempt

**Intrinsic feedback** Response-produced information that is available to learners from their sensory system both during and as a consequence of performance

**Invariant features** Relatively fixed underlying features that define a motor program

**Inverted-U principle** Relationship between arousal and performance in which there exists an optimal level of arousal for peak performance

**Key elements** Specific body movements that are observable and that affect the performance of a skill

**Knowledge of performance** Augmented feedback that provides information about the specific characteristics of the performance that led to the outcome

**Knowledge of results** Augmented feedback that provides the learner with information about the outcome of a response and is concerned with the success of the intended action with respect to its goal

**Learner-regulated feedback** Augmented feedback provided to a learner only when he or she requests it

**Learning** A relatively permanent change in a person's ability to execute a motor skill as a result of practice or experience

**Learning style** Individual preference for receiving and processing new information

**Manual guidance** Physically moving a learner through a goal movement

**Massed practice** Practice schedule in which the amount of time allocated to rest between sessions or practice attempts is comparatively less than the time a learner is engaged in practice

**Memory** The ability to store and recall information

**Modal strength** The preferred perceptual mode through which a learner takes in and processes information

**Motivation** An internal condition that incites and directs action or behavior

**Motor control** The study of the neural, physical, and behavioral aspects that underlie human movement

**Motor learning** The study of the processes involved in acquiring and refining motor skills and of variables that promote or inhibit that acquisition

**Motor program** An abstract representation of a movement plan, stored in memory, that contains all of the motor commands required for carrying out the intended action

**Motor skill** A goal-oriented act or task that requires voluntary body and or limb movement and must be learned

**Movement time** Interval of time between the initiation of a movement and its completion

**Moving target task** Task that requires the performer to anticipate the target's impending location

**Muscle spindles** Proprioceptors located between the skeletal muscle fibers in the muscle belly that indicate how much and how fast the muscle's length is changing

**Negative transfer** The learning of a new skill or its performance under novel conditions is negatively influenced by past experience with another skill or skills

**Open skill** A motor skill that is performed in an unpredictable, ever-changing environment

**Open-loop control** A mode of control whereby an action plan is generated that contains all of the information necessary to complete a response

**Outcome goals** Goals that are concerned with the final result of a competition relative to one's opponent

**Parameters** Flexible features that define how to execute a generalized motor program

**Part practice method** Teaching strategy in which the instructor breaks the skill down into natural parts or segments and learners practice those parts separately until they are learned and then integrate them to perform the skill in its entirety

**Perception** Process by which meaning is attached to information

**Perceptual-motor workspace** The individual's perceptual information sources and range of movement possibilities for a particular task

**Perceptual narrowing** The narrowing of attentional focus with increasing levels of arousal

**Performance** The act of executing a skill

**Performance goals** Goals that are concerned with self-improvement

**Performance plateau** A period of time during the learning process in which no overt changes in performance occur

**Phase shift** Change in the state of stability of a system causing a spontaneous reorganization into a new form

**Photoreceptors** Light-sensitive cells located in the eyes

**Positive transfer** The learning of a new skill or its performance under novel conditions is positively influenced by past experience with another skill or skills

**Post-feedback interval** Time from the provision of augmented feedback to the initiation of the next performance attempt

**Post-test** Skill performance test administered directly following a practice period, used to determine what the learner can do after practicing a skill

**Power law of practice** When learning a new skill, there tends to be a large initial improvement in performance, which slows later in practice (Newell & Rosenbloom, 1981)

**Precue** Clues in the environment that can assist a performer in anticipating

**Prescriptive feedback** Augmented feedback in which the practitioner offers a suggestion as to how to correct a performance problem

**Proactive interference** The interference of old memories with the retention of new ones

**Procedural knowledge** Information regarding skills, operations, and actions

**Procedural memory** The memory of information regarding how to do something

**Process goals** Goals that direct the performer's focus to achieving some technical element during skill execution

**Proprioception** The continuous flow of sensory information that is received from receptors located in the muscles, tendons, joints, and inner ear regarding movement and body position

**Proprioceptors** Receptors that provide information regarding body position and movement by detecting changes in muscle tension, joint position, and equilibrium

**Psychological refractory period (PRP)** Delay in responding to a second stimulus in a situation where two stimuli, each of which requires a different response, are presented in succession within a short period of time

**Quiet eye** The final fixation located on a specific target or object before the initiation of movement

**Random practice** Practice schedule in which the learner performs multiple task variations in a random order

**Rate limiters** Constraints that hinder or restrict the ability of a system to change

**Reaction time** Interval of time between the moment when a stimulus is presented and when a response is initiated

**Reflex** An automatic, involuntary response to stimuli

**Reflex arc** The simplest pathway by which a reflex occurs

**Regulatory conditions** Environmental factors that specify the movement characteristics necessary to perform a skill successfully

**Relative force** The concept that when the overall force used to execute a movement changes, the actual force characteristic of each component should change proportionally

**Response time** Time interval from the moment when a stimulus is presented to when the response is completed (combination of RT and MT)

**Retention test** Skill performance test given following a period of no practice that measures the persistence of improved skill performance

**Retroactive interference** Interference of new learning with the retention of older memories

**Schema** A rule or relationship that directs decision-making when a learner is faced with a movement problem

**Segmentation** Part practice technique in which the skill is separated into parts according to spatial or temporal elements

**Selective attention** The ability to attend to or focus on one specific item amid countless stimuli

**Self-organization** Spontaneous emergence of a movement pattern as a result of the interaction of ever-changing organismic, environmental, and task constraints placed on the learner

**Self-talk** Cues used by learners to guide themselves through an action or a movement sequence

**Semantic memory** The memory of general knowledge that is developed through experiences but is not associated with time

**Serial skill** A motor skill that is composed of a number of discrete skills whose integrated performance is crucial for goal achievement

**Simplification** Part practice technique in which the level of difficulty of the task or some aspect of the task is reduced

**Specificity hypothesis** The hypothesis that individuals inherit a large number of motor abilities and the inheritance of each ability is independent of the others

**Speed-accuracy tradeoff** The fact that an emphasis on speed in performance negatively affects accuracy and vice versa

**Spotting** Fixating one's visual attention on a specific spot during rotation of the body in order to reduce dizziness and remain oriented

**Stimulus** A change in the environment that evokes a response

**Stimulus-response compatibility** The extent to which a stimulus and its required response are naturally related

**Summary feedback** Augmented feedback in which the practitioner provides the learner with a summary of the performance after a certain number of trials are completed

**Task analysis** The breaking down of a skill into its component parts and corresponding underlying abilities

**Tau** Optic variable that provides time-to-contact information by taking the size of the retina image at any position of an object's approach and dividing it by the rate of change of the image

**Taxonomy** Model into which skills are classified

**Temporal anticipation** Prediction of when an event will occur

**Terminal feedback** Augmented feedback that is presented after the movement is completed

**Trait anxiety** An individual's propensity to perceive situations as threatening or non-threatening

**Transfer** Phenomenon in which the learning of a new skill or its performance under novel conditions is influenced by past experience with another skill or skills

**Transfer appropriate processing theory** Theory that we should expect positive transfer when practice conditions require learners to engage in problem-solving processes similar to those that the criterion task requires

**Transfer test** Test that measures the adaptability of a response, determined by testing the learner's ability to use a skill in a novel context or manner

**Variable practice** Practice schedule in which multiple variations of a given task are practiced

**Verbal cue** A word or concise phrase that focuses the learner's attention or prompts a movement or movement sequence

**Visual search** The process of directing visual attention while trying to locate critical regulatory cues in the environment

**Zero transfer** Past experience with another skill or skills has no influence on the learning of a new skill or its performance under novel conditions

**Zone of optimal functioning** Range of arousal levels that leads to optimal performance

# subject index